Primary Science

A Complete Reference Guide

Key Stages
1 & 2

Michael Evans

General Inspector – Science, Hampshire

JOHN MURRAY

Cover photograph: D. Roberts, Science Photo Library. False-colour X-ray of two sea horses, *Hippo campus*

Cartoons: Richard Duszczak

Line drawings: Taurus Graphics

Photographs: (*p. 170*) Unilab Ltd, (*pp. 181, 182*) Science Photo Library

First published in 1994
by John Murray (Publishers) Ltd
50 Albemarle Street, London W1X 4BD

Designed by Eric Drewery
Typeset by Wearset, Boldon, Tyne and Wear
Printed and bound by St Edmundsbury Press

A catalogue entry for this title can be obtained from the British Library

ISBN 0 7195 5233 8

Whilst every attempt has been made to raise awareness of any potential risks which may be involved with any substances or activities mentioned, teachers must ensure for themselves that any activity which is carried out with children is safe. Teachers will need to be guided by government Health and Safety at Work legislation and any local Safety rules and/or advice.

Other titles in the **Key Strategies** series

Planning Primary Science by Roy Richardson, Phillip Coote and Alan Wood
Physical Education A Practical Guide by Elizabeth Robertson

CONTENTS

INTRODUCTION

That science is a core subject within the National Curriculum is to be welcomed, since it identifies the subject as an entitlement for all children. However, the rapid introduction of science into the primary curriculum at Key Stage 2, in its present published form, has many implications relating to the levels of support which are needed to enable teachers to deliver it effectively and with confidence.

Teachers will be planning their work for the classroom based on the Programme of Study for science at Key Stage 2 and will assess pupils' achievements against the Statements of Attainment. Whilst doing this many questions may be raised about the intent of a particular word, phrase or idea. The depth to which ideas need to be developed within the classroom or indeed the deeper background knowledge required by the teacher are often in doubt.

This book aims to help teachers by providing support which will enable them to teach aspects of science at Key Stage 2 with a sense of confidence; including those topics with which teachers are at present unfamiliar.

The format of the book recognises that primary teachers are busy and is structured so that it may be used in a variety of different ways as follows:

A planning aid What ideas are there for teaching acids and alkalis? How can I introduce forces?

A reference guide Provides essential knowledge or understanding. What is an indicator? What is the difference between force and power?

An indication of the depth to which ideas should be taught What plants make good indicators? What living things can children study when learning about variation? What will they be doing at Key Stage 3?

A collection of investigations What investigations can be carried out relating to acids and alkalis?

A guide to the problems Children may encounter problems in developing particular ideas. What views do many children have about energy?

This book forms an ideal teaching companion and can be kept by the teacher's side for quick and accessible reference.

HOW TO USE THIS BOOK

The book consists of three sections.

1. **Developing An Approach To Teaching Science At Key Stage 2**
   A discussion of teaching and learning within the two aspects of science:

   ■ Developing knowledge and understanding (Sc2,3,4).
   ■ Developing procedural understanding (Sc1).

   The section provides an essential background to the framework of science in the National Curriculum. Investigations, and information about why it is important and helpful to consider childrens' own ideas when developing scientific knowledge and understanding, are explained.

3. **A To Z Reference Section**

   This is an A to Z glossary where the words found in **bold** type within the Programme of Study for Stage 2 are explained in detail, often with helpful diagrams.

   The glossary provides essential background knowledge for the teacher, and information about which concepts are appropriate for Key Stage 2 appears in tinted summary-boxes at the end of appropriate entries.

Attainment Target and strand

Development of key ideas.
Information about specific knowledge required at Key Stages 1, 2 and 3

The Programme of Study relating to the strand, with key reference words that are explained in section 3

Reference section highlighted in **bold** type

Pupils' own ideas. Information relating to pupils' ideas and where stumbling blocks to understanding may arise

Commentary and starting points. A series of suggested starting points derived from the Programme of Study

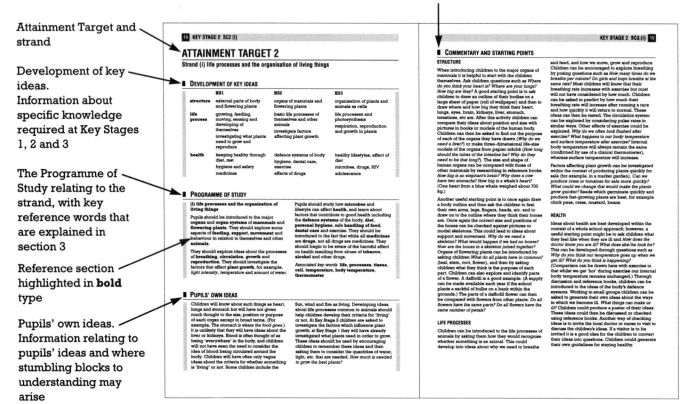

2. **Planning Activities At Key Stage 2**

A series of commentaries containing information to enable teachers to plan and teach science topics. Each commentary deals specifically with one strand, for example Attainment Target 2 strand (i) life processes and the organisation of living things, and highlights reference words in **bold** type, which can be found as entries in the A to Z reference section (section 3). Each of the twelve commentaries are supplemented with a series of starting points and ideas for Sc1.

1

Developing An Approach
To Teaching Science
At Key Stage 2

SCIENCE IN THE NATIONAL CURRICULUM – THE FRAMEWORK

Science can be regarded as both methods and a set of ideas. Science in the National Curriculum seeks to develop these two key aspects:

- Knowledge and understanding
  Attainment Targets 2 – 4; the ideas.
- Scientific investigation
  Attainment Target 1; the methods.

■ KNOWLEDGE AND UNDERSTANDING (CONCEPTUAL UNDERSTANDING)

This part of the National Curriculum deals with the key ideas which should help children explain and make sense of the world around them. It should help them answer questions such as *What are things made of? Why do materials behave in the way that they do? How do living things grow? What makes things go?*

In order to help understand and explain things through science we create models and pictures of our world and the things in it. This requires us to construct ideas, for example; the idea that energy is needed to make things go, that things are made of particles, and that in an electrical circuit something is flowing which we call current.

The understanding of these ideas and concepts such as force, mass, life and the Universe enables us to predict events and provides us with the ability to change things in predictable and desirable ways.

For example:

An understanding of bacterial growth can help prevent and cure disease.

An understanding of atoms and molecules can help us understand why some things dissolve and others do not, and can lead to the manufacture of new products such as detergents.

A knowledge and understanding of Newton's ideas of force, mass and acceleration has made space exploration possible.

■ SCIENTIFIC INVESTIGATION (PROCEDURAL UNDERSTANDING)

Scientific investigation is regarded as a means by which science tests its developing ideas. The results of investigations aid the development of scientific thinking which may eventually contribute to new knowledge and understanding.

Starting points for investigations are characterised by questions, such as:

> *I wonder why . . . ?*
> *What will happen if . . . ?*
> *What affects . . . ?*
> *Is there a connection between . . . ?*
> *What causes . . . ?*

Speculation about such questions can lead to predictions or tentative explanations (hypotheses), such as:

> *I think this will happen.*
> *I think it happens . . . because . . . .*

Ideas can be tested by designing experiments, considering the results and drawing conclusions about whether or not the predictions or explanations were correct.

Scientific investigation (Sc1) in the National Curriculum deals with procedures which should help children develop their own thinking as well as enabling them to appreciate the ways in which science is regarded to advance knowledge and understanding. It is anticipated that this should also lead to a simple understanding of the power and limitations of science.

CHILDREN'S LEARNING IN SCIENCE

An education in science seeks to develop these two key aspects:

- Knowledge and understanding.
- Scientific investigation.

■ KNOWLEDGE AND UNDERSTANDING (DEVELOPING A CONCEPTUAL UNDERSTANDING)

In order for us to 'operate' we create our own ideas about the world and the things in it to help us predict and anticipate the way things behave. These 'ideas' are constructed from our own experiences.

> When playing with different balls we notice that some bounce better than others and through experience we discover that rubber balls bounce better than most others. We use this 'idea' (things made of rubber bounce best) to help us anticipate the ways in which a ball may bounce when playing games so that we catch or hit the ball correctly.

Sometimes our lack of experience leads us to build an incomplete or even wrong model which we may not recognise as being wrong or incomplete because it works within the realm of our own experiences.

> The idea that rubber balls bounce best will serve us well if we come into contact only with rubber balls, hard plastic balls or wooden balls. Then one day someone bounces a 'supa' ball towards us and says *Catch*. We miss the ball because we did not anticipate it bouncing so high. Our 'model' no longer works, so we have to modify our ideas to take account of this new experience. So our new rule or idea might be

> that soft plastic bounces best (even better than rubber).

Scientific ideas are based on a wide range of experiences and sometimes conflict with children's own emerging ideas or models which they have constructed from their limited range of experiences.

> Young children tend to restrict their view of plants to things found in the garden. They tend to exclude things which science views as plants (for example, mature trees). Many children associate friction only with movement and do not consider that frictional forces exist if two surfaces are not moving relative to one another.

In order to help children acquire the accepted scientific ideas teachers need to take account of what ideas children may already have. An approach to teaching science which starts by finding out what children already think or believe about the aspect which is to be taught can help the teacher identify what direction needs to be taken or what issues should be addressed. This approach requires that the teacher becomes an effective questioner, and this will only come with practice. Throughout section 2 teacher-questions are provided in the starting points sections, and provide useful starting points in this process.

■ SCIENTIFIC INVESTIGATION (DEVELOPING A PROCEDURAL UNDERSTANDING)

Scientific investigation is a powerful procedure that can allow children to test their own ideas, models, and emerging understanding of the world around them. Performing scientific investigations encourages children to think so that they can be helped to understand better the key ideas of science.

At a very simple level this means asking children to first predict what they think will happen and then to test out their ideas and find out if they are right. They are more likely to learn, remember and understand if they are able to think about and try out ideas for themselves.

Obviously there is insufficient time and resources available when teaching science at Key Stage 2 to allow children to investigate every idea in every different circumstance. There are many good reasons why some ideas are best taught without requiring children to investigate. The teacher is crucial in exercising judgement about selecting the most appropriate approach for teaching a particular aspect of science. Neither can children be expected to perform investigations without help. They need to be taught a way to think through ideas and solve problems. They need a framework within which to operate. Teachers can best develop this framework and encourage this approach to critical thinking through the use of effective questioning.

A FRAMEWORK FOR DEVELOPING SCIENTIFIC INVESTIGATIONS AT KEY STAGE 2

Investigations can be regarded as consisting of three stages, each stage relating to one of the strands within Attainment Target 1.

Generating ideas and planning – strand (i)
At this stage children are encouraged to make predictions, consider what might cause certain things to happen and what might affect different events. They should also begin to make decisions about how they might test out their ideas. This is essentially a thinking stage: when discussing ideas in groups, with the teacher, and/or with others, and writing and drawing ideas on paper would be helpful.

Doing – strand (ii)
At this stage children will be carrying out their own tests that they have designed for themselves, considering whether or not they are fair, modifying their tests if they need to in order to obtain meaningful results. At this time children will be actively engaged in experimenting, observing and taking measurements. They may be working in small groups, in pairs, on their own or with the teacher. This can take time, depending on the nature of the investigation and how many aspects are being investigated.

Concluding – strand (iii)
At this stage children will be considering the results they have obtained, relating them to their original idea, prediction or hypothesis and drawing conclusions. This once again is predominantly a thinking stage, enabling children to reflect on what they have found out. Putting their ideas down on paper, comparing their results with others and discussing their findings can help develop their critical abilities.

SCIENTIFIC INVESTIGATIONS

Teachers can help children develop their abilities by prompting them with 'effective questions' which guide them through the process.

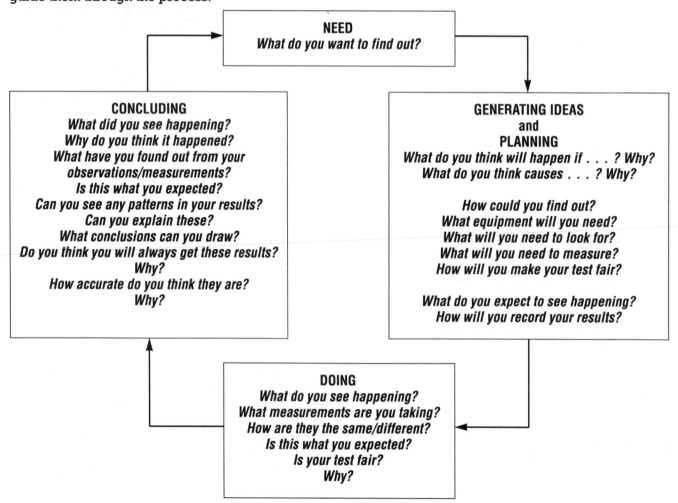

MANAGING SCIENTIFIC INVESTIGATIONS

Scientific investigation (Sc1) does not just mean 'practical work' in science. Performing investigations will require children to employ a range of practical skills, each of which needs to be taught and practised. However, scientific investigation is much more. It is a strategy for thinking scientifically. It is this strategy that needs to be carefully developed, which will enable children to approach and solve problems in a systematic and logical manner. It is also a very creative process and is a way of 'finding out'.

Developing children's approach to investigation needs careful management. It is important for children to recognise that there are important stages to any investigation. The first stage, about generating ideas, needs time. The use of effective teacher questioning is important here, and children need to be encouraged to write down or record in some way their predictions and/or hypotheses. This stage should not be rushed and sufficient time needs to be allocated for children to think about what they expect to happen and why. This stage is also important for the teacher since it is now that the misconceptions that children hold often reveal themselves. Encouraging children to 'brainstorm' ideas together as a class or small groups is valuable and will enable them to learn from each other. Once ideas have been generated children need further time to plan their investigation. The use of devices such as the photocopiable wallchart checklist (p. 10) or photocopiable planning sheet (p. 11) can help organise thinking and emphasises the need, where

appropriate, to consider how they will make their tests fair. It is also important to provide access to a range of equipment at this stage, for example different types of rulers – metre stick, ruler, tape measure, etc. – so that children can select the most appropriate instrument for each task.

In the second 'doing' stage, children will need to employ their practical skills such as observation and measuring. Once again questioning is important *What do you notice? How are they the same/different? What are you measuring?* Once again such standard questions can be provided on the wallchart. It is also important at this stage to provide sufficient time and recognise the need that children may have to reconsider what they are doing and try a different approach because their initial plan is not producing the information they wanted, or if they recognise that their test is not fair.

The third and final stage is about concluding and evaluating what they have done. As before children need to be encouraged through appropriate questioning. Questions such as *Can you spot any patterns in your results? What conclusions can you draw?* (or *What do your results tell you?*), will help children make conclusions which they need to be encouraged to write down. Responding to questions such as *How are you sure that your test was fair?* and *Are there any other conclusions you could draw from your results?* will help children evaluate what they have done. These questions can be provided on the wallchart.

2
Planning Activities At Key Stage 2

USING THE COMMENTARIES

In the following section each part of the Programme of Study for Key Stage 2 is addressed in turn, starting with that for scientific investigation (Sc1). The supporting commentary provides some general teaching ideas, followed by some photocopiable prompt sheets which can be used to structure pupil's thinking when they are engaged in scientific investigations.

The parts of the Programme of Study for Sc2, Sc3 and Sc4 are dealt with strand by strand, e.g. Sc2 strand (i) life processes and the organisation of living things.

■ On each occasion the Programme of Study is preceded by information indicating how ideas are developed across the three key stages. This should provide teachers with some indication of the depth of treatment required as well as providing information about learning in the other key stages.

■ The Programme of Study highlights reference words in **bold** type which can be found as entries in the A to Z reference section.

■ Following the Programme of Study, information is provided on common misconceptions and/or children's developing ideas.

■ A commentary is then provided which contains a number of suggestions for teaching that part of the Programme of Study, with some ideas for starting points.

■ Each commentary is supplemented by a number of ideas for scientific investigations which relate directly to each part of the Programme of Study under consideration. For each strand, some investigations are developed in more detail to be used as exemplar material. This consists of photocopiable childrens' stimulus sheets and teachers' notes.

ATTAINMENT TARGET 1

■ DEVELOPMENT OF KEY IDEAS

	KS1	KS2	KS3
strand (i)	making predictions	making predictions and hypotheses based on knowledge	making predictions and hypotheses based on scientific knowledge
strand (ii)	making observations beginning to measure	increasingly quantified observations carrying out fair tests	more precise observations and measurements controlling wider range of variables in fair test
strand (iii)	simple summaries beginning to draw conclusions, recognising the need to make tests fair	identifying patterns in results drawing simple conclusions beginning to recognise that there may be different ways of explaining results	drawing conclusions which recognise patterns recognising the limitations of the evidence evaluating the design of the experiment

■ PROGRAMME OF STUDY

Pupils should be encouraged to develop investigative skills and understanding of science through activities which:

- Help them to use and develop scientific knowledge and understanding.
- Encourage the raising and answering of questions.
- Foster understanding and practice of safety and care.
- Are within their everyday experience and provide opportunities to explore with increasing precision.
- Build on existing practical skills.
- Require an increasingly systematic approach involving the identification and manipulation of key **variables**.
- Involve the use of secondary sources as well as first-hand observation.
- Include the use of computers and simple electronic devices, such as digital watches, in their experimental work.

These activities should:

- Involve variables to be controlled in the development of 'fair tests'.
- Involve problems which can be solved qualitatively, but which increasingly allow for some **quantification** of the variables.
- Encourage the formulation of testable **hypotheses**, drawing on their developing knowledge and understanding.
- Develop skills of using equipment and measurement, encouraging them to make decisions about when, what and how to measure.
- Encourage systematic listing and recording of data, for example in *frequency tables* and *bar charts*.
- Promote the search for patterns in data.
- Foster the interpretation of data and evaluation against the demands of the problem.
- Involve the capture, transmission, storage and retrieval of information using computers and sensors.
- Encourage pupils to appraise their investigations and suggest improvements to their methods.

■ COMMENTARY AND STARTING POINTS

Scientific investigation is a 'process' which for assessment purposes is divided into three strands, each strand relating to a stage in the process.

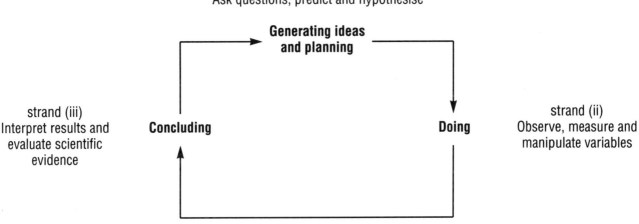

strand (i)
Ask questions, predict and hypothesise

**Generating ideas
and planning**

strand (iii)
Interpret results and
evaluate scientific
evidence

Concluding

Doing

strand (ii)
Observe, measure and
manipulate variables

Pupils will need to be made aware that when they are investigating they are going through a process which can be considered to consist of three stages. They need to know what these three stages are and what is expected of them at each stage. Teachers can guide children through these stages using a series of prompts or 'effective questions'. As a useful starting point it is often helpful to post questions identifying these stages on the wall, for example:

Starting point	What do you want to find out?
Stage 1	What do you think?
Stage 2	How could you find out?
Stage 3	What did you find out?

In order to make investigations manageable they need to start with a clear question or idea which needs to be investigated. These ideas can come from the children from something they notice or from the teacher put to the children as a challenge.

In order for children to demonstrate attainment at Level 3 and above, the investigations will need to involve variables. As a rule of thumb a question of the type *What factors affect . . . ?* or *What affects . . . ?* provides a useful starting point. Such questions should enable children to make *I think . . . because . . .* type responses. Some starting points for investigations:

- What affects the grip of training shoes?
- What factors affect how well plants grow?
- What do seeds need to germinate?
- Do woodlice prefer some conditions to others?
- What might affect the swing of a pendulum?

Introducing children to such investigations can usefully start by 'brainstorming' ideas with a group or the class. For example, one might expect

responses to *What affects how long a pendulum takes to swing?* such as *I think the length of the string will make a difference. I think the weight on the end will make a difference* and *I think the higher you let it go the longer it will take because it has further to go*, etc. Once children have suggested a range of ideas, they can be asked to consider how they might test one or each of them. For example, for *How could we find out if the length makes a difference?* a reply might be *We could try making pendulums with different length strings and time them – I think the longer the string the slower it will swing.* Such a response can be followed by *How will you make it fair?* which in turn could prompt thinking about designing a fair test with comments such as *By keeping the weight the same and letting it go from the same height* or *By keeping everything else the same*. Ideas can be further developed by further prompts.

Throughout this section, each strand contains a list of suggested starting points for investigations, together with some possible responses, some ideas for testing and some suggestions for conclusions.

Each investigation is linked to a part of the Programme of Study for either Sc2, Sc3 or Sc4. Each investigation has two sheets associated with it. The first is a photocopiable stimulus sheet for the child, the second is teachers' notes. The teachers' notes all follow the same format identifying ways in which the investigation can be introduced, equipment needed and the teachers' questions which will help promote and develop thinking.

Also provided is a planning sheet and a wallchart investigation checklist which can be photocopied and used as indicated on the teachers' sheets.

Scientific investigation

■ What are you trying to find out?

■ What do you think will happen?

■ Why do you think this?

■ How could you find out (if you are right)?

■ What will you need to look for/measure?

■ What equipment will you need?

■ How will you make your test fair?

■ What do your results tell you?

■ Is this what you expected?

Planning my investigation

Name _____

What I want to find out is _____
_____

What I think will happen is _____
_____
_____

I think this will happen because _____
_____
_____

My plan is _____
_____
_____
_____
_____
_____
_____
_____

What I am going to look for, count or measure is _____
_____
_____

The equipment I will need is _____
_____
_____

I will make sure my test is fair by _____
_____
_____

Doing my investigation

Name _____

What I noticed

The measurements I have taken

Concluding my investigation

Name _____

My results tell me

I expected/did not expect this because

I could have improved my investigation by

ATTAINMENT TARGET 2

Strand (i) life processes and the organisation of living things

■ DEVELOPMENT OF KEY IDEAS

	KS1	KS2	KS3
structure	external parts of body and flowering plants	organs of mammals and flowering plants	organisation of plants and animals as cells
life process	growing, feeding, moving, sensing and developing of themselves investigating what plants need to grow and reproduce	basic life processes of themselves and other animals investigate factors affecting plant growth	life processes and photosynthesis respiration, reproduction and growth in plants
health	keeping healthy through diet, rest hygiene and safety medicines	defence systems of body hygiene, dental care, exercise effects of drugs	healthy lifestyles, effect of diet microbes, drugs, HIV adolescence

■ PROGRAMME OF STUDY

(i) life processes and the organisation of living things

Pupils should be introduced to the major **organs** and **organ systems** of **mammals** and **flowering plants**. They should explore some aspects of **feeding**, support, **movement** and behaviour in relation to themselves and other **animals**.

They should explore ideas about the processes of **breathing**, **circulation**, **growth** and **reproduction**. They should investigate the factors that affect **plant growth**, for example, *light intensity*, *temperature* and *amount of water*.

Pupils should study how **microbes** and lifestyle can affect **health**, and learn about factors that contribute to good health including the **defence systems** of the body, **diet**, **personal hygiene**, safe **handling of food**, **dental care** and exercise. They should be introduced to the fact that while all **medicines** are **drugs**, not all drugs are medicines. They should begin to be aware of the harmful effect on health resulting from abuse of **tobacco**, **alcohol** and other drugs.

Associated key words **life processes, tissue, cell, temperature, body temperature, thermometer**

■ PUPILS' OWN IDEAS

Children will know about such things as heart, lungs and stomach but will have not given much thought to the size, position or purpose of each organ except in broad terms. (For example, *The stomach is where the food goes.*) It is unlikely that they will have ideas about the liver or kidneys. Blood is often thought of as being 'everywhere' in the body, and children will not have seen the need to consider the idea of blood being circulated around the body. Children will have often only vague ideas about the criteria for whether something is 'living' or not. Some children include the

Sun, wind and fire as living. Developing ideas about life processes common to animals should help children develop their criteria for 'living' or not. At Key Stage 2 children are asked to investigate the factors which influence plant growth; at Key Stage 1 they will have already investigated what plants need in order to grow. These ideas should be used by encouraging children to remember these ideas and then asking them to consider the quantities of water, light, etc. that are needed. *How much is needed to grow the best plants?*

■ COMMENTARY AND STARTING POINTS

STRUCTURE

When introducing children to the major organs of mammals it is helpful to start with the children themselves. Ask children questions such as *Where do you think your heart is? Where are your lungs? How big are they?* A good starting point is to ask children to draw an outline of their bodies on a large sheet of paper (roll of wallpaper) and then to draw where and how big they think their heart, lungs, eyes, brain, kidneys, liver, stomach, intestines, etc. are. After this activity children can compare their ideas about position and size with pictures in books or models of the human body. Children can then be asked to find out the purpose of each of the organs they have drawn (*Why do we need a liver?*), or make three-dimensional life-size models of the organs from papier mâché (*How long should the tubes of the intestine be? Why do they need to be that long?*). The size and shape of human organs can be compared with those of other mammals by researching in reference books. *How big is an elephant's brain? Why does a cow have two stomachs? How big is a whale's heart?* (One heart from a blue whale weighed about 700 kg.)

Another useful starting point is to once again draw a body outline and then ask the children to feel their own arms, legs, fingers, heads, etc. and to draw on to the outline where they think their bones are. Once again the correct size and positions of the bones can be checked against pictures or model skeletons. This could lead to ideas about support and movement. *Why do we need a skeleton? What would happen if we had no bones? How are the bones in a skeleton joined together?* Organs of flowering plants can be introduced by asking children *What do all plants have in common?* (leaf, stem, root, flower), and then by asking children what they think is the purpose of each part. Children can also explore and identify parts of a flower. A daffodil is a good example. (A supply can be made available each year if the school plants a sackful of bulbs on a bank within the grounds.) The parts of a daffodil flower can then be compared with flowers from other plants. *Do all flowers have the same parts? Do all flowers have the same number of petals?*

LIFE PROCESSES

Children can be introduced to the life processes of animals by asking them how they would recognise whether something is an animal. This could develop into ideas about why we need to breathe and feed, and how we move, grow and reproduce. Children can be encouraged to explore breathing by posing questions such as *How many times do we breathe per minute? Do girls and boys breathe at the same rate?* Most children will know that their breathing rate increases with exercise but most will not have considered by how much. Children can be asked to predict by how much their breathing rate will increase after running a race and how quickly it will return to normal. These ideas can then be tested. The circulation system can be explored by considering pulse rates in similar ways. Other effects of exercise could be explored. *Why do we often look flushed after exercise? What happens to our body temperature and surface temperature after exercise?* Internal body temperature will always remain the same (confirmed by use of a clinical thermometer), whereas surface temperature will increase.

Factors affecting plant growth can be investigated within the context of producing plants quickly for sale (for example, in a market garden). *Can we produce cress or tomatoes for sale more quickly? What could we change that would make the plants grow quicker?* Seeds which germinate quickly and produce fast-growing plants are best, for example chick peas, cress, mustard, beans.

HEALTH

Ideas about health are best developed within the context of a whole school approach; however, a useful starting point might be to ask children what they feel like when they are ill and *How does the doctor know you are ill? What does she/he look for?* This can be developed through questions such as *Why do you think our temperature goes up when we get ill? What do you think is happening?* (Comparison can be drawn here with exercise in that whilst we get 'hot' during exercise our internal body temperature remains unchanged.) Through discussion and reference books, children can be introduced to the ideas of the body's defence systems. Working in small groups children can be asked to generate their own ideas about the ways in which we become ill. *What things can make us ill?* Children could produce a poster of their ideas. These ideas could then be discussed or checked using reference books. Another way of checking ideas is to invite the local doctor or nurse to visit to discuss the children's ideas. If a visitor is to be invited it is a good idea for the children to convert their ideas into questions. Children could generate their own guidelines for staying healthy.

■ IDEAS FOR INVESTIGATIONS – Key Stage 2 Sc2 (i) life processes and the organisation of living things

Investigation *Starting point*	Strand (i) Generating ideas and planning *Pupil's suggestion*	Strand (ii) Doing *Pupil's activity*	Strand (iii) Concluding *Pupils could . . .*
Early in Key Stage 2			
What do plants need to stay alive?	*I think plants need/water/soil/warmth/rain/ light/food, etc. (If food is suggested prompt children to explain what they mean.)*	Set up fair tests to test their ideas.	Say which plants live/die and thus what conditions plants need.
What sort of people can jump furthest?	*I think tall people/young people/short people/people with long legs jump furthest.*	Compare jumps using fair tests using groups of tall/short, young/old, etc.	Say which groups jumped furthest and so tall people jump further, etc.
Later in Key Stage 2			
What affects how well plants grow?	*I think the amount of light/amount of heat/amount of water/colour of soil/amount of fertilizer, etc.* *I think the more light the better it will grow* *I think the more water the better it will grow, etc.*	Set up a series of plants under different light conditions/temperatures/soil colours, etc. and watch for 2–3 weeks, making sure each test is fair.	Say what they saw happening to each plant and that the more light there was the better the plant grew or the plants with a medium amount of water grew best, etc.
What affects how fast we can run?	*I think taller people run faster/people with longest legs run faster/lighter people run faster.* *(If strength or fitness is mentioned, prompt How can we measure strength/fitness?)*	Test a series of people of various heights over a course making sure the test is fair.	Make a chart of who covered the distance in what time and so who was fastest and what patterns there are, e.g. do people with longer legs run faster, etc.
What affects breathing rate?	*I think that the taller you are the slower you breathe/the bigger you are the slower you breathe, or I think the fitter you are the slower you breathe/the faster you run the quicker you breathe.*	Test a series of different people of different heights or weights, etc. A simple test for fitness could be to find out how many step tests can be done in a minute.	Make a chart of different breathing rates against height or weight, etc. State whether there are any patterns, for example the taller the person the slower they breathe or there is no connection between breathing rate and height or weight, etc.
What is the connection between pulse rate and breathing rate?	*I think that the quicker you breathe the quicker your pulse rate because I think that if you double your breathing rate you double your pulse rate. I think that people with faster breathing rates have faster pulse rates.*	Compare breathing rates and pulse rates of one person when they are standing still, after walking, after running slowly and running fast; or compare breathing rates and pulse rates of a number of different people.	Make a table of results, plot a graph, state whether there is a connection/pattern. (Are the points in a straight line?) Plot a scattergram of pulse rate against breathing rate for the different people. Is there a connection?

What affects how quickly we breathe?

■ Have you noticed that sometimes we breathe more quickly than normal?

■ Why do you think this is?

■ What do you think makes us breathe more quickly?

■ TEACHERS' NOTES

WHAT AFFECTS HOW QUICKLY WE BREATHE?

This investigation can be introduced when children are beginning to explore ideas about breathing. A good way of starting is to ask the children to measure their breathing rates. (How many breaths did they take in a minute?) The best way of doing this is to pair children and then to ask one child to count the number of breaths their partner takes in one minute. The breathing rates for the whole class can be recorded. This should demonstrate some differences in breathing rates of individuals.

Resources
■ stopclocks
■ watches
■ clocks
■ sandtimers

Questions to help develop thinking

Why do you think there is a difference?
What do you think might make a difference?
Write down as many reasons as you can why someone might breathe faster.

The intention is to encourage children to generate ideas which can be tested.

If volunteered ideas are scarce, some of the following further prompts may be useful.

Do you think tall people breathe slower?
Do you think boys breathe faster than girls?
Do you think running will make us breathe faster?
Do you think cycling will make us breathe faster?
Do you think walking will make us breathe faster?
Do you think watching television will make us breathe faster?

Once a number of ideas have been generated children can be encouraged to select one or more and to test each to find out whether it is correct. A planning sheet will help organise their thoughts.

Conclusions

Children should be encouraged to draw conclusions from their results making simple statements such as *Running makes me breathe faster than walking*. Patterns such as *The faster I run the faster I breathe* are also possible. It is equally important to state such conclusions as *How tall you are makes no difference to how fast you breathe*.

Children should discover that different people have different breathing rates, walking, running and cycling makes us breathe faster, and there is no apparent connection between height or sex or weight and breathing rate.

In adults slow breathing rates are linked to fitness; in children breathing rates can vary considerably.

Safety

Before asking pupils to exercise teachers need to be aware of any medical conditions (for example, asthma) which might place pupils at risk and should take appropriate action.

What is the connection between pulse rate and breathing rate?

■ When we exercise, our breathing rate goes up as our body needs more oxygen.

■ Have you noticed that our hearts seem to beat faster as well? Why do you think this is? Do you think there is a connection?

■ Our pulse is a measure of how fast our heart is beating.

■ What do you think is the connection between our pulse rate and breathing rate and why?

■ TEACHERS' NOTES

WHAT IS THE CONNECTION BETWEEN BREATHING RATE AND PULSE RATE?

This investigation could be introduced later in Key Stage 2 after children have already explored some ideas about breathing and have discussed ideas about the body needing more oxygen as it works harder. Children may well have already measured breathing rates and pulse rates; if not they will need to be shown how to do so. This investigation provides children with the opportunity to apply their knowledge about the body's need for more oxygen to help release more energy as it works harder. It may be logical to predict that the heart will quicken as the body works harder to ensure that the oxygen is delivered around the body more quickly, and because breathing rate increases so will the pulse rate. It will also provide the opportunity for children to identify any patterns in their results.

> **Resources**
>
> ■ stopclocks
> ■ watches
> ■ clocks
> ■ sandtimers
> ■ diagrams showing where and how to take a pulse
> ■ instructions for measuring breathing rates

Questions to help develop thinking

What happens to the air that we breathe in?
Where does the air go?
Why do we breathe more rapidly when we are running?
What is our pulse and what does it tell us?
Does our pulse rate go up when we run?
Why do you think this?
Do you think there is a connection between breathing rate and pulse rate?
What do you think the connection might be?

Questioning should encourage children to make statements such as:

I think that doubling the breathing rate will double the pulse rate, and increasing the breathing rate will increase the pulse rate by a lesser amount.

Children can use a planning sheet to organise their thoughts.

Conclusions

Children can be encouraged to draw conclusions which include simple patterns such as the faster the breathing rate the faster the pulse rate. They can also be encouraged to plot graphs of breathing rate against pulse rate. Children could discover that both breathing rates and pulse rates can easily double after exercise, at rest the breathing rate is much less than the pulse rate (in adults breathing rates of about 30 breaths per minute and pulse rates of about 70 per minute are common), and there is a connection between breathing rate and pulse rate.

Safety

Before asking pupils to exercise teachers need to be aware of any medical conditions (for example, asthma) which might place pupils at risk and should take appropriate action.

ATTAINMENT TARGET 2

Strand (ii) variation and the mechanisms of inheritance and evolution

■ DEVELOPMENT OF KEY IDEAS

	KS1	KS2	KS3
variation	similarities and differences between themselves and some animals and plants sorted into broad groups	investigate and measure similarities and differences in locally occurring plants, animals and themselves make and use simple keys	wider range of animals and plants consider trends and norms
evolution	recognise that some life forms are extinct	introduce fossils	consider causes of variation and extinction
inheritance	taking care of living things	introduce ideas of inheritance	introduce the gene and mechanisms for inheritance and selective breeding

■ PROGRAMME OF STUDY

(ii) variation and the mechanisms of inheritance and evolution

Pupils should investigate and measure the similarities and differences between themselves, animals and plants and fossils.

They should be introduced to how **plants** and **animals** can be preserved as **fossils**.

They should have the opportunity to develop skills in identifying locally occurring **species** of animals and plants by observing structural features and making and using simple **keys**.

They should be introduced to the idea that information is passed from one **generation** to the next.

Associated key words **major groups** (**animals** and **plants**), **gene, selective breeding**

■ PUPILS' OWN IDEAS

Young children will often have a narrow view of 'animal', only accepting vertebrates or mammals as belonging to this group, and not insects, worms, slugs, snails or humans. At Key Stage 2 children should have experiences which involve a wide range of animal life. Teacher's language can often be helpful here, for example by saying . . . *This is an insect, a type of animal.* The same is true of children's view of 'plant'; since they will often not regard trees or vegetables as plants, they once again need to be encouraged to think of the term plant in a wider scientific view.

At Key Stage 1 children would have considered differences and similarities between themselves and some other living things. At Key Stage 2 they are asked to investigate and measure these. Children find it easier to recognise differences than similarities. Also at Key Stage 2 these ideas should develop into making and using keys.

■ COMMENTARY AND STARTING POINTS

VARIATION

In developing ideas about variation in living things as many different species as possible should be investigated. Some variation to look for in themselves is: eye colour, height, weight, length of ear lobe, tongue rolling ability, hair colour, hand span and foot size. Ask *Is there a connection between hair colour and eye colour? Do the tallest people always have the biggest feet? Do taller people have the largest hand spans?* to help children investigate variations amongst themselves and build on earlier studies at Key Stage 1 where they will probably have drawn bar charts of eye and hair colour for the class. Also at Key Stage 2 there should be more opportunities to measure variations.

Variation in other animals might include: pattern on snail shells, size of snails, and on a trip to the zoo, stripes on a zebra and patterns on a tiger. Ask *Are all snail shell patterns the same? How many different variations are there? Is there a connection between size and pattern? Do all zebras have the same pattern of stripes? Can you tell them apart?* to help children investigate variation amongst other animals.

Variation in plants could be: different patterns on clover leaves, leaf shape of dandelions, length of oak leaves, tree height, and leaf shape, colour or size.

Investigations can be initiated by asking such questions as *Are all clover leaves the same? How many different patterns on the leaves can you spot? How many different dandelion leaf shapes are there? Is there a connection between shape and size?*

Asking such questions as *Is there a connection between snail shell colour or pattern and where they live?* can also lead to ideas about how living things are suited to the surroundings (Sc2(iii)).

Investigating habitats (Sc2 strand(iii)) provides many opportunities to identify species using keys. Children can also make their own simple yes/no or branching keys which allow others to identify the organisms they have found.

EVOLUTION

A useful starting point when considering how fossils are formed is to look at a collection of fossils or fossil models and discuss ideas about how they might have been formed. This can lead to children being challenged to make their own 'fossils' using leaves, shells, Plasticine, clay, and plaster of Paris (see **fossil**).

INHERITANCE

A good starting point for introducing the idea that information is passed on through generations is to look at family histories for similarities in eye colour or hair colour. Obviously care needs to be exercised with this activity to avoid problems. Sensitivity needs to be exercised with children from single parent families and adopted children.

Asking questions such as *What leaf patterns will the seed from this clover plant produce? Will the seeds from the tallest sunflower produce the tallest sunflowers next year?* also provide good starting points for developing ideas on the passage of information from one generation to another.

■ IDEAS FOR INVESTIGATION – Key Stage 2 Sc2 (ii) variation and the mechanisms of inheritance and evolution

Investigation *Starting point*	Strand (i) Generating ideas and planning *Pupil's suggestion*	Strand (ii) Doing *Pupil's activity*	Strand (iii) Concluding *Pupils could . . .*
Early in Key Stage 2			
Is there a connection between shoe size and height?	*I think taller people have bigger feet.*	Compare shoe size and height by taking a series of measurements of children in the class or children in different years and perhaps some teachers.	Children could list their results in a table, plot their measurements on a class scattergram. State whether they see a pattern.
Is there a connection between leaf size and shape in dandelion leaves?	*I think that the bigger leaves have rougher edges/are more wavy (more serrations).*	Measure the size of some dandelion leaves and count the number of serrations.	List the results in a table and state whether they see a pattern. Do bigger leaves have more serrations?
Will the size of a seed affect how tall a plant grows?	*I think that the longer/fatter the seed the taller the plant will grow. I think it will make no difference.*	Try planting long seeds in one half of a tub and short seeds in the other, label which is which and let them grow, measuring height of plants after 2–3 weeks; making sure that their test is fair, for example they give both halves same amount of water, same amount of light/warmth, etc.	Make a chart showing short seed heights and tall seed heights and state that there is no difference in the average height of plants from each type of seed, or that they see a pattern.
Later in Key Stage 2			
Which sunflower seeds will make the best plants? (Does anything about the seed affect how well it will grow?)	*I think that the fatter seeds/the larger seeds/the seeds with the thicker coats/the more stripes will make the best plants.*	Test their ideas, making sure their tests are fair, for example keep the amount of water the same/the light the same. Also if they are comparing stripes that they keep the size the same, etc.	Make a chart of their results, stating whether they see a pattern or not, and say whether this was what they expected.
Does our size affect how we move?	*I think that the taller we are the faster we can run/the shorter we are the faster we can run. The taller we are the higher we can jump.*	Test their ideas by designing fair tests by comparing children within the class measuring height, distance jumped, or time taken to run 30 metres.	Make a scattergram of their results stating any patterns they observe.
What differences (or variations) in seeds might affect their germination rates?	*I think the size/the thickness of the coat/the length might make a difference.*	Design fair tests to test their ideas. Controlling such factors as amount of water/light/heat, etc., as well as other variations within the seed. When investigating length, thickness of coat must be the same (about).	Design their own charts/graphs showing comparison, stating any patterns they see, and possible explanations. Is this what they expected?
What might affect leaf size of dandelions? What might affect size of clover leaves (or oak leaves?)	*I think that where they grow/how much Sun they get/how damp it is/the type of soil will affect the size.*	Children could measure leaves in different places noting the conditions they find them in. In for example sunny areas/dark areas (noting whether the areas were similar in other ways – same degree of dampness, etc.).	Design their own charts/graphs noting any patterns and consider different interpretations of the evidence.

Do you think there is a connection between the height of a person and their shoe size?

- We know that some people are taller than others and we know that some people take bigger shoe sizes.

- Do you think that taller people take bigger shoe sizes or do you think height makes no difference?

- Why do you think this?

■ TEACHERS' NOTES

DO YOU THINK THERE IS A CONNECTION BETWEEN THE HEIGHT OF A PERSON AND THEIR SHOE SIZE?

This investigation can be introduced when children are exploring variation by investigating similarities and differences between themselves. It encourages children to look for patterns and identify connections. Having tried this activity children could be asked to suggest other connections, for example *Do blue eyes and fair hair always go together?* Such activities can help children discover more about variation and make predictions drawing on their developing knowledge and understanding.

> **Resources**
>
> ■ metre rules
> ■ tape measures
> ■ chalks and boards on which to mark heights

Questions to help develop thinking

Do you think that taller people have bigger shoe sizes?
Do you think there is a connection?
Why do you think that?
How could we find out if you are right?
What will we need to measure?
How many people will we need to measure?
Do you think we might get a different answer if we measured more people?
How will we record our results so that they show what we need to know?
What other connections do you think there might be?
Do you think taller people have darker hair, longer arms and bigger heads?
Is there a connection between hair colour and eye colour? Do people with blue eyes have fair hair?

Children can use a planning sheet to organise their thoughts.

Conclusions

Children can be encouraged to make conclusions in simple general terms. *Taller people tend to have larger feet.* They should also be encouraged to recognise that their findings (which may differ from the above) may not be valid with older people or if a wider range of children were included. Children should find that such a general pattern exists although growing children will exhibit wide variations and the hypothesis may not be true for the group of children tested.

What affects how quickly a seed will germinate?

- Have you noticed that some seeds seem to germinate faster than others? Why do you think this is?

- Look at the seeds provided. In what ways are they different? Which seeds do you think will germinate first and why? Write down your ideas like this: 'I think that .... seeds will germinate first because ....'

- Make a plan of how you could find out if you are right. Use your Planning Sheet to help you.

■ TEACHERS' NOTES

WHAT AFFECTS HOW QUICKLY A SEED WILL GERMINATE?

This investigation can be introduced when children are exploring variation or growth. It will encourage pupils to look for differences amongst seeds and consider whether or not these have an influence on germination rate. They might for instance consider the size of a seed, weight of a seed, thickness of coat or whether the coat is torn or damaged. Broad bean or sunflower seeds (which have numbers of stripes as an additional variation) are suitable. Children should be provided with a collection of seeds of the same type (they could on another occasion investigate the effect of type on germination rate) and be given time to handle the seeds, compare and perhaps measure them.

Performing this investigation should help children realise that water needs to penetrate the seed coat before germination can take place.

Questions to help develop thinking

Do you think that all the seeds will germinate at the same time? Why not?
Which will germinate first? Why?
Do you think size, weight, shape, thickness of the seed coat or its colour/number of stripes will make a difference to the germination time?
How can you find out if you are right?
How will you make sure your test is fair?
How many seeds will you need to test?
How will you know when the seed has germinated? What will you look for?
What will you need to measure – if anything?

Conclusions

Children can be encouraged to make simple conclusions such as *The colour of the seed coat makes no difference to how quickly the seed germinates*. They should be encouraged to appreciate that such apparently 'negative' results are important. They should find that the variables listed, such as colour, number of stripes, size, weight appear to make no difference to germination rate. The condition of the seed will affect its rate of germination; for example whether its seed coat is damaged. The age of the seed will also make a difference.

Resources

- ■ seeds – broad bean, sunflower, chickpea, sweetpea, pea, runner bean
- ■ electronic kitchen scales (sensitive to at least 0.5g)
- ■ rulers
- ■ paint colour chart (to match shades of colour)
- ■ water supply
- ■ measuring jugs
- ■ seed trays
- ■ soil
- ■ damp cloths
- ■ blotting paper
- ■ jam jars

ATTAINMENT TARGET 2

Strand (iii) populations and human influences within ecosystems

■ DEVELOPMENT OF KEY IDEAS

	KS1	KS2	KS3
habitat	study plants and animals in their local habitats	environmental conditions competition	variety of habitats factors affecting population size
human activity	humans change environment	consider effects of types of human activity on the environment pollution	wider range of activity and its effect on air and water quality

■ PROGRAMME OF STUDY

(iii) populations and human influences within ecosystems

Pupils should explore and investigate at least two different **habitats** and the **animals** and **plants** that live there. They should find out how animals and plants are suited to these locations and how they are influenced by **environmental conditions** including **seasonal changes** and **daily changes** and measure these changes using a variety of instruments. They should develop an awareness and understanding of the necessity for sensitive collection and care of **living things** used as the subject of any study of the **environment**.

They should study aspects of the local environment affected by human activity, for example *farming*, *industry*, *mining* or *quarrying* and consider the benefits and detrimental effects of these activities.

They should be made aware of **competition** between living things and their need for food, shelter and a place to reproduce.

They should study the effects of **pollution** on the survival of living things.

Associated key words **ecosystem**, **survival**, **predation**, **life processes**

■ PUPILS' OWN IDEAS

Children tend to think that smaller animals and plants are always younger and that the larger organisms are older. Thus when studying how light or shade might affect the size of a leaf within a particular species care needs to be taken that the children appreciate that these plants are not just different ages (link with variation).

Children also do not often think of food being a scarce commodity for animals since they think that animals can move to where there is food,

hence competition between animals is often only thought of in terms of them fighting each other. Competition between plants tends to be easier for children to accept because the plants cannot move.

Children also tend to think of pollution as something that kills and rarely will they have considered how pollution may affect organisms in other ways, for example how noise might disturb animals' breeding behaviour.

■ COMMENTARY AND STARTING POINTS

HABITAT

Before visiting a habitat, asking children questions such as *What do you think lives there? What do you expect to find?* and *Why?* can help them to begin to appreciate that there are good reasons why different plants and animals are found in different places and that this may have something to do with how they are suited to their environment. Children can then explore the habitat, trying to find and identify as many different organisms as possible in order to confirm their ideas. Habitats such as a school field, wall, waste ground, individual tree, soil, leaf litter, hedgerow, meadow, woodland, pond, ditch, stream, seashore and sand dunes will provide a wide range from which to select. Questions such as *What conditions do you think woodlice prefer?* or *What sorts of plants can we find in sunny and shady places?* can also help children focus on the ideas that organisms live where the conditions suit them.

Setting up a patch garden consisting of different squares, each containing a different soil such as peat (acid), lime (alkaline), clay (poorly drained) and sand (well drained), and planting each square with the same plants will also help develop the idea that plants are suited to different conditions. Some plants are better suited to certain soils. Cabbage and kohlrabi prefer lime soil, onions and parsnips prefer acid soil, carrots and lettuce prefer sandy soil, and broad beans and cauliflower prefer clay soil. Children can sow seeds and over a period observe the way in which the plants grow in the different conditions. *Do you think the plants will grow the same in each soil? Which do you think will be the best soil? Why do you think that?* can provide useful starting points for this exploration. This can also provide children with the opportunity to measure the acidity of soils (using an indicator such as red cabbage solution), the temperature of soil and the water content of each type of soil. (Links with Sc3(i) and Sc3(iv).) Choosing a particular habitat (for example, the school field, soil, or a tree) and asking children to think about what changes they would expect to see in the spring, summer, autumn or winter, making a note of their predictions by writing or drawing, can provide a useful starting point for exploring seasonal changes. These predictions can be stored and retrieved at different points in the year for children to check their ideas, and record any differences from those which they expected. *What will the weather be like in summer and spring? How do you think this might affect the living things we found? What changes do you expect to see?* are all useful prompts.

HUMAN ACTIVITY AND COMPETITION

When exploring habitats children can be encouraged to look for differences in the sizes of one type of plant and to think about why this should be so. For example plantain plants can be found with large leaves and with small leaves. The large-leaved plants are often those which are found among other tall plants or in the shade, where they are competing for resources such as sunlight. The ideas of competition can be further developed by sowing different quantities of cress seeds in containers of the same size. Questions such as *Do you think the plants will all grow to look the same? Why do you think that?* can help children to think about the idea of competition. Observing how these plants develop with questions such as *Why do the plants look different? Why are some tall and spindly?* will also help. Children can also be encouraged to think about competition between animals within a habitat through questions such as *How many rabbits, foxes, and caterpillars do you think live here? Why? Why don't you think there will be more?*

Encourage children to speculate with prompts. *What will happen if . . . ?* can provide a good starting point which will help children appreciate how human activity may affect living things in different habitats. *What do you think would happen to the living things we found in the meadow if a local company discovered gravel below the surface and began quarrying . . . ? What changes would the quarrying bring about?* (For example, noise, vibration and removal of soil.) *How would each of these affect the living things we found?* Simulations and discussions about the siting of a new quarry or mine provide good opportunities to discuss the benefits and detrimental effects of the activity. The effects of pollution on living things can be studied initially through the use of news stories and pictures of disasters such as oil spills where the effects are obvious. Ideas about the effects of pollution can be further developed by considering how less obvious situations might affect living things without necessarily killing them, for example smoke and dust from factories coating the leaves of plants thus reducing their ability to photosynthesise. The children might also consider how this might affect other living things in the food chain.

IDEAS FOR INVESTIGATIONS – Key Stage 2 Sc2 (iii) populations and human influences within ecosystems

Investigation / Starting point	Strand (i) Generating ideas and planning / Pupil's suggestion	Strand (ii) Doing / Pupil's activity	Strand (iii) Concluding / Pupils could . . .
Early in Key Stage 2			
Where would these cress seeds grow best and best?	I think that these cress seeds would grow best in the Sun/in the warm/in moist soil.	Set up their cress seeds in different places making sure that their tests are fair (i.e. same type/amount of soil (if used) same container/same number of seeds, etc.).	Say in which places the cress grew best and whether this is what they expected and saying how they made sure their test was fair.
Where would you find most daisies?	I think I would find most daisies in the open/in a field/in a wood.	Visit different places recording how many daisy plants they find in similar sized areas (for example, 20 paces by 20 paces).	Say where they found most daisies growing and whether this is what they expected.
How might the length of daylight affect the growth of plants? (or seedlings?)	I think that the seedlings would grow best during long days because they need sun to grow.	Set up an investigation where they leave some seedlings in the Sun for the whole day, some for one hour, some for two hours, and some for four hours, measuring the height of the seeds after one week and two weeks.	Say which plants grew best and why they did so (related to sunlight).
Later in Key Stage 2			
What sorts of conditions do woodlice prefer?	I think that woodlice prefer damp/dark/dry/light.	Design a series of fair tests involving woodlice and lunch boxes, one half dry or one half in the light the other half in the dark. Watch to see where the woodlice spend most of their time.	Make a chart or graph of their results, stating any patterns they see, for example the woodlice spent most of their time in the . . . so this means that woodlice prefer the . . . .
What affects where moss grows?	I think that the amount of light/the temperature/amount of water present might affect where moss grows.	Visit places where moss grows and record conditions comparing them with similar nearby areas where no moss grows, for example light levels, moisture, temperature, etc.	State in which conditions moss was more frequently found growing and suggest possible reasons/interpretations of these results.
Near smoky factories what might affect how well plants grow?	Plants which grow near factories might be smaller because they get covered with dust so do not get so much Sun.	Visit places where plants are near smoky chimneys and where they are not. Compare leaf surfaces and leaf size.	Make a chart of average leaf size against place where found. State any pattern observed and why they think it happened, perhaps what other causes might there be.
Why do you think cress seeds bend when they grow?	I think cress seeds bend towards the light/the warmth, etc.	Design and carry out fair tests to test their ideas, measuring the bend (for example, towards light or towards warmth) using a simple home-made scale or protractor.	State under what conditions the cress seeds were seen to bend and draw conclusions about the causes.
What affects the size of plants in a wood/field?	I think that plants in the wood will be bigger because there is less Sun/will be smaller because there is less Sun/will be bigger because it is sheltered.	Visit different areas recording the sizes of the plants, noting other conditions which might have an effect, for example damp/dry, etc.	State what they observe and any conclusions they could draw, together with other possible interpretations.
What differences might the time of day make to conditions either side of a hedge?	I think that late in the day the North side of the hedge will be colder/will be darker.	Visit hedges at different times of day, take appropriate measurements using light meters/thermometers, etc., record these against the direction hedge is facing, for example N, S, E or W.	State whether the conditions are different and why they think this is. Could there be any other reasons?

What affects how well plants grow?

- In order to keep plants healthy we need to care for them. We need to find the best conditions for them to grow.

- What do you think affects whether a plant, such as a tomato plant, will grow well or not?

- Write down your ideas as a series of statements of the type:
  'I think the tomato plant will grow well with .... because ....'

- Now make a plan of how you could test one (or all) of your ideas.

■ TEACHERS' NOTES

WHAT AFFECTS HOW WELL PLANTS GROW?

This investigation can be introduced as a starting point for children when considering the conditions necessary for plant growth. It will encourage them to make predictions and generate hypotheses based on either everyday experience (knowing that you need to water plants because they have seen this being done at home) (*Level 3*) or some scientific knowledge (knowing that plants need the Sun in order to make food or grow) (*Level 4*). This will enable them to make statements such as *Plants will grow best in bright conditions because they need the Sun to grow (or make food)* (a hypothesis) or *Plants will grow best when the soil is moist*. Young tomato plants are good for this experiment since they respond reasonably quickly to lack of water, light and temperature.

Children could use a planning sheet to help organise their thoughts.

Questions to help develop thinking

What do you think affects how well plants grow?
  (supplementary prompts *Do you think the amount of water, the amount of light or how hot it is will make a difference? What about the type of soil they are in?*)
How can you find out if you are right?
How will you make your test fair?
What will you need to look for or measure?
How often will you need to check your plants?

Conclusions

Children should be encouraged to make statements such as *Plants grow best in brighter light.* Children should find that the light intensity, the amount of water and the temperature influence how well plants grow. Plants need to be kept warm (not too hot nor too cold) and must have sufficient water (overwatering is just as damaging as underwatering).

Resources

- tomato plants (about 7 cm tall. They can be grown easily and cheaply from seed)
- different light conditions (windowsill, dark cupboard, shaded areas, areas at different temperatures but with constant light
- light meter (photographic or similar)
- measuring jugs for water
- rulers and string for measuring
- thermometers

What conditions do woodlice like best?

- You may have noticed that woodlice seem to be found in some places rather than in others.

- What sorts of conditions do you think woodlice prefer?

- Why?

- Can you think of ways of testing your ideas to find out if you are right?

- How will you make sure your test is fair?

■ TEACHERS' NOTES

WHAT CONDITIONS DO WOODLICE LIKE BEST?

This investigation can be introduced as children are finding out about the suitability of living things to their environment. It also helps develop children's awareness of the need to handle living things with care. Woodlice can generally be found under piles of logs or damp stones. A supply can usually be quickly gathered. They can be kept quite safely for a day or two in margarine tubs. Children can be encouraged to make predictions about the sorts of conditions woodlice prefer and then design ways of testing their ideas. This usually involves the construction of some sort of choice chamber where the woodlice can choose their conditions by moving into different areas, for example dry or damp, dark or light.

Questions to help develop thinking

Where do you think woodlice can be found?
Where do you think they prefer to live?
    (Prompts if children have no ideas *Do you think they prefer damp or dry, light or dark, warm or cold?*)
How could you find out if you are right?
How could you make use of these margarine tubs and paper to provide the woodlice with a choice of conditions?
How will you know when the woodlice have made a choice?
How will you make your test fair?
What will you need to look for?
Will you need to measure anything?
How will you record your results?
How many times will you need to do the test to know you are right?

Conclusions

Children should be encouraged to draw conclusions based on their observations, but also to recognise that to be sure then the test needs to be repeated. Different group results in the class can be compared. Children should find that woodlice tend to prefer dark, warm areas but there will be differences.

Resources

- woodlice (about 7 or 8 per pupil-group)
- black paper (to provide blackout)
- desktop lamp (which can provide warmth or light)
- blotting paper (damp and dry)
- plastic trays with dry or damp areas or half-covered with dark-coloured paper to provide dark and light areas to act as choice chambers
- scissors
- rulers
- string
- glue
- Sellotape

ATTAINMENT TARGET 2

Strand (iv) energy flows and cycles of matter within ecosystems

■ DEVELOPMENT OF KEY IDEAS

	KS1	KS2	KS3
energy transfer	plants are the source of all food	green plants use Sun's energy food chains	food pyramids and biomass
recycling	some waste decays, some does not	investigate factors involved in decay	cycling of materials in biological communities biodegradable and non-biodegradable

■ PROGRAMME OF STUDY

(iv) energy flows and cycles of matter within ecosystems

They should be introduced to the idea that **green plants** use **energy** from the **Sun** to produce **food** and that **food chains** are a way of representing feeding relationships.

They should investigate the key factors in the process of **decay** such as **temperature**, moisture, air and the role of **microbes**.

They should build on their investigations of decay and consider the significant features of **waste disposal** procedures, for example, in sewage disposal and composting, and the usefulness of any products.

Associated key words **ecosystem, food pyramid, biomass, biodegradable**

■ PUPILS' OWN IDEAS

Children tend to think that plants get their food from the soil and whilst they may appreciate that the plants need the Sun to live they do not connect this with the Sun's rays providing energy for the plant to make its own food. Even when older children have been taught about photosynthesis, often their views that plants get food from the soil still persist.

When considering what happens to living things when they die and decay, young children often think that plant matter just disappears; later they may consider that it enriches the soil but not that it becomes the soil and is recycled. Some children think that this rotting material is eaten by animals. At Key Stage 2 pupils are gaining experience which should form a basis for beginning to develop their ideas about recycling at Key Stage 3.

At Key Stage 1 children will have considered what sorts of things decay; at Key Stage 2 they will consider what factors affect decay.

■ COMMENTARY AND STARTING POINTS

ENERGY TRANSFER

Children can be introduced to the idea of food chains following the exploration of a habitat. They can label cards with the names of the animals and plants they have found and then find out what eats what using books, other children, or the teacher as sources of information. They can be encouraged to place the animals in order with arrows in between showing the idea of a food chain. Children can be challenged to see who can make the longest chain, or the most food chains. Once this has been done children can make mobiles to illustrate the different food chains within a habitat. Alternatively children could be provided with ready-made cards, perhaps representing the organisms found in a domestic garden and then be asked to make up a number of different food chains, for example:

cabbage → snail → thrush → cat

plant material in soil → earthworm →
    blackbird → fox

rose → greenfly → ladybird

lettuce → caterpillar → frog → fox

lettuce → caterpillar → hedgehog → fox

Through these activities children should be able to see that at the start of each food chain there is always a plant. *What do all these food chains have in common? What is always at the beginning of the food chain?* can help develop this appreciation. *Where does the plant get its food?* can prompt discussion that will enable children to be introduced to the idea that plants make their own food using energy from the Sun. This is a difficult concept and is developed at Key Stages 3 and 4.

Playing a game whereby each child holds one card and then finds something (someone) 'to eat' and also takes their card, can help consolidate the idea that material and energy is passed along a chain. Each time someone loses a card they are out of the game. The game can continue until only a few children (top predators) remain. These children will have a number of cards in their hands. *Did the fox eat the lettuce or the plant material in the soil?* can help children begin to appreciate that the organism at the end of the food chain does not eat everything in that chain. Comparing the 'hands'

that each predator has can also help children appreciate that feeding relationships are more complex than simple chains and that one organism can exist in a variety of different chains. *What would happen if there were no foxes or no snails?* can help develop the ideas.

RECYCLING

Investigations concerning decay are best left to the latter part of the key stage. Children can be challenged to consider what affects how things decay. *What affects how quickly this apple or piece of bread will decay?* could lead them to suggesting ideas about whether it is warm or not, whether it is damp or not and perhaps whether it is exposed to the air or not. The ideas suggested by the children can be used to set up a series of different investigations. *How can we find out if that is true? What will we need to do? What will we need to look for? How will we make our tests fair?* are useful prompts to promote further thinking.

When setting up any investigations involving decay any local *Health and Safety guidelines* (for example, LEA) involving microbes must be followed. If teachers are unsure of the risks involved advice must be sought before attempting any such work. It is advisable to set up the pieces of apple or pieces of bread in sealed plastic bags. These must never be opened and should be disposed of in dustbins at the end of the experiment. Children must not handle decaying material. Bags can be set up in warm places and cold places, containing moisture or not. Air can be partially excluded by placing the piece of apple or bread at the bottom of a tin of dry sand or wrapping tightly in cling film within a plastic bag although this is not easy. Children may suggest other factors which may not affect decay; these too could be investigated. Other suggestions may include light or dark, etc.

After considering and learning about the key factors in decay, children can be challenged to suggest the best conditions for composting, how we may get rid of household rubbish. *Can you find a way of making compost quickly? Can you suggest a way in which we can deal with household waste so that none of it needs to be buried in landfill sites?*

■ IDEAS FOR INVESTIGATIONS – Key Stage 2 Sc2 (iv) energy flows and cycles of matter within ecosystems

Investigation *Starting point*	Strand (i) Generating ideas and planning *Pupil's suggestion*	Strand (ii) Doing *Pupil's activity*	Strand (iii) Concluding *Pupils could . . .*
Early in Key Stage 2			
What sorts of things decay?	*I think that anything we eat decays, but plastic doesn't, nor does metal or cloth.*	Set up tests by placing plant material alongside contrasting materials, for example, plastic, metal. (Do not use meat and do not allow children to handle decaying food. Wrap in bags and dispose of properly).	Write down what they saw and say how this relates to their original idea. Is this what they expected?
How could we make something decay more quickly or more slowly?	*I think we could make things decay more quickly by warming them up or keeping them wet.*	Set up tests where foods (apples, oranges, bread) are placed in warm places, cold places. The bread is wet, the bread is dry. These tests can be made fair by making sure the same size pieces are used and other conditions are constant. Place food in sealed plastic bags.	State what they saw happening and what conclusions they draw (why they think it happened) and how they made the test fair.
What would happen if we left these plants in the dark?	*I think these plants would die or shrivel.*	Try leaving some of the same plants in the dark and some in the light, making sure that both are watered in equal amounts and are at the same temperature to make the investigation fair.	State what they saw happening and what conclusions they draw (why they think it happened) and how they made the test fair.
Later in Key Stage 2			
What affects how quickly things decay?	*I think that the temperature, the amount of water present and the air present will make a difference.*	Design fair tests to test their ideas. Choose the range of temperatures which are appropriate. Make sure only plant material is used in sealed plastic bags.	State what they saw happening, draw conclusions which relate to the prediction, and state any other possible interpretations of their results.
What affects how many aphids are found in a garden?	Before posing this question children will need to have been taught where aphids appear in food chains, and what they feed on. (Sap from growing tips of plants.) *I think that more aphids will be found in warmer weather. More aphids will be found in damp conditions/dry conditions. More aphids will be found in gardens with more rose bushes/where there are fewer ladybirds.*	Decide what needs to be looked for; where, when, and how often, how they will record what they see. Visit gardens at different times of year to record conditions, numbers of aphids found, numbers of ladybirds present.	From their results identify any patterns they see, suggesting reasons for these and offering possible alternative reasons.

What sorts of things decay?

■ You will have noticed that when thrown away some things tend to rot or decay and some do not.

■ What sorts of things do you think decay and what sorts of things do you think do not?

■ Do you know what causes decay?

■ Can you find out and use this information to help you decide?

■ TEACHERS' NOTES

WHAT SORTS OF THINGS DECAY?

At Key Stage 1 children will have been asked to consider how far waste products decay, and why some wastes do not decay. The intention here is that the work should remind them of these ideas and take them a stage further by widening the materials to include all types of substance and begin to find out what causes decay and to link this with the sorts of things that undergo decay.

This investigation is suitable for lower Key Stage 2. It can be followed at a later stage by considering what affects the speed at which something decays (see pages 43–4).

> **Resources**
>
> ■ materials (vegetables, fruits, leaves, wood, etc.) Do not use any animal material, e.g. meat
> ■ plastics
> ■ rubber
> ■ metal
> ■ rock
> ■ plastic bags
> ■ Sellotape
> ■ scissors

Questions to help develop thinking

What sorts of things do you think decay? Why?
Can you decide which of these substances will decay and which will not and why?
How can you find out if you are right?
What will you need to do?
How will you make sure your test is safe? (You must not touch or sniff anything that is rotting.) Would putting things in a sealed plastic bag help?
How will you know whether something is rotting or not?
What will you need to look for?
How long will it take?

Conclusions

Children need to be encouraged to draw simple broad conclusions such as *Things we eat decay, while other things do not decay. Plant material decays, while metals, plastics and rocks do not decay.*

Safety

Great care needs to be exercised when performing any investigations involving microbes since many (even those found on fruit) can be hazardous to health. Any rotting material must be kept in sealed bags and disposed of in a dustbin without removing it from the bag. Do not keep rotting food for longer than is necessary and on no account use meat or animal products in such investigations. Children must not be allowed to handle rotting materials. If teachers are in any doubt about the risks involved advice must be sought from an authoritative body, for example LEA.

What affects how quickly things decay?

■ You will have noticed that some things decay and some do not, and that sometimes things seem to decay more quickly. For example apples sometimes decay quickly and sometimes slowly. What makes a difference to how fast an apple decays?

■ What do you think affects how quickly things decay? What ideas do you have? Write them down.

■ For example, I think things will decay more quickly

when they are _____

because _____.

■ Make a plan of an investigation you could do with pieces of apple which could help you find out if you are right.

SAFETY NOTE

! You must not handle rotting apple, so check with your teacher that when you set up your investigation the pieces of apple are in sealed plastic bags.

■ TEACHERS' NOTES

WHAT AFFECTS HOW QUICKLY THINGS DECAY?

This investigation can be introduced in the latter half of the Key Stage when pupils are considering decay as a key to the process of recycling. As part of their investigations on the key factors in the process of decay children can be encouraged to consider how they might increase the rate of decay. They may suggest warmth, water content, and presence or absence of air. Each of these can be investigated using apple pieces in sealed plastic bags. The plastic bags can be inflated with air before sealing with Sellotape. If children know about microbes as the cause of decay then some may suggest removing the microbes from the apple, for example by boiling the apple to kill the microbes.

Resources

- apple pieces
- plastic bags
- Sellotape
- thermometers
- access to water
- safe places to leave sealed bags for 1–2 weeks

Questions to help develop thinking

What do you think will make something decay more quickly? Why? (Do you think the temperature, moisture, air might make a difference? Why?)
How can you find out if you are right?
What will you need to do?
How will you make sure your test is safe? (You must not touch or sniff anything that is rotting.) Would putting things in a sealed plastic bag help?
How will you know whether something is rotting or not?
What will you need to look for?
How long will it take?
How will you make sure the test is fair?

Conclusions

As a result of their investigations children should be able to state that temperature and the presence of air and water have an effect on the rate of decay. Substances will decay more rapidly in warm conditions yet, if the temperature is too high, decay will slow down and may be prevented.

Safety

Great care needs to be exercised when performing any investigations involving microbes since many (even those found on fruit) can be hazardous to health. Any rotting material must be in sealed bags and disposed of in a dustbin without removing it from the bag. Do not keep rotting food for longer than is necessary and on no account use meat or animal products in such investigations. Children must not be allowed to handle rotting materials. If teachers are in any doubt about the risks involved advice must be sought from an authoritative body, for example LEA.

ATTAINMENT TARGET 3

Strand (i) the properties, classification and structure of materials

■ DEVELOPMENT OF KEY IDEAS

	KS1	KS2	KS3
physical properties	similarities and differences, including shape, colour, texture	grouping according to characteristics including strength, hardness, mass, solubility	main classifications of materials, properties include density, thermal and electrical conductivity
chemical properties	–	acidity and alkalinity, indicators	acids, alkalis, pH grouping as element, compound, mixture and in Periodic Table
processes	dissolving, squashing, pouring, bending, etc	dissolving, filtering, evaporating, chromatography, purifying some mixtures	dissolving, reactions, filtration, distillation, separating and purifying mixtures

■ PROGRAMME OF STUDY

(i) the properties, classification and structure of materials

Pupils should investigate a number of different everyday **materials**, grouping them according to their characteristics. **Properties** such as **strength**, **hardness**, **flexibility**, compressibility, **mass (weight)**, volume and **solubility** should be investigated and related to everyday uses of the materials.

Pupils should be given opportunities to compare a range of **solids**, **liquids** and **gases** and recognise the **properties** which enable **classification of materials** in this way.

Pupils should test the **acidity** and **alkalinity** of safe everyday **solutions** such as *lemon juice*

using **indicators** which may be extracted from plants such as *red cabbage*.

Pupils should know about the dangers associated with the use of some everyday materials including hot oil, bleach, cleaning agents and other household materials.

Experiments on **dissolving** and **evaporation** should lead to developing ideas about **solutions** and **solubility**. They should explore ways of **separating and purifying mixtures** such as muddy water, salty water, and ink by **evaporation**, **filtration** and **chromatography**.

Associated key words **melt, solidify, physical process, aqueous, neutral**

■ PUPILS' OWN IDEAS

At Key Stage 1 children will have been considering characteristics of objects such as size, colour, shape and texture. At Key Stage 2 they are asked to consider more the characteristics of the material of which the objects are made, for example whether the material is hard, flexible or soluble, as well as 'object' properties of volume and mass. Previous experience involving solubility and solutions may well have been limited and children are unlikely to have considered

where, for instance, sugar goes when it is stirred into tea. Children will often use the word *melting* incorrectly to describe dissolving, and often use these words interchangeably. When considering solids, liquids and gases children often do not relate these three as being different forms of one substance. For example, when water changes to steam, steam is sometimes called air, air and steam being regarded as the same thing.

■ COMMENTARY AND STARTING POINTS

PHYSICAL PROPERTIES

Children could start to explore the properties of materials by considering what material they would choose to do particular jobs and why they would choose it. For instance, they could be asked to select from a range of materials provided which they would use to make the walls, the roof, or the floor of a building. *Which material would be good for flooring? Why? What would be good to line walls with? Why?*

When considering compressibility children could be asked to handle a variety of balls and to say which they think would bounce the highest – solid balls or balls filled with air (tennis balls). Many children will describe the 'best bouncers' as those that are the squashiest, i.e. those filled with air (gases can be compressed much more easily than solids).

ACIDS, ALKALIS AND INDICATORS

Acids can be introduced by asking children to taste lemon juice, lime juice, vinegar and acid drops (sweets) (all are acids). *How would you describe their taste? Are their tastes similar? What do they all have in common?* (Acids have a sharp, sour taste.) These substances are also similar in the way they behave. *What happens when we mix these solutions with baking powder?* Show children what happens when you mix baking powder with lemon juice and then ask them to predict what will happen when you mix vinegar and lime juice. Weak citric acid solution could also be introduced here as a new acid. (Acids make baking powder fizz.) *What happens when an indicator paper such as litmus is placed in lemon juice?* (Acids turn litmus red.) Once again, show children lemon juice and then try the others asking children to predict what will happen. A way of introducing indicators is to look at the effect of vinegar and lemon juice on the colour of plant materials. Try rose petals and red cabbage leaves. The indicator can be made by grinding some of the plant material with a little water in a pestle and mortar and then decanting the liquid. Alternatively the material can be put into boiling water. This works especially well with onion skins. Children should not be allowed to use boiling water without close adult supervision. Water can be boiled in saucepans on cookers. Once the children know how to make an indicator they can be challenged to find the 'best indicator' by exploring a range of different plant materials. *What would you need to make a good indicator? What plants do you think would make good indicators? Why? What colour changes would you expect?* (Plant indicators tend to be red in acid and blue in alkali.) Having found their best indicator children could then be encouraged to use it to discover which common materials are acid and which are alkaline. *What sorts of things are acids? What sorts of things are alkalis?* Another challenge is to ask the children to consider how they would tell whether something was neither acid nor alkaline but neutral. Neutral substances do not affect the colour of indicators.

SOLUTIONS AND SOLUBILITY

One way of developing ideas about solutions and solubility is to ask children to dissolve some salt in water. *Where does the salt go? Can we get it back? If so, how? What ideas do you have?* are all useful starting points. Children can also be asked *How much salt can you dissolve in a glass of water? How might you be able to dissolve more?* Younger children may count the number of spoonfuls added whereas older children may weigh amounts on kitchen scales and measure the volume of the water in measuring jugs or measuring cylinders. How well different substances dissolve can also be explored, for example the mass of sugar that dissolves in a known volume of water compared with the mass of salt, or the mass of Epsom salts (magnesium sulphate), or baking powder.

SEPARATING AND PURIFYING MIXTURES

Children can be challenged to think of ways of purifying muddy water or getting the salt back from salty water, or even recovering the water, although this would require some method of condensing the water vapour from evaporation or from steam when the salt solution is boiled. Salt solutions can be boiled in a saucepan on a cooker, under close teacher supervision. Great care must be taken since as the water is boiled away the remaining salt will 'spit' out of the pan. Place a lid on the pan and provide safety goggles for children and teachers.

Children can be shown the technique of chromatography using a black felt-tip pen, water and blotting paper and then asked to find out the colours which make up other felt-tip pen colours. *Which colours do you think are mixtures? Why? Make a list of the colours you think are present in each of the felt-tip pen colours, then find out if you were right using chromatography.* It is important to encourage children to realise that this is a technique for separating mixtures rather than merely a way of making pretty patterns.

The green colour from plants can also be separated, although nail varnish remover or methylated spirits are better solvents than water in this case. If this is attempted care must be exercised since both solvents are flammable.

■ IDEAS FOR INVESTIGATIONS – Key Stage 2 Sc3 (i) the properties, classification and structure of materials

Investigation / Starting point	Strand (i) Generating ideas and planning / Pupil's suggestion	Strand (ii) Doing / Pupil's activity	Strand (iii) Concluding / Pupils could . . .
Early in Key Stage 2			
Which washing-up liquid is best?	I think thick/runny/green/lemon liquids are best because that is the one Mum buys and I know it makes more bubbles/the bubbles last longer.	See how many teaspoons of oil a tablespoon of washing-up liquid will dissolve or which liquid makes bubbles or which one washes the most plates. They can consider how they make the test fair.	Say what happened and which one they now think is the best, with a reason.
Which type of carrier bag is best?	I think plastic/paper/square/long/thin ones are best because they are stronger (plastic is stronger than paper)/carry more/stretch more.	Set up fair tests to test the strength of the different carrier bags.	State what they saw happening, which one is therefore the strongest and how they made the test fair.
Which is the best material from which to make a kite?	I think paper/tissue paper/thin plastic (PVC)/nylon (as in sail cloth) is best because it is stronger/lighter/will catch more wind/will not break in the wind.	Set up fair tests to test their ideas. Investigations with wind can use hair driers to supply a constant source of wind.	State what they saw happening, which one is therefore the best and how they made the test fair.
Can you find a way to dissolve sugar in tea more quickly?	I think I can dissolve the sugar more quickly by stirring/shaking/using a bigger cup/making the tea hotter.	Design their own fair tests making decisions about what to use and how many tests to do.	Say what they saw happening, from their results identify any patterns and whether these were what they expected.
Which sort of ball is the best bouncer?	I think that rubber/plastic/tennis balls make the best bouncers because they are squashy/contain air/are hard/soft.	Design their own fair tests, making decisions about what to use, how many results to take, and how to record their results.	Say what they saw happening, what their results tell them, identifying any patterns and whether this is what they expected.
Later in Key Stage 2			
What affects how well sugar dissolves?	I think that stirring/temperature of the water/how much water there is/whether the sugar is in lumps/granulated/caster will make a difference.	Design their own fair test making decisions about what to use, how many results to take.	State what they see happening, why they think it happened and what patterns they notice and whether this is what they expected.
What affects the strength of the material used to make a carrier bag?	I think that the type of material/the thickness of the material/the length of the material might make a difference because . . . (for example, the thicker the material the stronger it is).	Design a series of tests to investigate each of their ideas, making sure each is fair.	From the results identify any patterns they may find. The thick plastic bags were stronger than paper bags, stating whether or not this is what they expected. Also any other possible causes.
What affects how stiff bed springs are?	I think that the length/thickness/type of material/number of coils will make a difference.	Design a series of tests to test each of their ideas making sure each is fair.	From the results identify any patterns they may find, for example the thicker the spring the stiffer it is, stating whether or not this is what they expected. Also any other possible causes.
What affects how stretchy or flexible hair is?	I think that blond/brown/thin/thick/long/short/girl's/boy's hair will be more stretchy (or strong).	Test their ideas using a series of fair tests; the hair can be suspended and weights hung on the bottom, the stretch being measured or pulled with a forcemeter.	From the results, identify any patterns they may find, stating whether or not they expected. Also any other possible causes.
What affects how well balls bounce?	I think the type of material/the size of the ball/the surface it drops onto/the height it drops from will affect how high it bounces.	Design a series of fair tests to test each idea in turn (or some of them).	From the results, plot graphs identifying any patterns linking these to their prediction(s).

Which washing-up liquid is best?

- You have probably seen many adverts which claim that one washing-up liquid is better than another. Are these adverts correct?

- What do you think makes a good washing-up liquid?

- You will first have to decide what 'best' means. Is it the liquid that produces the most lather per drop, or the one which dissolves the most vegetable oil or butter?

- Can you predict which of the washing-up liquids will be best? Why is it best?

- Can you now think of a way of finding out if you are right?

■ TEACHERS' NOTES

WHICH WASHING-UP LIQUID IS BEST?

This investigation can be introduced when children are developing their ideas about dissolving, perhaps after they have discovered that substances such as fats (butter, vegetable oils) do not dissolve in water. The idea that adding washing-up liquid or soaps to water helps to dissolve grease and fats should be developed. This is an appropriate activity for early Key Stage 2. A variety of washing-up liquids can be purchased easily; compare ones which are viscous (concentrated), green, yellow, contain additives (for example, lemon), cheap, expensive, or are thin. Children need to be shown how they can add one or two drops of each liquid to water and shake to produce a lather, or how they can shake with a little oil to disperse the oil within the water.

> **Resources**
> - different washing-up liquids
> - droppers (e.g. eye droppers)
> - measuring jugs
> - measuring cylinders
> - washing-up bowls
> - access to water
> - fats (butter, cooking oil, etc.)

Questions to help develop thinking

Which do you think will be the best washing-up liquid? Why?
(*Do you think those containing lemon will be better than those that do not? Are green-coloured liquids better? Are concentrated liquids better. Why?*)
How can you find out if you are right?
Could we use the amount of lather the liquid produces as an indicator?
How would we measure it? Could we use the amount of vegetable oil that the liquid can make disappear as an indicator?
How can you make your test fair?

Conclusions

Children can be encouraged to make statements such as *More concentrated liquids produce more lather.* A recent *Which?* report found that Fairy Liquid did wash more dishes than other liquids. It is important to stress that conclusions which state apparently negative findings are important. *Whether a liquid contains lemon or not appears to make no difference.*

Safety

Children need to be reminded that washing-up liquid can irritate eyes and with some people it can irritate the skin.

!

What affects how well sugar dissolves?

■ We stir sugar in our tea to make it sweet. The sugar dissolves in the tea. Have you tried dissolving sugar in water?

■ Have you ever thought about how you could make the sugar dissolve more quickly in the water?

■ What do you think will affect how well sugar dissolves in water? Why?

■ Write a list of your ideas below and think of a way of testing them. Use a Planning Sheet to help you.

■ TEACHERS' NOTES

WHAT AFFECTS HOW WELL SUGAR DISSOLVES?

This investigation can be introduced when children are developing their ideas about dissolving. It could be introduced in the context of a hot drinks manufacturer receiving complaints about his drinks not being sweet enough. *He knows the sugar is being added to the tea and coffee but why isn't it dissolving? How can he make the sugar dissolve more quickly?* This can be introduced at any point in the key stage but is probably best introduced later when children will have more ideas on which to build. The effect of temperature can be investigated using water from a kettle at different temperatures, for example 30°C, 40°C, 50°C, 60°C.

Resources
■ sugar (granulated, caster, lumps, icing)
■ thermometer
■ stopclock
■ measuring jugs
■ measuring cylinders
■ electronic kitchen scales
■ washing-up bowls
■ plastic cups
■ sponges
■ paper towels
■ spoons
■ stirring rods

Questions to help develop thinking

What do you think affects how well sugar dissolves?
Why do you think that?
    (supplementary prompts *Do you think temperature, amount of water, amount of stirring, state of sugar (lumps, granulated, powder) will make a difference?*)
How could you find out if you are right?
What equipment will you need?
What will you need to measure?
How will you make your test fair?
How will you know when the sugar has been dissolved?

Conclusions

Children should be encouraged to state conclusions of the type *Temperature does affect how well sugar dissolves, the higher the temperature the more easily the sugar dissolves.* Children should find that temperature, rate of stirring and particle size will affect how quickly the sugar will dissolve, and that stirring will have the most effect. Caster sugar will dissolve more quickly than granulated or lumps of sugar but icing sugar sometimes aggregates as lumps. Sieving the icing sugar can help to prevent this.

Safety

Great care should be taken when using hot water. There is no need to use hot or very hot water. Water up to 60°C is hot enough; even at this temperature water can cause burns. Close adult supervision must be given.

ATTAINMENT TARGET 3

Strand (iii) chemical changes

■ DEVELOPMENT OF KEY IDEAS

	KS1	KS2	KS3
material	natural and manufactured, e.g. ice water, wax, wood, clay	raw materials and origins	range of sources of raw materials
changing materials	effect of heating and cooling on ice, water, wax	effect of heating causing permanent change on some everyday materials	wide range of chemical reactions including combustion, salt formation, electrolysis, oxidation and reduction
	permanent change when heating dough, wood	chemical changes with plaster of Paris/water, baking powder/vinegar	factors which affect rate of chemical reaction
		iron rusting and combustion	chemical reactions form new materials

■ PROGRAMME OF STUDY

(iii) chemical changes

Pupils should explore the origins of a range of materials in order to appreciate that some **occur naturally** while many are made from **raw materials**.

They should investigate the action of **heat on everyday materials** resulting in permanent change; these might include cooking activities and firing clay.

Pupils should explore **chemical changes** in a number of everyday materials such as those that occur when mixing **plaster of Paris**, mixing **baking powder** with **vinegar** and when **iron** rusts.

They should recognise that **combustion** of **fuel** releases energy and produces **waste products**, including gases.

Associated key words **chemical reaction, rusting and oxygen** (*see* **chemical change**)

■ PUPILS' OWN IDEAS

The word material is often regarded by young children to mean just cloth or fabric. Later their idea of 'material' will often be related to the ingredients for making things: they will not tend to use it in its wider sense. They will not think of gases (such as air) or liquids (such as water) as materials. Their views of natural and man-made are also often not the same as those expressed here. Often, for instance, children will consider the wool in a ball of wool to be man-made because someone has spun the wool, or that a roofing slate is man-made because someone has shaped it. When materials are changed by burning children often think that the material just disappears. When materials are changed very few children will consider whether the material can be treated in such a way as to convert it to its original state.

■ COMMENTARY AND STARTING POINTS

MATERIALS

At Key Stage 1 children will have considered which of the materials they were using were man-made and which were natural. This idea is developed at Key Stage 2. A useful early starting point is to ask children to consider what different materials their homes are made from (building, fittings, walls and floors) and where each material comes from. *How many different materials can you find in your home? Where do you think they come from?*

Children will probably be able to suggest that wood comes from trees, that the wool in the carpet comes from sheep, and that pottery in the tiles comes from clay. Their thinking can be developed in other areas by asking them to suggest what certain materials look like: for example, when some children suggest concrete on the floors comes from cement, further prompting may bring answers such as the cement comes from crushing stones. Further useful prompts are *Where does the cement come from? What do you think the cement looks like?* Naturally the children will need to be told about some ideas. *Glass is made by melting sand, and metals come from special rocks called ores.* Children will also need to have opportunities to handle, observe and comment on a wide range of different materials, linking them to their uses (link with Sc3 strand (i)). A useful collection of materials could include: wool from a sheep, a ball of wool, raw cotton from the plant, a patch of woven cotton material, a patch of nylon, lumps of chalk (rock), gypsum, limestone, flints, shells, clay, brick, dressed building stone, sandstone, sand, iron ores (haematite, pyrites), copper ore, scraps of different metals (such as iron, copper, aluminium, zinc, steels) samples of different types of glass, lumps of plaster, lumps of cement, pebbles, different woods, scraps of different plastics (such as nylon, PVC, Bakelite, polypropylene), slate (rock), a roof slate and roof tile.

Children should be encouraged to handle these and observe them using magnifying glasses, looking at their structure and similarities and differences. Care needs to be exercised when handling glass, when gloves should be worn and eyes protected. They could be encouraged to sort them into 'man-made' and 'natural' and to discover using books the stages the manufactured materials go through linking the stages with arrows. For example:

gypsum rock → crush rock → heat powder → add water → wall plaster

CHANGING MATERIALS

Children will need to appreciate that heat can change things permanently (a chemical change). When cooking things or firing clay useful prompts include *What do you see happening? What changes are occurring? How are they now different? What has changed? What have they become?* If the school does not have access to a kiln, the possibility of Raku pottery could be explored making use of a simple brick-built outside charcoal 'kiln'. Outside small bonfires can also be used to explore the effects of heat on wood, coal, coke and charcoal. Teachers can explore with children the making of charcoal outside using wood and covering the 'fire' with turfs.

Other chemical changes which can be explored are:

Mixing plaster of Paris with water. *What do you notice/feel when the water is mixed?* (It gets hot) *What other changes can you see? Can we get back to the original plaster of Paris? What are your ideas? Try them out to see if they work.*

Mixing baking powder with vinegar. *What do you notice/see happening? What changes can you see? Can you get back the vinegar and the baking powder? How? Try out your ideas. Did they work?*

Iron rusting. Children can observe iron nails rusting when left in a saucer containing some water. They can also be shown some rusty metals and asked *What changes can you see happening? Can we get the metal back? How could we stop the metal from rusting? What is needed to make things rust?* Children could then try out their investigations.

Children should soon realise that these changes produce new substances which cannot easily be changed back into the original substances.

Other chemical reactions which can be referred to include the mixing of cement with water, the mixing of model-making resins, the burning of substances in fireworks, the use of descalers in kettles.

Children should not handle cement powder, resins, fireworks or descalers.

IDEAS FOR INVESTIGATIONS – Key Stage 2 Sc3 (iii) chemical changes

Investigation *Starting point*	Strand (i) Generating ideas and planning *Pupil's suggestion*	Strand (ii) Doing *Pupil's activity*	Strand (iii) Concluding *Pupils could . . .*
Early in Key Stage 2			
What do you think will happen if you heat these materials?	*I think that these materials will burn/shrink/go black/get hot/not change.*	Make a note of their observations whilst a series of different materials are heated.	State what they saw and whether this is what they expected. State what sorts of materials burn/don't change, etc.
Can you find a way to make clay strong?	*I think you could make it strong by drying it/ heating it/squashing it/squeezing it/pressing it.*	Try out each of their ideas in turn.	State what they did, what they saw happening and whether or not they made it strong.
Later in Key Stage 2			
What affects how quickly potatoes cook? How could we cook potatoes more quickly?	*I think you could cook potatoes more quickly by using more water/using less water/ chopping the potatoes into smaller pieces/ leaving potatoes as large pieces/adding salt to the water/using a bigger gas ring/boiling the water faster.*	Make decisions about how they will test their ideas, what size to use/how many pieces/how much water, etc., and how they will make their tests fair. The boiling can be carried out by adult or under close supervision.	State what their results show, whether there are any patterns, for example the smaller the potatoes the faster they cooked, and whether this is what they expected.
What affects whether an egg is hard boiled or soft boiled?	*I think the size of the egg/the amount of water/ how hot the water is/how long it boils will make a difference.*	Test each of their ideas in turn making sure they control all other variables (making the test fair).	State which factors affect how quickly the egg will cook and which have no effect. Relate this to what they expected.
What affects how quickly iron rusts?	*I think iron will rust more quickly when it is in water/when it is in sea water/when it is hot/ when it is moist/when it is exposed to the air.*	Design a series of fair tests. Nails can be used for iron.	State what they saw happening, in which conditions the nails rusted more quickly, and draw conclusions about the factors needed to make iron rust.
What affects how quickly bread dough rises?	*I think that the hotter the temperature/the wetter the mixture/the smaller the lump, the quicker the dough will rise.*	Design a series of fair tests making decisions about the range of temperatures to be tested or the range of 'wetness' of the mixture, perhaps measured by extra spoonfuls of water.	State what they saw happening and any patterns they may have identified, for example the warmer the dough was, the quicker it rose.
Which is the best material for keeping soup hot?	*I think that expanded polystyrene cups/hard plastic/pottery/glass will keep the soup hottest.*	Design a fair test to test their idea, making decisions about the amount of soup, how to measure the temperature and how often, etc.	Draw graphs of their results showing how each cupful of soup cooled down. Draw conclusions about which material is best from the pattern in the graph.

What affects how quickly iron rusts?

■ You will have seen rusty objects made of iron. Rust on car bodies, for example, is a real problem. Some cars seem to rust more quickly than others.

■ Why do you think this is?

■ What affects how quickly iron rusts?

■ What are your ideas? Use a Planning Sheet to collect your ideas and suggest ways in which you could use some iron nails to test each of your ideas.

■ TEACHERS' NOTES

WHAT AFFECTS HOW QUICKLY IRON RUSTS?

This investigation is best carried out towards the end of Key Stage 2.

It can be introduced when children are exploring rusting as an example of a chemical change. Children may have been taught about rusting, including how the rusting process only takes place in the presence of water and air. This investigation develops these ideas further. Children can use nails cleaned previously using emery paper to ensure that the rust shows quickly.

Questions to help develop thinking

What do you think affects how quickly iron rusts?
Why do you think that?
   (supplementary prompts *Do you think temperature, amount of water, presence of air, salt in the water will make any difference?*)
How could you find out if you are right?
What equipment will you need?
What will you need to measure?
How will you make your test fair?
How will you know when the iron has rusted?

Conclusions

Children should be encouraged to draw conclusions based on their observations. They should find that raising the temperature will increase the rate of rusting and that provided both are present the volume of water or air has little effect. Salty water will also make the nails rust more quickly.

Resources

- iron nails
- plastic containers with lids
- water
- salt
- thermometers
- measuring cylinders

ATTAINMENT TARGET 3

Strand (iv) the Earth and its atmosphere

■ DEVELOPMENT OF KEY IDEAS

	KS1	KS2	KS3
weather	observe changes in weather effects of weathering	observations and recording of weather including measurements weathering	factors which influence and cause different weather/meteorological symbols weathering
water	–	water cycle as a result of observations on weather	properties of water, water cycle, effect of water on Earth's surface
rock	observe/compare natural materials	investigate natural materials rock, mineral soil	rock cycle, geological processes, age of Earth, soil forming processes

■ PROGRAMME OF STUDY

(iv) the Earth and its atmosphere

Pupils should have the opportunity to make regular, **quantitative** observations and keep records of **weather** and the **seasons** of the **year**. This should lead to a consideration of the **water cycle**.

Pupils should investigate **natural materials** (**rocks**, **minerals**, **soils**), sort them by simple criteria and relate them to their uses and origins.

They should be aware of local distributions of some types of natural materials (sand, soil and rock).

They should observe through fieldwork how weather affects their surroundings, how **sediment** is produced and how soil develops.

They should consider the major **geological events** which change the surface of the **Earth** and the evidence for these changes.

Associated key words **weathering, erosion, transport**

■ PUPILS' OWN IDEAS

By Key Stage 2 children will already have observed local changes in the weather, the effects of weathering (for example, the effect of rain on a window frame or frost in the local churchyard).

At this stage children will often express ideas such as the frost brings the cold, rather than thinking that the frost might be a result of the cold. Early in Key Stage 2 children may readily accept the idea of water cycling and will often be able to express ideas about clouds, rivers and evaporation as matters of fact rather than appreciating the processes involved. It is generally within their experience that things dry up more quickly on warmer days, so asking questions such as *Will a puddle dry up more quickly on a warm or cold day?* could

stimulate thinking that it is the heat from the Sun which evaporates the water. These ideas are developed at Key Stage 3.

By Key Stage 2 children will probably have collected and displayed a range of natural materials such as rocks, stones, soils, leaves, twigs and seeds. They will have been encouraged to look for similarities and differences through sorting and grouping activities and to describe simple properties of the objects such as colour, texture and size. If they have observed soils closely they may well have some ideas about what soils are composed of but it is unlikely that they will have considered how the soils were produced. *Where do you think the bits in the soil have come from?* can stimulate thinking.

COMMENTARY AND STARTING POINTS

WEATHER

When introducing children to observing and keeping records of the weather it is useful to provide a purpose for doing so. *What do you think the weather will be like tomorrow? Why? How do you think the weather person finds out? How good are you at predicting the weather? Who has the best system?* can provide a stimulating context. The quantitative observations referred to in the Programme of Study are those which involve a degree of measurement such as daily rainfall, windspeed, temperature and wind direction. Children can be encouraged to understand the purposes and appropriateness of forms of recording (Sc1) with questions such as *What do you need to record? How often do you need to record – each day or each week? Who needs to know about your results? Which would be the best way of recording? Can you design a way?* 'Weather watching' provides an excellent opportunity to integrate science with technology by asking the children to design and make their own weather recording instruments.

Such activities can be developed by asking the children to predict what they think the typical air temperature, wind speed, wind direction or rainfall might be in different seasons. *How warm do you think it is on a summer's day/winter's day?* can help develop estimating skills. A useful mnemonic is, '5, 10 and 21 winter spring and summer sun' (temperatures are in degrees Celsius). *How much rain falls in a winter month? Is this the same for every country? How could you find out?*

WATER

Weather watching can be followed by asking children questions to develop their ideas about the water cycle by linking these with their observations. *Where do you think the water in the rivers comes from? Where do rivers go? Where do clouds come from? Can water pass through rocks? What happens to the water in puddles when they dry up?* This could lead to children creating their own posters to explain their ideas and develop their ideas of a water cycle.

ROCKS

Pupils could be encouraged to collect rocks, soils and stones which occur locally (for example, from gardens). These can be displayed and compared. Soils from different gardens and areas of the school can be compared for colour, texture, grain size, humus content and water retention. Children could design their own tests for these. When comparing soils a useful technique is to shake a little soil in a jar full of water. The soil will separate into bands, the heavier larger particles settling first, humus floating on the top. It is far better, however, to ask children to think of their own ways of finding out what soil is made of. They may suggest using magnifying glasses, shaking in sieves, etc.

Fieldwork could include:

> Looking at streams and rivers and asking *Where do you think the sand, mud, stones in the stream have come from? Why are the stones round? Where in the stream are the biggest, smallest stones found? Why do you think this is?*

> Looking at buildings, statues and gravestones and asking *Which do you think are the oldest? Why? How can you tell? What do you think causes the wearing away of stone and brick? How could you find out? Which are the best building materials? Why?*

When children investigate natural materials they should be involved with activities which are derived from *Sc1 Scientific Investigation*. Pupils could investigate the permeability of different rocks and soils. *Look closely at the rock, soil; how are they the same, different? Which do you think would let the most water through? Why? How could you find out?* Children could investigate how hard different rocks are. *Look carefully at the rocks: which do you think are the hardest? How could you find out? Can you put them in order of hardness?* Such investigations could lead the children to consider which rocks are the best for building and why. For example, soft rocks are useful because they are easy to work, hard rocks withstand damage better, non-porous rocks are least likely to be affected by weathering.

Major geological events include faults, folding, earthquakes and volcanoes erupting. As an introduction to these ideas children could be asked to consider the land around them and features on the world landscape such as mountain ranges. *Why are there mountains in that part of the world but not this one?* Through books, videos and pictures children could be asked to find out where earthquakes and volcanoes appear. They should also look at pictures showing folding in rocks and asked to consider why they think the rocks are like this. Models can be made to represent this with layers of Plasticine.

IDEAS FOR INVESTIGATIONS – Key Stage 2 Sc3 (iv) the Earth and its atmosphere

Investigation *Starting point*	Strand (i) Generating ideas and planning *Pupil's suggestion*	Strand (ii) Doing *Pupil's activity*	Strand (iii) Concluding *Pupils could . . .*
Early in Key Stage 2			
Is there a connection between wind and rain?	I think that the more windy it is the more rainy it is. I think more rain comes with westerly/ northerly, etc., winds.	Make decisions about how they will measure the wind strength, direction and the rainfall. Collect data over a number of windy and rainy days.	State what their results tell them and how this relates to what they expected.
Is damp seaweed (or opening fir cones) a good predictor of rain?	I think the more bendy or moist the seaweed is the more likely it will rain. I think the more open a fir cone the more likely it will rain.	Try recording the condition of the seaweed/ fir cone on different days, making a prediction about the weather and recording the actual weather on the following days.	Look for patterns in the results. How often are they good predictors?
Is there a connection between soil colour and where we find it?	I think you can find darker soils under trees/ lighter soils near rivers/darker soils near the top/darker soils in woods/darker soils in fields, etc.	Collect soil from different places and consider the colour in light of their predictions.	State their observations and relate these to their original predictions. Is this what they expected?
Can we grow things equally well in different soils?	I think plants grow better in dark soils/heavy soils/sandy soils/sticky soils.	Plant seeds in a range of tubs containing different soils making sure that their tests are fair by controlling the other factors.	State what they saw happening and what conclusions they can draw.
Can you find a way to make a vibration (Earthquake) detector?	I think vibrations of the table are detected best by the movement of thin strips of paper/thick strips of paper/thin wires/thick wires/card.	Try making different thickness strips of paper vibrate, and different materials, then choose the one which shows most movement.	State which material/strip detected most vibration and say why they thought this happened.
Later in Key Stage 2			
What affects how well soils drain? or What affects how much water soils can retain?	I think lighter/darker/sticky/sandy/clay/acid/ grainy/smooth soils drain best. I think clay/sandy/loam/chalky dark/light soils can hold most water.	Design a series of fair tests to test each of their ideas in turn. A measured volume of water can be poured through the same amounts of soil held in a funnel. The amount of water which passes through can be collected.	State what they found out from the results and what conclusions they could draw. Is this what they expected?
What affects how well rocks absorb water?	I think grainy/shiny/sandy/hard/soft/ big/ small rocks absorb most water.	Design fair tests (using same size rocks, etc.) to test absorption of water. Place rock in water and measure increase in mass/loss of water from the bowl, etc.	State their results and draw conclusions which relate to their original predictions. State how they made their tests fair.
What affects how quickly water evaporates?	I think puddles which are deeper/shallower/more spread out evaporate more quickly. Windy/dry/wet/hot days make water evaporate more quickly.	Design a series of fair tests to test each idea, choosing a range of variables to be tested, for example different depths, different surface areas.	State what the results are, identifying any patterns which appear and how these relate to the original idea.

What affects how quickly water evaporates?

■ Some puddles seem to disappear very quickly whilst others seem to last a long time. Why do you think this is? Why is there a difference?

■ What affects how quickly a puddle evaporates and why?

■ Write down your ideas in sentences of the type:
'I think puddles that are .... will evaporate more quickly because ....'

■ How could you find out if you are right? Can you design some tests to check your ideas using water and different containers in the classroom?

■ TEACHERS' NOTES

WHAT AFFECTS HOW QUICKLY WATER EVAPORATES?

This investigation should be carried out later in Key Stage 2.

It can be introduced when children are exploring ideas about the water cycle as part of their work on the Earth and atmosphere. Puddles can be simulated by pouring water into different shaped and sized containers. These containers can be placed in different places (for example, hot or cold) according to the ideas suggested by the children. Children may need to be guided to the idea that in order to test their ideas about how quickly a puddle will evaporate they may need to 'model' a puddle (using different containers). In order to find out how different conditions may affect the evaporation rate we need to control the conditions (for example, puddles in hot or cold places).

Questions to help develop thinking

What do you think makes the water in puddles evaporate?
How could we make it dry up more quickly?
    (supplementary prompts *Do you think the size of the puddle will
    make a difference? Do you think the depth of the puddle will have an
    effect? Do you think how hot it is will make a difference? Do you think
    how windy it is will make a difference?*)
What do you think will happen?
Why?
How will you find out if you are right?
How will you make your test fair?
What will you need to look for?
Will you need to measure anything?
How can you record your results?

Conclusions

Children could discover that the higher the temperature (of water or air) the faster the water will evaporate, also the more spread out the water (greater surface area) or the faster air blows across that surface the faster the rate of evaporation. Some children may suggest that evaporation is affected by light or dark (rather than heat from the Sun): by investigation they should discover that this is not the case.

Safety

If kettles are used to heat water make sure that children do not handle containers containing very hot water. Water which is the temperature of a hot bath is sufficient and a lot safer.

Resources

- containers (different shapes and sizes)
- measuring jugs
- measuring cylinders
- thermometers
- tape measures
- metre rules
- rulers
- hair driers (to simulate wind)
- kettle (to provide hot water)

What affects how well soils drain?

- Some soils appear to allow water to drain through them quickly and easily, while others do not.

- Why do you think this is?

- In what ways are the soils different?

- How does this help explain why soils drain at different rates?

- Write down your ideas. Use statements of the type: 'I think soils that are .... will drain more easily because ....'

- Think up some ways in which you could test out your ideas. You could use a Planning Sheet to help you.

■ TEACHERS' NOTES

WHAT AFFECTS HOW WELL SOILS DRAIN?

This investigation can be introduced as part of children's explorations of the Earth and in particular the investigation of natural materials. To gain the most from this investigation it would be appropriate for it to follow activities which had enabled children to appreciate that soil was made up of a mixture of things including rock fragments of different sizes (including clays and sands), and humus. It would also have been helpful for them to have analysed previously different soil samples, for example a clay soil and a sandy soil.

Questions to help develop thinking

In what ways are soils different?
Which of these differences might affect how well a soil drains? Why?
Which soil do you think will drain more quickly? Why?
How could you find out if you are right?
How will you tell which one has drained more quickly?
Will you need to measure anything?
How will you make your test fair?
Will you need to repeat your test?
How will you record your results?

Conclusions

Children should discover that soils with the larger particle sizes (i.e. sandy soils) allow water to drain more quickly; clay soils tend to become waterlogged. The reason for this is that the spaces between the larger particles are greater so drainage is easier. The amount of humus in a soil will also affect its drainage properties. Soils containing large quantities of humus will drain well once the humus within the soil is thoroughly wetted.

Safety

If using soils from outside, then it is advisable to ask children to wear gloves and certainly to wash their hands after use. Soil can be contaminated with many dangerous microorganisms, for example from the faeces of cats and dogs.

Resources

- soils (sand, loam, clay, peat, composts, gravel, etc. Soils can be made up using different combinations of these)
- soil sieves
- jars
- newspaper
- hand lenses
- funnels
- washing-up bowls
- stopclocks
- measuring jugs
- rulers

!

ATTAINMENT TARGET 4

Strand (i) electricity and magnetism

■ DEVELOPMENT OF KEY IDEAS

	KS1	KS2	KS3
circuit	bulb, buzzer, battery conductors	range of components variable resistor/heating magnetic effects	wider range of components electrical measurements of current, etc. develop ideas of current as a flow of charge electrostatics
mains	use and dangers	dangers and safety measures	measuring and costing of use
magnet	effect of magnets on materials	properties of magnetic materials magnetic effect of electric current	magnetic fields, principles and uses of electromagnets
micro-electronics	–	sensing, switching, control, logic gates	systems approach, logic, decisions, control circuits to solve problems

■ PROGRAMME OF STUDY

(i) electricity and magnetism

Pupils should have the opportunity to construct simple **circuits**. They should investigate the effects of using different **components**, of varying the flow of **electricity** in a circuit and the **heating** and **magnetic effects**.

They should plan and record construction details of a circuit using drawings and diagrams.

They should learn about the dangers associated with the use of **mains electricity** and appropriate safety measures. They should investigate the properties of **magnetic** and non-magnetic materials.

They should begin to explore simple circuits for sensing, switching and control, including the use of **logic gates**.

Associated key words **circuit diagram, microelectronics, sensor, relay** (*see* **component (electrical)**), **variable resistor**

■ PUPILS' OWN IDEAS

At Key Stage 1 children will have made simple circuits involving bulbs and batteries and may well be able to construct more complex circuits. Children often hold their own views about electric current. These sometimes firmly held views can often interfere with the child's ability to construct circuits. For instance one common view amongst the children is that current goes from the battery to the bulb where it is used up. This will often mean that children will only see the need for one wire. This may happen even if they have been shown previously that two are needed. Children will need many frequent practical experiences which involve making circuits in a variety of contexts to help them modify their views. It is very important for children to realise the different nature and dangers of mains electricity. It has been known for children realising that 'more electricity' is needed to make a device (such as a motor) work to connect it to the mains supply. No practical work involving mains supply should be undertaken.

Many children (and adults!) hold views that 'metals are magnetic' rather than ferrous (iron and steel). This probably arises because in their experience the metals they frequently come into contact with are iron and steel. Once again there is a need for activities involving magnets and different metals, for example brass, aluminium, copper and iron.

!

■ COMMENTARY AND STARTING POINTS

CIRCUIT

Children should have many opportunities to construct circuits with batteries, wires and simple components such as bulbs, buzzers, motors and switches to help develop their ideas. They should be allowed to explore these by handling the components and trying to make bulbs light and motors work. Later they should be prompted to think about how they will construct their circuits. *Can you draw a picture to show how you will connect your circuit?* These opportunities could arise in a variety of technological contexts. Early in Key Stage 2 children might be making and designing a variety of their own switches, for example a switch which only works when you press it, a switch you can leave on or off, a switch you cannot leave on, a two-way switch changing from one part of a switch to another. They should also be able to use a variety of 'bought' switches, including two-way, reed (operated by a magnet) and dimmer switches.

Later on children could design more complicated switching arrangements, for example to control 'hall and landing lights' and sets of traffic lights. These are not easy for children.

Children should also be given opportunities to explore and investigate their own ideas about circuits. The following questions provide useful starting points. *How many batteries will you need? How many bulbs will you need? Where will you put the switch? Do you think it makes a difference if the switch comes before the bulb or after the bulb? How could you find out? How could you make the bulb brighter? What things could you change in your circuit? Do bigger batteries always make the bulb brighter? What happens to the brightness of the bulb if we use a long piece of wire? Will this battery light a bulb in the next room?* (needs a long length of wire).

Children can also learn a lot about circuits by fault finding. Presenting children with circuits which do not work and asking them *I don't know what's wrong with this, why doesn't the bulb light? Can you find out?* can provide children with good opportunities to develop their ideas about circuits.

When a current passes through a wire it creates a magnetic field around it. Children could be asked to place compasses on top of wires connecting a bulb to a battery and asked to switch their circuit on. Ask *What do you notice happening? What does it tell you about the wire when electricity is flowing through it? What would you expect to happen to a nail if you coiled the wire round it and switched on the current? Find out.* Children can also be asked what other changes they notice when electricity passes through a wire. They might suggest that sometimes wires get hot. Short-circuiting wires (connecting one end of a battery to another without being connected to an electrical component can make these wires very hot (heating effect of electrical current). It is dangerous to do this to rechargeable batteries since it is possible for them to explode. These batteries should not be used for open circuit work by pupils (there is a risk of short-circuiting). A short-circuit can be a serious fault and can waste a lot of electrical energy: batteries will often get very hot when they are short-circuited. It is important for children to have the opportunity to discover short-circuits and their effects for themselves.

MAINS

The idea of short-circuits and electrical current 'taking the easiest path' can provide a very good starting point for discussing safety issues about mains electricity and how short-circuits from wires which have been tugged loose in plugs can start fires. The need for an Earth wire can be discussed. Children need to be shown how to remove a plug from a wall safely (switching off first) and told never to touch the bare metal of the plug or touch a switch when they have wet hands.

MAGNET

Children should have opportunities to discover that objects made of iron (or nickel) are attracted to a magnet. At Key Stage 2 they will need to be provided with a range of different metals, for example iron, aluminium, copper, brass, zinc and magnesium. (Be careful about tin cans since they are made of iron with a thin coating of tin on their surface (tinplate). Tin cans will be attracted to a magnet because of the iron content.) Knowing about the magnetic properties of iron will allow children to sort things into those made of iron or not.

MICROELECTRONICS

The purchase of microelectronics kits is invaluable. The MFA (Microelectronics For All) decisions module will enable children to explore the use of light, temperature, moisture, magnetic sensors and control outputs through the use of logic gates: AND, NOT, OR. Using a decisions board children can solve a range of problems by designing appropriate circuits involving gates, relays, bulbs and buzzers. For example *Design a circuit to automatically switch on a light when it gets dark, or a fan when it gets hot.*

IDEAS FOR INVESTIGATIONS – Key Stage 2 Sc4 (i) electricity and magnetism

Investigation *Starting point*	Strand (i) Generating ideas and planning *Pupil's suggestion*	Strand (ii) Doing *Pupil's activity*	Strand (iii) Concluding *Pupils could . . .*
Early in Key Stage 2			
What materials does a magnet attract?	*I think that iron/metals/silvery metals are attracted to magnets.*	Try testing different materials with a magnet.	State what they saw happening. Which metals are attracted to magnets and whether this was what they expected.
How can you measure the strength of a magnet?	*I think the stronger magnets will pick up more paper clips/lift heavier weights/pull heavier weights along the table.*	Try out their methods on a strong magnet and a weak magnet, making decisions about how to perform the tests.	Say which test works best and why they think this is so. Is this what they expected?
What affects the strength of a magnet?	*I think that the material the magnet is made of/the size of the magnet/the type of magnet (horseshoe/bar) will affect its strength.*	Design a series of fair tests comparing a range of different magnets, making decisions about how many different sizes to test, which materials, and how many types to test.	State what they have found out from their results and identify any patterns. For example, the bigger the magnet the stronger it was.
Which materials allow electricity to pass through them?	*I think that iron/copper/aluminium/metals/plastic/wood/glass allow electricity through.*	Make a test circuit which perhaps includes a bulb, wires, battery and a gap in which to test each of the materials. Children could consider the fairness of this test by making all the materials the same size.	State which materials let electricity through and how this matched their predictions.
Later in Key Stage 2			
What affects the strength of an electromagnet?	*I think that you can make the electromagnet stronger by using more batteries/using less (more) wire/using thicker wire/using a bigger iron nail.*	After being shown how to make an electromagnet they could design fair tests to test an idea, making decisions about the number of different measurements to take. (For example, how many different turns of coil, how many different thicknesses of wires.)	State what they have found out from their results and identify any patterns. For example, the more coils the stronger the magnet, the more batteries the stronger the magnet.
What affects the brightness of a bulb in a circuit?	*I think you could make the bulb brighter by using more batteries/using shorter (longer) wires/connecting the bulb to a different side of the battery.*	Test each of their ideas using fair tests where appropriate, designing their own circuits.	State what they found out, in each case drawing the circuit they used and saying how they made the test fair, identifying any patterns.

What affects the strength of a magnet?

- Have you noticed that some magnets are strong and others are weak?

- Why do you think this is?

- What do you think affects the strength of a magnet?

- Can you make a list of the things that might make a difference?

- Now look at the magnets you are given. Which magnet do you think will be strongest and why?

- Can you find a way of comparing the strength of the magnets that is fair?

■ TEACHERS' NOTES

WHAT AFFECTS THE STRENGTH OF A MAGNET?

This investigation should be carried out early in Key Stage 2 in conjunction with investigating the properties of magnets and magnetic materials.

Children will probably have experience of magnets and will know they can be different strengths. The children can be challenged to think of what they think might make a difference to the strength of a magnet. Ideas might range from colour of the magnet to the material it is made from. A wide range of different magnets is needed for this investigation.

It is a challenge for children to think of a way of comparing or measuring the strengths of magnets. In the past children have suggested a wide range of ideas such as the number of paper clips lifted, the distance between a magnet and a pin placed on a desk when the pin begins to move, the distance between a standard magnet and the magnet when the standard magnet moves, the size and shape of the magnetic field as revealed by sprinkling iron filings around the magnet, or the reading produced on a top-pan balance when the magnet repels a standard magnet placed on top of the scales as it is brought close.

Resources
■ magnets (bar, horseshoe, circular, steel, ceramic)
■ paperclips
■ iron filings
■ kitchen scales

Questions to help develop thinking

Which do you think is the strongest magnet?
Why?
  (supplementary prompts *Do you think the colour, size, shape, material or weight of magnet will make a difference?*)
How can you find out if you are right?
How will you measure the strength of a magnet?
How will you make your test fair?
How can you record your results?

Conclusions

The extent of the conclusions that children will be able to draw about the strength of magnets will depend on the type of magnets investigated. They should be able to conclude that strength is independent of size, colour and shape and dependent on the type of material from which the magnet is made.

What affects the strength of an electromagnet?

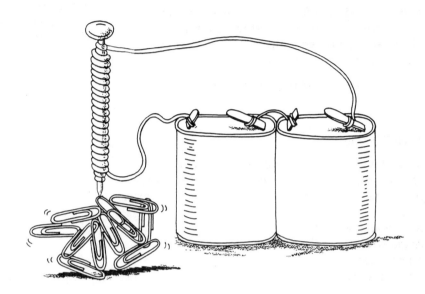

■ Electromagnets can be made by winding some covered wire tightly around an iron nail and then connecting the ends of the wire to a battery, as shown in the picture.

■ Make one for yourself and test it. How strong is it? Think how you will measure its strength.

■ How could you make your electromagnet stronger?

■ What things could you change?

■ What things do you think might make a difference? Write down a list.

■ How could you find out if you are right?

■ How will you make your test fair? You could use a Planning Sheet to help you.

■ TEACHERS' NOTES

WHAT AFFECTS THE STRENGTH OF AN ELECTROMAGNET?

This investigation is best carried out near to the end of Key Stage 2 in conjunction with investigating the magnetic fields of an electric current. It is best introduced after children have experienced a magnetic field produced by a coil.

Once the children have watched the effect on a compass of an electric current flowing through a coil of insulated wire wrapped around an iron nail, they can then make simple electromagnets and be challenged to think of ways to make them stronger.

Competitions could be held between groups to make the strongest electromagnet.

> **Resources**
>
> ■ wires (copper and iron of different lengths)
> ■ batteries (1.5 V, 4.5 V, 6 V)
> ■ nails (6", 4")
> ■ paper clips

Questions to help develop thinking

What do you think affects the strength of an electromagnet? Why?
　　(supplementary prompts *Do you think the length of nail, thickness, length of wire, type of wire, thickness of wire or number of batteries will make a difference?*)
How could you find out if you are right?
How will you measure the strength of the electromagnet?
How will you make your test fair?
How will you record your results?

Conclusions

Children should discover that the more turns of wire in the coil and the more batteries the stronger the magnetic field that is produced.

ATTAINMENT TARGET 4

Strand (ii) energy resources and energy transfer

■ DEVELOPMENT OF KEY IDEAS

	KS1	KS2	KS3
resource	fuels at home and in school	global energy resources, renewable/non-renewable	fuel/oxygen systems, energy from the Sun, nuclear energy, fossil fuels biomass as fuel
transfer	feeling hot and cold link with thermometer readings	feeling hot and cold investigating changes when heating investigating movement	introduce concept of energy transfer principle of energy conservation ways of measuring energy (unit joule)

■ PROGRAMME OF STUDY

(ii) energy resources and energy transfer

Pupils should investigate **movement** using a variety of devices, for example, toys and models, which are self-propelled or driven and use **motors**, **belts**, **levers** and **gears**.

Pupils should investigate the changes that occur when familiar substances are heated and cooled, and the concepts of **hot and cold** in relation to their **body temperature**.

They should survey, including the use of secondary sources, the range of **fuels** used in the home and at school, their **efficient** use and their **origins**.

They should be introduced to the idea that **energy sources** may be **renewable** or **non-renewable** and consider the implications of limited **global energy resources**. They should be introduced to the idea of **energy transfer**.

Associated key words **temperature, thermometer, biomass, joule**

■ PUPILS' OWN IDEAS

Children tend to think of hot and cold as two distinct variables, i.e. cold can pass into things making them colder just as heat can make things hotter. They need to be encouraged to think of cold as something lacking 'hotness' and that things get colder when heat is removed.

Children will often think that only living things possess energy, while others connect energy

only with movement, and see no reason to consider where energy comes from or where it goes. Often the words 'fuel' and 'energy' are used interchangeably.

Children need to be encouraged to appreciate that when things happen (not only movement) energy transfers are taking place and that fuels are sources of energy, and are not themselves energy.

■ COMMENTARY AND STARTING POINTS

ENERGY RESOURCES

Ask children *What are fuels? Why do we need fuels? How many different fuels do you each use at home? What is each source used for? How many homes use gas for heating or cooking?* Electric current is not a fuel but is a convenient way of transferring energy from a fuel (for example, coal or gas) in the power station to the home.

After surveying different fuels and their use at home, the types and use of fuels in the school can be explored. The size of the school's energy bill could be compared with a typical bill from a house. Children should begin to realise that the majority of available energy from fuels is used for heating. Through discussion and the use of books children near the end of the key stage could begin to find out about the ways in which we can prevent heat from 'escaping', in simple terms.

Where do you think the heat goes? Some children could be encouraged to draw-up an action plan for the school and reduce its energy bill over the next quarter using simple measures, for example closing doors and turning off the lights. These could be tried out to see what effect they might have over a period of a week or two. The energy use can be checked by reading the school's electricity or gas meters.

Such activities should begin to develop the idea that energy resources can be used efficiently. It is not until Key Stage 3 that children deal with formal ideas about energy efficiency.

Children can be introduced to renewable forms of energy by being challenged to think about where they would get their energy from if coal, oil, gas and nuclear fuel supplies were exhausted. Design activities which involve children in making things, such as windmills to make use of the energy from winds or paddle wheels to make use of the energy from waves and tides are also useful ways of developing ideas about renewable sources of energy.

ENERGY TRANSFER

Children can be introduced to movement by exploring a wide range of differently powered toy cars or models (see **movement**). Ask *what makes it go? How fast does it go?* and *How could you make it go faster?* For example, with a cotton reel tank children could be asked *What makes it go? How could you make it go faster? How far will it go with 20 winds, and with 40 winds? What is the steepest slope it can climb?*

Later children can investigate movement from starting points such as *What affects how fast toy cars roll down slopes? What affects how fast a sailing boat travels? Is there a connection between sail size and the speed of turning of a windmill? What affects how fast a water wheel turns?*

Providing children with a range of models and toys which use gears, pulleys and levers and asking them *Can you see how energy is transferred from the source (for example, the battery) to the wheels? Can you follow its path? Can you see how the gears can change the direction of movement?* can help develop their ideas about energy transfer. Finally children can be asked to make energy chains to show how energy is transferred in a range of simple toys (see **energy transfer**).

When everyday substances such as water, wax and wood are heated children can be prompted with questions such as *What do you expect to see happen? What do you notice? Why did the (substance) get hotter? How can we cool it down? What do you expect to see happening as it cools?* Children should be encouraged to use thermometers to check the temperatures of things that feel hot and cold.

Early in Key Stage 2 children can be provided with some jugs containing water at different temperatures, for example from cold to just above luke-warm (not too hot). Then ask *How good is your sense of touch?* The children can then use their sense of feel to place the water in the jugs in order of 'hotness'. Their order can be checked by measuring the temperature of the water in each jug using a thermometer.

Only luke-warm water should be used. Teachers need to check that the temperature of the water is safe for children to feel.

!

■ IDEAS FOR INVESTIGATIONS – Key Stage 2 Sc4 (ii) energy resources and energy transfer

Investigation *Starting point*	Strand (i) Generating ideas and planning *Pupil's suggestion*	Strand (ii) Doing *Pupil's activity*	Strand (iii) Concluding *Pupils could . . .*
Early in Key Stage 2			
Why do some rooms feel colder than others? (Do some have more windows etc.?)	*I think that rooms with more windows/no carpets/bare walls/more doors/more outside walls feel colder. Big rooms feel colder.*	Try taking the temperature in different areas of the room where they think it will be colder or warmer to test their ideas.	List the temperatures in a table and state whether their prediction was correct.
How can we make a toy car travel faster across the floor?	*I think we could push the car harder/push the car on a hard floor, not carpet.*	Try out their ideas making their tests fair, for example by keeping the 'push' the same but changing the surface.	State what they saw happening, how this matched their expectations and how they made the tests fair.
How can a model windmill be made to turn faster?	*I think you can make a windmill turn faster by blowing harder/using bigger sails/changing the shape of the sails (making them square/ longer).*	Designing fair tests to test their ideas, by changing only one thing at a time, for example size or shape. A hair drier can be used to simulate wind.	They could state which made the windmill turn fastest and how they made the test fair.
Later in Key Stage 2			
What affects how far a jar will roll beyond a slope?	*I think that the weight of the jar/what is in it/the size of the jar/the steepness of the slope/the type of surface will make a difference.*	Roll jars down different slopes making sure that each test is fair by changing only one variable at a time, deciding the range of measurements to be taken (for example, how many different slopes).	State which factors affect the speed at which the jar rolls, and identify any patterns from the range of results. State how these are related to their predictions.
What affects how fast a cotton reel tank can climb a slope?	*I think the steepness of the slope/the type of surface/how much we wind the tank will affect how quickly it climbs the slope.*	Design fair tests which change only one variable at a time. Make a choice about the range of measurements to be taken.	State which factors affect the climb of the tank, and identify any patterns from the range of results. State how these are related to their predictions.
What affects how fast a sail boat will travel?	*I think the shape of the hull/the size of the sail/the shape of the sail will affect how fast it travels.*	Design fair tests which change only one variable at a time. Make a choice about the range of measurements to be taken. The boats can be sailed down a gutter filled with water (stopped at either end); the wind can be simulated by a hair dryer.	State which factors affect the speed of the boat, and identify any patterns from the range of results. State how these are related to their predictions.

What affects how far a jar will roll beyond a slope?

■ What will affect how far a glass jar will roll, after it has gone down a slope?

■ Make a list of your ideas.

■ Plan an investigation to test your ideas. Use your Planning Sheet to help you.

■ How will you make the tests fair?

■ How will you record your results? Use your 'Doing my Investigation' Sheet to help you.

■ TEACHERS' NOTES

WHAT AFFECTS HOW FAR A JAR WILL ROLL BEYOND A SLOPE?

This investigation should be carried out later in Key Stage 2 in conjunction with investigating movement and exploring the idea of energy transfer.

Children can be asked to think about whether the jar has any energy at the top of the slope and then how much energy they think the jar will have if it is placed half-way down the slope.

This can provide a useful introduction to the task and will provide them with the opportunity to make statements such as *The jar will roll further when starting from higher up the slope because it has more energy*.

Resources

- glass jars
- jars filled with liquid, sand, golden syrup
- slopes (adjustable)
- metre rules
- tape measures
- marker pens

Questions to help develop thinking

What do you think will affect how far a jar will roll beyond the slope?
    (supplementary prompts *Do you think the steepness, size of jar, weight of jar, what it is filled with, distance up the slope, will make a difference?*)
Why do you think that?
How can you find out if you are right?
How will you make your test fair?
What will you need to measure?
How will you record your results?

Conclusions

Children could find out that the steepness of the slope will affect the distance rolled beyond the slope, as will the weight of the jar. The substance in the jar will also affect how far the jar rolls; for instance a liquid will make the jar roll more slowly than anticipated because of movement within the jar.

How can a model windmill be made to turn faster?

- Model windmills can be made with cardboard sails. Can you make one like the one in the picture?

- Try out your windmill. Does it work?

- How could you make your windmill turn faster? Make a list of the things you could change that might make a difference.

- How could you find out which ones in your list do make a difference?

- Plan a series of tests to check out your ideas.

- Make sure your test is fair.

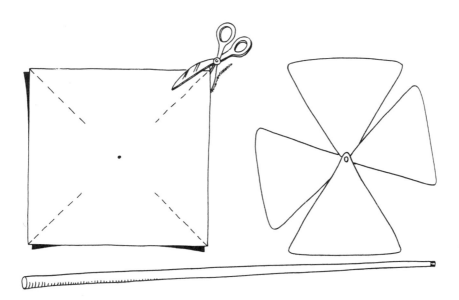

■ TEACHERS' NOTES

HOW CAN A MODEL WINDMILL BE MADE TO TURN FASTER?

This investigation can be introduced when children are exploring movement or renewable and non-renewable sources of energy.

Children will need to be shown how to make a simple windmill using card or paper. They could try changing the thickness of card, angle of the blades, size of blades, or if using a hair drier, the speed of the 'wind'.

Questions to help develop thinking

What do you think affects how fast a windmill turns?
What could you change that might make a difference?
Why do you think that?
How could you find out if you are right?
How could you judge how fast the windmill is turning?
How could you make your test fair?
Will you need to measure anything?

Conclusions

Children should find that the size of the blades, the angle of the blades, and the 'wind' speed will alter the speed at which the sails on the windmill rotate.

Resources

- paper
- card (different thicknesses and sizes)
- hair drier (variable speeds)

ATTAINMENT TARGET 4

Strand (iii) forces and their effects

■ DEVELOPMENT OF KEY IDEAS

	KS1	KS2	KS3
Force	experiencing forces as pushes and pulls, which make things move, stop and change shape floating and sinking	comparing effects of forces measuring forces factors involved in floating and sinking friction, speed balancing systems	forces involved in simple machines, lever, pulley, etc investigating movement measuring speed, pressure relationship between force, work and power turning forces

■ PROGRAMME OF STUDY

(iii) forces and their effects

Pupils should explore different types of **forces** including **gravity** and use measurements to compare their effects in, for example, *moving things* and *bridge building*.

They should investigate the strength of a simple structure. They should be introduced to the idea that forces act in opposition to each other, that one force may be bigger than another, or equal to it, and that the relative sizes and directions of the forces can affect the movement of an object.

They should investigate the factors involved in floating and sinking.

They should explore **friction** and investigate the ways in which the **speed** of a moving object can be changed by the application of forces. This work should be set in everyday situations, for example, **road safety, transport** (including *cycling* and *sailing*), **balancing systems** and **hydraulic mechanisms** in *model making*.

Associated key words **resultant force, pressure, work, power**

■ PUPILS' OWN IDEAS

Young children will use the word force loosely and interchangeably with words such as pressure, power and energy. They tend to associate the idea of force with strength and will tend to think that it is only things that are moving that 'have a force'.

They tend not to consider that systems in equilibrium have forces acting within them. Even in balancing systems, when the forces

counteract each other, there is a tendency to think they just 'disappear'.

The idea of gravity is often confused with ideas about the surrounding air. Some children will express views such as *Gravity is caused by the air pressing down on us*. Hence they may express the view that *There is no gravity in space because there is no air.*

■ COMMENTARY AND STARTING POINTS

TYPES OF FORCES

Forces can be described to children as 'pushes' and 'pulls'. The children could then be asked to experience a range of different forces, recording whether they think they were big, medium or small forces. Forces to try could include: pulling two magnets apart, pushing a polystyrene tile under water, lifting a brick, stretching a spring, squashing a spring, kicking a ball.

They could also be asked to pull a series of different model toys up slopes and asked *Which one needed the biggest pull or force to move it up the slope?* This can be followed by asking children *Can you think of a way to use a rubber band to measure the size of the 'pull', or force, in order to check your ideas?* Larger forces will make the rubber band stretch more: children could use this effect making up their own scale for measuring 'pulls'.

Children could also be challenged to find a way of measuring pushes (for example, using bedsprings, foam rubber or similar). Later force meters calibrated in Newtons could be introduced and used to measure the size of range of other forces. *How much force is needed to open a door? How much force is needed to turn on a tap?*

STRUCTURES

Children can be introduced to forces and structures by showing them how to fold a sheet of paper to make a square section tube, a triangular section tube and a cylindrical section tube (see **structures**). *Which do you think will support the heaviest load? Why?* They can then be asked to test their ideas, making sure it is a fair test. Children could then be challenged to use this new information to make the strongest bridge possible from three sheets of newspaper.

Children could also look at photographs of many different structures such as bridges, the interiors of cathedrals, giant cranes and asked *What can you tell me about the shapes? Are there any common shapes? Why do you think this is? Are some shapes stronger than others? How could we find out?* Asking questions such as these will help promote thinking and should help children identify arches and triangles as 'strong' shapes that can help to 'spread' force.

FLOATING AND SINKING

Children can be reminded of their experiences at Key Stage 1 by being asked to push polystyrene tiles under water and feel the effects. *What do you feel when you push the tile under water? Is the water pushing back? What do you think you will feel if you push the tile in sideways? Do you think it will make a difference?* Children can also weigh things in water and weigh things in air using forcemeters. *What do you think floating things weigh in water? What do you think the things that sink weigh in water and air? Do you think that there will be a difference? If so, why?*

Children could then be asked to use these experiences to make a lump of Plasticine float *How many floating shapes for Plasticine can you find?* Children could then be challenged to investigate the factors affecting floating and sinking. *What affects whether something floats or sinks?*

MAKING THINGS MOVE

Children can be introduced to the idea of friction by sliding objects down a slope. *Why do some objects slide down a slope faster than others? What is stopping some things from sliding down? What sorts of objects slide easily down slopes? What have they in common?* Friction can be introduced as the force which is pushing or pulling on things preventing them from moving. Children could investigate movement using rubber-band powered models, for example cotton reel tanks, and running them up slopes. *How could we make the tank go faster? What do you think affects how fast the tank is going?* are useful starting points when children might suggest the number of turns of the rubber bands, the number of rubber bands used, the thickness of the rubber band, the size of the tank, etc. Children can also explore friction and movement in relation to their own bicycles. *How do your brakes work? How could you make them work better?* and *What affects how fast you go on your bike?* are also useful starting points.

The idea of balancing and opposing forces can easily be introduced through playground experiences such as riding see-saws and pushing each other on swings or roundabouts. Children can be asked to pair up and push each other (hands against hands) so that they are pushing with equal force (they do not move). The children must take care with each other. They could then be asked to predict what would happen if one of them started pushing with a bigger force and then what would happen if someone pushed with a smaller force *What do you think would now happen if someone pushed you from the side? Which way do you think you would move? Try it. Were you right?* Experiences such as these should enable children to explore ideas about resultant forces. Children pushing against each other when on roller skates or sitting on skate boards can also provide useful experiences provided they are carefully supervised. Some of these activities are best attempted in a physical education lesson under careful supervision.

!

■ IDEAS FOR INVESTIGATIONS – Key Stage 2 Sc4 (iii) forces and their effects

Investigation Starting point	Strand (i) Generating ideas and planning *Pupil's suggestion*	Strand (ii) Doing *Pupil's activity*	Strand (iii) Concluding *Pupils could . . .*
Early in Key Stage 2			
What will happen if we wind up the rubber band for 10, 20, 30 or 40 turns in a cotton reel tank?	*I think the more you wind the tank the further/faster it will go.*	Test out their ideas measuring how far it goes or how long it takes to cover 10 cm.	State what they saw happening and list the measurements in a table. They could draw a bar chart and try to identify any patterns, for example the more you wind the rubber band the further the tank goes.
When playing marbles how can you make a marble go the furthest?	*I think you could throw your marble harder/hit it from close by/hit it straight.*	Test their ideas whilst trying to make their tests fair, for example by throwing with approximately the same force and by the same child.	State what they saw and what they discovered and how they made their test fair.
Which sorts of objects float and which sink?	*I think things made of wood/light things/things with air in will float. Heavy things will sink.*	Test each of their ideas, making sure that where appropriate their tests are fair.	State what they discovered, listing their results in a table. Relate their findings to what they expected.
Later in Key Stage 2			
What affects how well an object floats?	*I think what something is made of/how heavy it is/what shape it is will affect how well it floats.*	Design some fair tests to test each of their ideas, changing one variable each, for example time, shape, or material.	State what they discovered and how they made their test fair.
What affects the strength of a bridge?	*I think what the bridge is made of/the length of the span/the thickness of the beam will affect how strong the bridge is.*	Design a series of fair tests comparing a range of different bridges, making decisions about how many different sizes to test, which thicknesses, etc.; select appropriate measuring instruments.	State what they discovered, identifying any patterns, for example *The longer the bridge the . . .*, and saying whether these were what they expected.
What affects the 'pull' of a rubber band?	*I think that shorter/thicker/wider/longer rubber bands are harder to pull.*	Design a series of fair tests, choosing a range of variables to investigate.	Plot graphs of their results, stating any patterns in their results.
Is there a connection between the size of a muscle and the force with which it pushes or pulls?	*I think that thicker arms can lift heavier weights. I think longer muscles can lift heavier weights.*	Measure the circumference of children's arms and ask them to lift a constant weight, just using a bent arm; or measure arm length and repeat experiment.	Plot a scattergram of muscle size against mass lifted; identify and state any pattern in their results.
What affects how strongly a training shoe grips?	*I think that the material/the pattern/how much sole is in contact with the ground will affect the grip.*	Try different training shoes on a tilting slope. The slope can be slowly increased until the shoe begins to slide. Fair tests can be carried out to test their own ideas.	List their results in a table and then draw charts or plot graphs depending on how many results are taken. Patterns can be identified.

What affects the grip of training shoes?

■ You will probably have noticed that training shoes have different-shaped grips on the sole. Good grips make good training shoes. Are some better than others?

■ What do you think affects how well a training shoe grips on to a surface?

■ Write a list of the things that you think might make a difference.

■ Use the idea shown below to find out if you are right.

■ How will you make your test fair?

A simple way of finding the grip of training shoes is to place one on a plank and slowly lift it until it starts to slide. The angle gives a measure of the 'grip'.

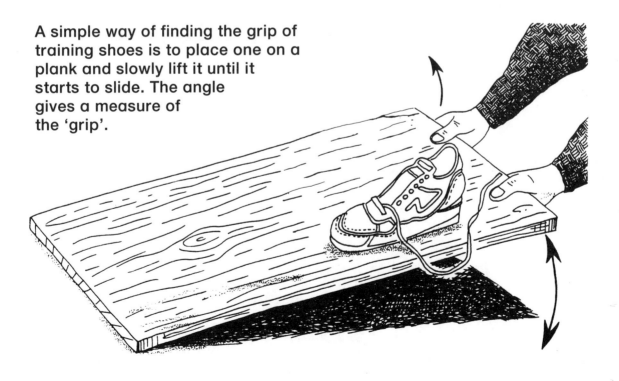

■ TEACHERS' NOTES

WHAT AFFECTS THE GRIP OF TRAINING SHOES?

This investigation can be introduced when children are exploring forces, and in particular friction. This activity may be used as an introduction to friction or as a follow up activity to others which have investigated the factors affecting friction.

In this investigation the children can test out and apply their new knowledge. Children may suggest that the 'tread' pattern, the material from which it is to be made, and size of the sole may make a difference. They may also suggest that the weight of the trainer may make a difference.

Children can use trainers of their own and those of their friends. Alternatively, they can make 'model' trainers with different tread patterns, modelled in Plasticine.

> **Resources**
> - different trainers (with different treads)
> - weights
> - a 'slope'
> - tape measures
> - metre rules
> - protractors (or clinometers)
> - Plasticine
> - balance

Questions to help develop thinking

What do you think will affect how strongly a training shoe grips?
Why do you think that?
How could you use a slope to find out if you are right?
How will you make the test fair?
Will you need to measure anything?
How will you make your measurements?
How will you record your results?
What results do you expect? Why?

Conclusions

As a result of their investigations children should discover that the grip has nothing to do with the tread pattern but that friction between two surfaces is dependent on mass.

ATTAINMENT TARGET 4
Strand (iv) light and sound

■ DEVELOPMENT OF KEY IDEAS

	KS1	KS2	KS3
light	explore light sources shadow, reflection and colour	investigate formation of shadows explore reflection and effects of light through lenses, water prisms and colour filters light travels faster than sound	electromagnetic spectrum transmission, absorption, reflection, refraction and dispersion of light the eye and optical devices
sound	experience range of sounds reflection of sound (echoes) making sounds (music)	sound created by vibration, travels to ear via variety of materials sounds are reflected pitch, loudness, timbre	the ear, audible range, defects of hearing, sound travels as waves control of sound/noise in the environment

■ PROGRAMME OF STUDY

(iv) light and sound

Pupils should learn that **sounds** are heard because they travel to the **ear** and that they can do so via a variety of materials.

They should learn that sounds are made when objects **vibrate**, and investigate how sounds are changed in **pitch**, **loudness** and **timbre** by changing the characteristics of the vibrating objects, for example by changing length, tension, thickness of material of the vibrating object, or the way it is made to vibrate as exemplified by using musical instruments.

They should be aware of the obtrusive nature of some sounds in the environment.

They should learn about the **reflection** of both light and **sound** and relate this to everyday effects (**mirrors**, **echoes**).

They should learn that light travels faster than sound by considering natural events such as **thunderstorms**.

They should explore the effects produced by shining light through such objects as **lenses**, **colour filters**, water, **prisms**.

They should also investigate the formation of **shadows** and represent in drawings their ideas about how light varies in terms of brightness, colour and shade.

Associated key words **wave** (*see* **ear**), **eye**, **electromagnetic spectrum**, **refraction**, **dispersion**

■ PUPILS' OWN IDEAS

Children tend to think of sound as a direct result of their own actions. They may not readily relate the cause of the sound to the vibration of a material, rather that they have caused the sound.

They also do not tend to think of sound travelling but rather that as soon as it is made it is heard. When this is considered they tend to think that in order for it to be heard it must not be obstructed rather than thinking sound needs a medium to travel through, for example air, water or wood.

Young children tend to think of light as just being 'there'; they do not always associate light with a source. Children have many different ideas about why they see things. Some explain their ideas by saying that light comes from their eyes, whilst others think that the light from a light bulb in a room first goes into their eyes, then out again, striking the object that is seen; rather than saying that we see because the light from a source is reflected off the object into our eyes.

■ COMMENTARY AND STARTING POINTS

SOUND

Children can explore a variety of ways of making sounds by making different objects vibrate. A good starting point is to challenge children to find as many different things to vibrate as possible, for example rulers, rubber bands, drum skins, air in bottles (blowing across them). Children can then be challenged to discover the factors affecting the sound produced from a rubber band or a similar vibrating string. They could be provided with a variety of rubber bands and/or nylon/steel guitar strings and asked *What do you think affects the highness or lowness of the note produced? What else about the note changes as you use different strings? Can sound travel through wood, water or space?* to help them to start thinking about the need for a medium within which sound can travel. *Have you heard whale calls? How far do they travel? Can you hear someone tapping a table top with your ear to the table?*

Children can be introduced to echoes by taking them into the school hall or reminding them of experiences such as walking through subways or caves. The idea that sound can be reflected can be developed further by challenging children to make 'sound mirrors'. Hard, smooth surfaces reflect sound best. Metal dustbin lids can sometimes be used to reflect sound to the ear. The lid is held behind the ear and directed towards the sound you want to hear. The shape of the lid tends to bounce the sound to a central spot (similar to a parabolic reflector with light). Children could try their own shapes and materials. *Which is best?*

Another useful starting point for exploring noise is to first explore the sounds around them in and around school by going on a noise or sound walk. Try walking to different areas, ask them to close their eyes and make a note of all the sounds they hear and what they think is making them. *Which is the loudest part of the school? Why do you think that is? Where are the quietest parts?*

Children can try to find out how well they can do things or not. For example they can try solving a series of maths additions or multiplications in a quiet atmosphere and in a noisy one (for example, loud music or shouting). *In which environment did you get most right? Why do you think this is?* They can then be asked to consider how the noise at airports might affect the people who work there, especially those who are responsible for safety.

LIGHT

A darkened room or corner of a room is needed. Strong light sources should be provided, such as a torch, desk-top light or beam from a slide projector. A narrow light beam can be produced by taping a piece of cardboard with a slit cut in it over a torch.

Children can explore shadows by being asked to make shadows of their friends on the wall and then challenged to change the size of the shadow. Useful starting points are *Where will you need to shine the light from in order to make a shadow of your friend on the wall? How could you make the shadow bigger or smaller? Why do you think the shadow gets bigger when the torch is nearer your friend?*

Children could be encouraged to anticipate what they would expect to see when a beam of light is shone through different materials. They could try shining a torch or slide projector beam through a goldfish bowl full of water from the side. *What happens to the light beam as it shines through the water?* Try viewing a fish tank full of water from the side whilst shining a torch from above. *What happens to the light beam as it enters the water?* Try also shining a torch beam through blocks of plastic, glass and prisms. Light beams can be seen to bend; prisms can also produce spectrums. Try placing prisms and tanks of water on OHPs and in front of slide projectors. 'Rainbows' can be produced on the ceiling and walls using these methods.

Reflection can be introduced by asking children to predict where a beam of light will appear when it is shone onto a shiny surface. *If we shine light into the mirror from here where do you think it will go? How can I use the mirror to reflect the light beam from the torch onto the wall?* This can be developed further by asking children how they could use mirrors to see things. *Can you use a mirror to see what is behind you? Can you use a mirror to see round corners?* This can be further developed by making things involving mirrors such as periscopes or even kaleidoscopes.

Children can 'model' the idea of reflection at a flat surface by rolling a ball or marble at a wall and watching the angle it bounces off and then using a narrow beam from a torch at the same angle and observing the angle at which the beam is reflected from a mirror placed in front of the wall. *What angle do you expect the ball to bounce off when rolled from here? At what angle will you expect the light beam to bounce off?*

Children need to develop ideas that we see things because light is reflected off objects into our eyes. Such ideas can be developed by first introducing children to a shoebox in which a number of small objects are placed. A hole is made and the children asked to look in. *Can we see in the dark? Can you see the objects?* Other holes can be made in the other sides of the box. *What do you see now? What causes the differences you see?* Children could then be encouraged to explain why they see a book on a table when the only light in the room is the Sun streaming in through their window. They could be given drawings showing the Sun, the book on the table and themselves and encouraged to add lines to the drawings to show how they see the book. Some older children might be able to design an investigation to find out whether their ideas are correct.

IDEAS FOR INVESTIGATIONS – Key Stage 2 Sc4 (iv) light and sound

Investigation / Starting point	Strand (i) Generating ideas and planning / Pupil's suggestion	Strand (ii) Doing / Pupil's activity	Strand (iii) Concluding / Pupils could . . .
Early in Key Stage 2			
What do you think will happen if we shine red light on coloured objects?	I think the coloured things will look red/look different colours/turn blue.	Try shining light from a torch covered in red on coloured objects and recording the colour seen.	Say what colours the objects appeared under red light and how this relates to what they expected.
Using mirrors can you find a way to see behind you?	I need to hold the mirror in front of me/to the side of me/behind me.	Try positioning the mirrors as suggested and draw pictures to show what they saw.	State where the mirror has to be in order to see behind or to the side and say whether this is what they expected.
Can we hear some sounds better than others?	I think I can hear loud sounds/high sounds best.	Try listening to high notes/low notes made on a recorder at increasing distances across a playground.	State what they discovered and whether this was what they expected.
Can you find a way to make your notes higher/lower (using a drinking straw whistle or bottles containing water)?	I think I can make notes higher by making the straw longer/shorter/using a wider straw, etc.	Try cutting the drinking straw to different lengths, choosing how many different lengths to test.	Identify any pattern, for example the shorter the straw, the higher the note.
Later in Key Stage 2			
What factors affect the pitch of a note (using a stringed instrument or a drinking straw whistle)?	I think I can make higher notes by tightening the string/shortening the string/using thinner string/using metal 'strings'.	Design fair tests using musical instruments such as guitar/violin/recorders. Choose a range of different variables from instruments available.	Record their observations in charts or tables and state any patterns they identify, for example the tighter the string the higher the note, the thicker the string the lower the note.
What makes a good string telephone? (Which factors affect how well sound travels through the telephone?)	I think that the type of 'string' (wire/string/thread)/the thickness of the string/the way in which it is fixed to the cup/the size of the cups/the material the cup is made from will make a difference.	Try making different telephones with different combinations of the variables. Make the test fair by only changing one variable at a time. Choose a suitable range of variables in order to identify any patterns, for example 4 or 5 different thicknesses rather than 2.	State any conclusions in terms of patterns, saying how these relate to their original predictions.
What affects how well a surface reflects light (or sound)?	I think light (or sound) is best reflected from shiny/hard/smooth surfaces.	Design a series of fair tests involving a range of different surfaces to confirm their ideas. They need to consider how well they can measure the amount of light reflected (perhaps using a light meter) or sound (using a microphone connected to a tape recorder with a sound level indicator).	State the results in a table or chart, depending on the range of materials tested, and draw conclusions which relate to the prediction.
What affects how much light bends when it travels through things?	I think that the type of material (plastic/water/glass)/the angle of the beam/the thickness/depth of the material will make a difference.	Design a series of fair tests using a darkened room (or cupboard) to test their ideas choosing the range of variables to measure and select an appropriate instrument with which to measure the degree of bend (ruler, protractor).	List their results in a table or chart, identifying any patterns.

What makes a good string telephone?

■ String telephones can be made from string and plastic cups. Look at the picture below.

■ Try making one for yourself. Can you hear your partner? (You will need to keep the string tight!)

■ How could you improve your string telephone?

■ What do you think affects how well sound travels through the telephone?

■ Make up some sentences like:
'I think that making the telephone with .... will make the sound travel better because ....'

■ Can you think of a way of testing your ideas? Use your Planning Sheet to help you.

■ TEACHERS' NOTES

WHAT MAKES A GOOD STRING TELEPHONE?

This investigation can be introduced when children are exploring sound and in particular when finding out that sound can travel through a variety of materials.

When the string telephone is introduced to children, they may suggest that the length, thickness and type of the material (for example, wire or string), the type of cup (plastic or paper) and the size of the cup may make a difference.

Questions to help develop thinking

What do you think affects how well sound travels along the telephone?
What could you change that might help sound travel better?
Why do you think this?
How could you find out if you are right?
How will you make sure your test is fair?
Will you need to measure anything?
How will you be able to tell that sound is travelling better?
How will you record your results?

Conclusions

The conclusions that children come to will depend largely on the materials used in their investigation. They should find that the type of material and its thickness alters the sound. The size of the cup will also affect the sound. They may also discover that the method by which the string is fixed to the cup makes a significant difference to the sound achieved.

Resources

■ cups (plastic or paper)
■ string (different lengths and thicknesses)
■ wires (different lengths and thicknesses)
■ scissors
■ paper
■ card
■ glue

ATTAINMENT TARGET 4

Strand (v) the Earth's place in the Universe

■ DEVELOPMENT OF KEY IDEAS

	KS1	KS2	KS3
Earth and Universe	day, season and weather changes, relate to the passing of time observe changes in length of day, position of Sun and Moon	track position of Sun, observe position of bright planets and Moon and night sky planetary movement explanations for day/night/year length and phases of the Moon	Solar System, galaxy, Universe introduce idea of gravitational force human exploration of Space and use of satellites

■ PROGRAMME OF STUDY

(v) the Earth's place in the Universe

Pupils should track the path of the Sun using safe procedures such as a **shadow stick** or **sundial**.

They should study, using direct observations where possible, the **night sky** including the position and the appearance of bright **planets** and the **Moon**.

They should learn about the motions of the **Earth**, **Moon** and **Sun** in order to explain **day and night**, **day length**, **year length**, **phases of the Moon**, **eclipses** and the **seasons**. They should be introduced to the order and general movements of the planets around the Sun.

Associated key words **Solar System, Universe, galaxy, gravity, satellite**

■ PUPILS' OWN IDEAS

At Key Stage 1 children will have been introduced to the Earth as a spherical body. They may even say we are living on a spherical Earth but they often have a view that somehow we all live in the sphere or on the top half of it. Ideas about day and night are mixed, with some children persisting with the view that at night the Sun is covered by clouds or hills rather than being caused by the rotation of the Earth.

Young children have ideas about relationships between the Sun, Earth and Moon which place the Earth at the centre.

They also have many different ideas about how long it takes for the Earth to rotate, to orbit the Sun, or for the Moon to orbit the Earth, which are not linked to times of day/night/year, etc.

When discussing movements teachers can help by asking questions which direct pupils to make the link *If day and night is caused by the Earth spinning on its axis how long does it take for one complete revolution . . . ?*

■ COMMENTARY AND STARTING POINTS

TRACKING THE SUN

A useful starting point when tracking the path of the Sun across the sky is to look at the shadows produced by climbing frames, trees or posts in the playground at the beginning of the day and then ask children to predict how they think the shadows will 'move' during the day. Any suggested changes can be marked with chalk on the playground *Where do you think the shadow will be at mid-day and in the late afternoon? Why do you think that? Can you mark the positions of the shadows? How big do you think these shadows will be at mid-day, in late afternoon? Why do you think that?* On no account must children look directly at the Sun.

NIGHT SKY

First study sky maps showing the star constellations in books. At night children can be encouraged to find some of these in the sky and report back the next day to the class. Listen to the weather forecasts and choose a clear night. Some constellations are very difficult to find and children can be encouraged to come up with their own pictures. *Can you make your own constellation? You can do this by drawing imaginary lines between the stars. What patterns can you find?* Some of these bright 'stars' will be stars, some distant galaxies and some of the brighter ones, planets.

Children can be encouraged to be 'cosmic detectives' by distinguishing between stars and planets using simple 'rules of thumb'. *If it twinkles it is a star and if it moves it is a planet.*

Children can be encouraged to make their own star map of a small group of stars and then look at them after a week and then after a second week. If one of the 'stars' has moved in relation to the others it is a planet. The position and shape of the Moon can be traced and recorded by the whole class over a period of a month. *What was the shape of the Moon last night? Where was it and how high was it last night at 6pm?* This can be recorded on a wall chart.

EARTH, MOON AND SUN

The idea of day and night arising from the rotating Earth can be introduced simply by asking children to work in pairs. A child becomes the 'Earth person' and another the 'Sun person'. The 'Sun' holds a torch and shines it at 'Earth'. 'Earth' turns slowly round: at times they are in the light (day), at times in the 'dark' (night).

The movement of the Earth and Moon around the Sun can be modelled using a bright light source to represent the Sun, for example a desk-top lamp or slide projector beam, and then a globe for the Earth and a suitably sized ball used to represent the Moon. The globe can be moved around the light with the other ball (Moon) moving around the Earth. Children can look where the light falls and where shadows form. Practice is needed to get the best results. A strong light source and a darkened room are needed. Children can then repeat this in smaller groups using torches, tennis balls and small footballs. *Can you see which part of the Earth is in day/night as you spin the Earth? Can you see when the poles (top or bottom) of the tilted Earth get daylight all the time/none of the time?* Children could be encouraged to make posters to explain the different aspects, for example day, seasons. Different groups can make different contributions.

PLANETS

Children could be introduced to the movement of planets by making papier mâché models of individual planets and then use books to help them make a mobile to show how they move around the Sun.

They should be encouraged to notice that the planets all move in the same direction and are in the same plane (like a flat plate with the Sun at the centre). The exception is Pluto. *What do you notice about the movement of the planets? In which direction is each moving? What does their orbit look like? Is it a circle or an ellipse?* are useful prompts.

■ IDEAS FOR INVESTIGATIONS – Key Stage 2 Sc4 (v) the Earth's place in the Universe

Investigation Starting point	Strand (i) Generating ideas and planning Pupil's suggestion	Strand (ii) Doing Pupil's activity	Strand (iii) Concluding Pupils could . . .
Early in Key Stage 2			
What affects day length?	I think that days are longer in the summer/ winter.	Study tables of lighting-up times and match the times against different months.	Children could identify any pattern by comparing lighting-up times on the first day of each month and show this on a bar chart. They should state whether they expected their results.
What affects how high the Sun is in the sky?	I think that the Sun is higher in the sky in the afternoon/morning/at mid-day/during the summer.	Using suitable methods, observe the Sun at different times of the day/year, logging its position on a chart.	Write or illustrate what happens to the height of the Sun during a day and/or from season to season.
What affects how brightly a torch shows up an object?	I think the thing is brighter when the torch is stronger/when the torch is closer/when the thing is white.	Children could try out their ideas making their tests fair by changing only one variable at a time.	State what they saw happening and what this means and how it relates to their original ideas. Is this what they expected?
What affects the length of a shadow?	The length of a shadow is affected by how tall the thing is/the time of day/the height of the Sun in the sky. I think that the longer shadows appear when the Sun is low in the sky.	Design a fair test using a stick outside or modelling the Sun using a torch and stick in a darkened room. In the latter case, by choosing a wide range of different heights they could investigate by how much the length of the shadow changes when the height is, for instance, doubled.	List results in a table and then plot results as a graph, with either time against length of shadow or height of torch against length of shadow. Any patterns in their results can be identified.
Later in Key Stage 2			
What affects the size of a crater (on the Moon)?	I think that bigger craters will be formed by bigger meteorites/falling faster/in softer ground.	Design investigations where they drop Plasticine/marbles or polystyrene balls onto different surfaces such as sand, gravel, mud, clay, etc. They can make the tests fair by only investigating one variable at a time.	They can list their results in tables and plot graphs and then identify any patterns and state whether these are what they expected.

What affects the length of a shadow?

■ Have you noticed that sometimes shadows are long and sometimes short?

■ What do you think affects the length of a shadow?

■ Write down your ideas.

■ Can you use a torch and stick to check your ideas?

■ How will you make your test fair?

■ TEACHERS' NOTES

WHAT AFFECTS THE LENGTH OF A SHADOW?

This investigation can be introduced when children are about to track the path of the Sun across the sky.

This will serve as a link between what they have done at Key Stage 1 and Key Stage 2.

It is a very simple investigation and it can be treated this way; however the complexity can be increased for those children who immediately suggest that the height of the Sun will affect the length by asking them to suggest how they might double the length of the shadow, or treble the length, i.e. what is the relationship between height and length?

Resources

- sticks (different lengths)
- metre rules
- string
- tapes
- torches

Questions to help develop thinking

What do you think affects the length of a shadow?
What could we change that might make the shadow longer?
Why do you think this?
How could you find out if you are right?
How will you make sure your test is fair?
Will you need to measure anything?
How will you record your results?

Conclusions

Children should be able to conclude that the length of the stick (tree) and the height, or angle, of the torch (Sun) will make a difference to their results. They should also be able to identify simple ways in which they can use torches in fair ways to test their ideas.

3

A To Z Reference Section
A Guide To The Key Scientific Ideas
Contained Within The Programme Of Study
At Key Stage 2

ACIDITY

Many unripe fruits and some ripe fruits have a natural sharp, sour taste. Sourness (one of the four fundamental tastes; the others being sweet, salt and bitter) is sensed on the sides of the tongue, explaining why people often 'suck their tongues' when tasting the juice of a lemon or vinegar.

The Latin word *acidus* derived from *acere* means sour. Acid is the term given to a substance which, often characterised by a sour taste, has other properties which makes it very useful to man.

As early as medieval times vinegar (an acid) was known to corrode certain metals by gradually dissolving them.

It was also recognised that some chemical reactions would only proceed in the presence of vinegar.

The subsequent discovery of stronger acids, such as hydrochloric, nitric and sulphuric acids, which reacted more quickly with many more substances, contributed greatly to industry.

The majority of reactions in the chemical industry make use of acids. In Victorian times such importance was placed on sulphuric acid that the quantity of sulphuric acid a country manufactured was regarded as an indicator of its economic wealth. Still today sulphuric acid is termed a 'barometer chemical'. Acids are a very important group of substances. Typically acids are substances which:

- Have a sharp, sour taste.
- Change the colour of indicators.
- Neutralise alkalis.
- React with metals to form salts.
- Contain hydrogen.

Acid substances only behave as acids when they are in solution (dissolved in water). For example, citric acid crystals only change the colour of wet indicator paper.

Substances and the acid they contain; suitable for study at Key Stage 2

- Acid drops (sweets) contain citric acid.
- Vinegar – use white wine vinegar preferably – contains acetic acid.
- Lemon juice contains citric acid.
- Orange juice contains citric acid.
- Apple juice contains malic acid.
- Lime juice contains citric acid.
- Sour milk contains lactic acid.
- Yoghurt contains lactic acid.
- Beer contains a mixture of acids.

- Wine contains a mixture of acids
- Tea contains tannic acid.
- Coca-Cola contains carbonic acid (dissolved carbon dioxide), phosphoric and citric acids.
- Lemonade contains carbonic acid (dissolved carbon dioxide) and citric acid.
- Rain water contains carbonic acid (dissolved carbon dioxide).
- Acid rain ('polluted' rain) contains carbonic acid (dissolved carbon dioxide), sulphuric and nitric acids.
- Citric acid (purchase from home brew and health food shops). (Citric acid crystals are classed as an *irritant*. Children should not be allowed to handle these. A solution is safe to handle.)
- Tartaric acid (purchase from home brew and health food shops) (also found in grapes).
- Vitamin C (ascorbic acid) (purchase as a powder) found in fruit and vegetables in small amounts.
- Certain soils contain a mixture of acids.

At Key Stage 3 children will use acids such as:

- Hydrochloric acid.
- Nitric acid.
- Sulphuric acid.

These are all strong acids.

Recognising acids – testing for acids using indicators

It is not always obvious that a substance is an acid. It would certainly be unsafe to rely on taste to identify an acid by its typical sourness. A simple way to identify an acid is to use an indicator. These are solutions of dyes or strips of dyed blotting-type paper carrying dye, which change colour according to whether an acid or an alkali is present.

An acid turns litmus (a standard indicator made from lichens) red, and changes the colour of Universal indicator (another standard indicator) within a range of colours depending on the pH value (a measure of the degree of acidity).

pH value	Colour of Universal indicator
1	red
2	orange-red
3	orange
4	pale orange
5	yellow
6	light green
7 (neutral)	dark green

Many coloured plant materials can act as indicators, changing colour in the presence of an acid. For example, red cabbage solution turns from purple to bright red in an acidic solution and blue in an alkaline solution. Flower petals and vegetables can behave in similar ways (*see* indicators). Growing hydrangea plants act as indicators, turning blue in alkaline soil and red in acidic soil. Gardeners can change the colour of their hydrangea plants by adding peat to make the soil more acidic or by adding lime to make the soil more alkaline.

Acids

Measuring acidity on the pH scale

Different acids can have different strengths. Some acidic solutions may be described as strongly acidic, whilst others are weakly acidic. Strongly acidic solutions tend to be more reactive than weakly acidic solutions. The pH value of a solution describes its relative strength. The pH scale ranges from 0 to 14. Acidic solutions can take a range of values between 0 and 7. A pH value of 1 indicates a strongly acidic solution and a pH value of 6 indicates a weakly acidic solution. Vinegar has a pH value of approximately 3 and is considered to be weakly acidic. The pH value of an acidic solution can be determined using an indicator such as Universal indicator which changes to a different colour for each pH value (*see* indicators, pH).

The pH scale:

0	1	2	3	4	5	6	7	8	9	10	11	12	13	14

← **increasing acidity** — **neutral** — **increasing alkalinity** →

milk
beer
vinegar
orange juice
gastric juice
lemon juice
sour milk
Coca-Cola
apple juice
yoghurt
lemonade
acid rain

strongly acidic ←——→ **weakly acidic** ←→ **neutral**

Typical reactions of acids

Acids and a metal

Metals can react with acids, and when they do so they react in a typical way. In an acidic solution a reactive metal will 'fizz'; and gradually 'dissolve'. A chemical reaction takes place in which hydrogen gas is evolved (the 'fizz') and a solution of a type of substance called a salt is produced (*see* salts). Acids produce hydrogen in this way because all acids contain hydrogen atoms which are chemically joined to other atoms within the acid. The reaction of a metal with an acidic solution can be summarised as follows:

acid + metal → salt + hydrogen

The extent and the speed of this reaction depends on a number of factors:

1. The metal involved.
- Some metals do not react with acid, for example copper, silver and gold.
- Some metals are more reactive than others.

Examples:
- Magnesium (metal pencil sharpeners) reacts quickly.
- Aluminium (pans) can react reasonably quickly but surface tarnish can prevent reaction.
- Zinc (galvanised metal sheet) reacts moderately.
- Iron (nails, screws) reacts slowly.
- Copper (pans, ornaments) will not react with acidic solutions.

The state of the metal will also make a difference. For example, iron filings will react more quickly than iron nails, because of the increased surface area with which the acid reacts.

2. The acid involved.
- The strength of an acid will make a difference; acetic acid (in vinegar) is a weak acid and hydrochloric acid is a strong acid. Weak acids will show little if any activity with many metals.

- The concentration of the acidic solution will alter the speed of the reaction. More concentrated solutions will react more quickly.

3. The temperature.

- Reactions will proceed more quickly if the acidic solution is warm.

In general, acidic solutions suggested for use in Key Stage 2 contain weak acids and will show little, if any, obvious activity with metals. For example, vinegar is a dilute solution of a weak acid (acetic acid) and reacts only very slowly with metals such as iron. If left overnight in vinegar an iron nail or screw will appear much brighter and will probably show a collection of bubbles on its surface.

Acids and a carbonate
Carbonates are chemical compounds, some of which are found in rocks. Typically when carbonates are placed in acidic solutions they fizz, producing the gas carbon dioxide. In this process the acid itself is neutralised; a type of salt is produced together with water. Carbonates are a group of substances which react with acids to produce a salt, water and carbon dioxide gas. The reaction can be summarised as follows:

acid + carbonate →
    salt + water + carbon dioxide

Typical carbonates:
Calcium carbonate   limestone, chalk, in eggshells, in coral.
Sodium hydrogencarbonate   bicarbonate of soda or sodium bicarbonate, in baking powder.
Sodium carbonate   washing soda.

When bicarbonate of soda is placed in vinegar it fizzes, slowly disappearing as it reacts. If more bicarbonate is added, it too will fizz until eventually all of the acid will have been used up and neutralised. The solution will now contain a dissolved substance, a salt called sodium acetate:

acetic acid + sodium hydrogencarbonate →
    sodium acetate + water + carbon dioxide

If a little red cabbage solution (purple) is added to the acid at the start of the reaction it will turn red indicating that vinegar is an acid. As the bicarbonate is added and reacts with the acid the red cabbage indicator will gradually change colour becoming more greeny-blue as the acid is neutralised. If all of the acid is used up and some bicarbonate

remains then the red cabbage indicator will turn blue showing the bicarbonate to be alkaline in solution (*see* indicators).

Lemon juice, containing citric acid, will react in the same way to produce a solution containing sodium citrate. Notice that the name of the salt (the substance formed) depends on the type of acid used (*see* salts).

Acids, alkalis and bases
A base is a substance which will neutralise an acid, so it can be considered to be the opposite of an acid. Alkalis are soluble bases (dissolve easily in water). A base and an alkali react with an acid to produce a neutral solution of a salt. Often no gas is given off, so it is not always obvious that a reaction has taken place, although sometimes the solution does get noticeably warmer. The reaction can be followed by adding a few drops of indicator which will change colour as the acid is neutralised by the base or alkali.

Most common alkalis are hydroxides such as caustic soda (sodium hydroxide), caustic potash (potassium hydroxide) and lime (calcium hydroxide). These are hazardous (*corrosive* or *irritant*) and must not be handled by children.

Milk of Magnesia is a suspension of magnesium hydroxide in water and is alkaline (pH 9), and will neutralise acids such as lemon juice or vinegar. The reaction can be followed by adding a small amount of indicator such as red cabbage solution (purple) which will change to a blue colour as the solution changes from acidic to neutral or to alkaline. The reaction can be summarised as follows:

acid + alkali → salt + water

Examples of neutralising reactions
Acid indigestion
Gastric juice is found in the stomach and aids the digestion of food. Its main constituent is hydrochloric acid (pH 2). Indigestion is caused by excess acid in the stomach (often referred to as acid indigestion). It is alleviated by taking antacids (anti-acids) such as Milk of Magnesia, Rennies, Tums, or bicarbonate of soda.

All these remedies are bases, and so help to neutralise the acid in the stomach relieving the symptoms of indigestion.

The remedies either contain hydroxides, as in Milk of Magnesia, or mixtures of carbonates and hydrogencarbonates (bicarbonates) as in Rennies.

Typical chemicals used in the manufacture of antacids are magnesium hydroxide, aluminium hydroxide, magnesium carbonate, calcium carbonate and sodium hydrogencarbonate (can be found listed on the side of packets).

The effectiveness of each brand can be compared by measuring how much antacid it takes to neutralise a constant volume of lemon juice, using red cabbage solution as an indicator.

Insect stings
Bee stings are acid. Treating with bicarbonate of soda will neutralise the stings and reduce inflammation. Wasp stings are alkaline so the recommended treatment is vinegar which will neutralise the sting. Ant stings contain formic acid. They can be treated in a similar way to those of bees.

Showerhead and kettle descalers
Showerheads and kettles tend to build up limescale deposits in hardwater areas. Deposits are caused by dissolved hydrogencarbonates in tap water being deposited as carbonates, mainly calcium carbonate. Since it is a carbonate it can be reacted with an acid to remove it. Hence descalers tend to contain acids such as formic acid. This reacts with the carbonate which fizzes producing carbon dioxide and calcium formate, a soluble salt.

Fizz
Sherbet and liver salts (for example, Andrews) are powders which contain both a carbonate and an acid (citric acid). When mixed with water they react and produce a 'fizz' (carbon dioxide gas).

Raising agent
Baking powder contains a mixture of an acid (sometimes tartaric acid) and sodium bicarbonate (sodium hydrogencarbonate). When wet and warmed baking powder releases carbon dioxide gas, which bubbles through a cake mixture during cooking, causing it to 'rise'. Carbon dioxide gas is released by a combination of reactions. The action of heat on carbonates releases carbon dioxide, and the reaction between an acid (when wet) and the carbonate also releases carbon dioxide.

Note: baking powder contains more sodium bicarbonate than acid. When it is mixed with water it produces an alkaline solution.

ALCOHOL

Alcohol found in beers, wines and spirits is a chemical called ethanol and is a drug. Ethanol is produced by fermentation, a process in which yeast acts on natural sugars found in foodstuffs.

Beer is made by fermentation of sugars in malted barley, and wine is made by fermentation of sugars in grapes. Beer contains approximately 5% alcohol and wine approximately 12%. One glass of wine has approximately the same alcohol content as half a pint of beer.

    1 unit of alcohol = half a pint of beer
    = 1 glass of wine = 1 measure of spirit

The Health Education Council has recommended that men should drink no more than 21 units of alcohol a week and women no more than 14 units.

Alcohol is both physically and psychologically addictive. It is a depressant and affects the body by reducing inhibitions, impairing judgement and perception, lowering alertness, reducing muscular co-ordination and raising blood pressure. Consumption of large amounts of alcohol can lead to damage of the liver and kidneys and an increase in blood pressure, which can cause damage to the heart.

The liver is a site of detoxification for the body's toxins such as alcohol. Drinking alcohol over many years can lead to the liver cells becoming inflamed and dying, leaving scarred areas (cirrhosis).

At Key Stage 2 children should be aware that alcohol is a drug which is addictive and which affects behaviour, reduces co-ordination and alertness, and can cause careless driving. High levels of alcohol intake can damage the liver, kidneys and heart.

ALKALINITY

Substances can be classified as acidic, alkaline or neutral (*see acidity, neutral*). Alkalis are substances which can be loosely regarded as 'opposites' to acids. An alkali reacts with an acid to form a neutral solution. An alkali is a soluble hydroxide (dissolves in water readily) such as sodium hydroxide (caustic soda) or potassium hydroxide (caustic potash) or ammonium hydroxide (ammonia solution).

However, in general use, the word alkaline is often applied to substances which are not soluble and which should be more correctly referred to as bases. These are substances which neutralise acids and may be hydroxides, oxides or carbonates; for example, bicarbonate of soda (sodium hydrogencarbonate) is a basic substance but is often referred to as an alkali.

> It is appropriate at Key Stage 2 to use the term alkali in a general way and to refer to any substance as being alkaline if it dissolves in water to give a solution of pH greater than 7.

Alkaline substances are often used as kitchen cleaning solutions because of their ability to dissolve grease. This means that they will be harmful to the skin since they dissolve and react with the skin's natural oils. Many soaps, cleaners, and some detergents are alkaline. Alkalis are also particularly damaging to the eyes so great care must be exercised to prevent splashes to eyes. Even apparently safe substances can cause irritation to eyes.

In general alkaline substances will:

- Change the colour of indicators.
- Neutralise acids.

> **Substances and the alkali they contain; suitable for study at Key Stage 2**
>
> - Milk of magnesia (magnesium hydroxide).
> - Antacids (indigestion remedies such as Rennies, Tums, Bisodol) (mixture of carbonate and hydroxide).
> - Bicarbonate of soda (sodium hydrogencarbonate (sodium bicarbonate)).
> - Baking powder (sodium hydrogencarbonate) (see baking powder).
> - Health salts (Andrews) (sodium hydrogencarbonate).
> - Soap (many soaps are mildly alkaline).
> - Washing powder.*
> - Bath salts (mixture of carbonates).
> - Kitchen cleaners* (some contain ammonia).
> - Bath cleaners* (many are alkaline).
> - Floor cleaners* (some contain ammonia.)
> - Glass cleaners* (some contain ammonia).
> - Antiseptics (such as Dettol).

*If it is intended to use any of these cleaners teachers will need to ensure that these substances are safe to use. There may be local safety rules governing their use either adopted by the governing body of a school or the Local Education Authority. In any case it is advisable that children wear gloves (plastic, disposable) and eye protection (goggles) when handling such cleaners. Many of these cleaners irritate the skin; this should be indicated on the label in the form of a 'Hazard sign'. Advice concerning precautions to take when using the cleaner should also be displayed on the packet. It is advisable to check with the Local Education Authority if there is any doubt about the safety of a particular brand.

Children should not handle caustic soda (sodium hydroxide), oven cleaner (which often contains sodium hydroxide) or dishwasher powder since these are strongly alkaline and are corrosive. Alkalis are extremely hazardous to the eyes.

Recognising alkalis – testing for alkalis using indicators

A simple way to identify alkalis is to use indicators. These are solutions of dyes or strips of absorbent paper carrying dye, which change colour according to whether an acid or an alkali is present. Many alkalis will, for example, turn litmus (a standard indicator made from lichens) blue; they will also change the colour of Universal indicator (another standard indicator) into different colours depending on the pH value (the degree of alkalinity).

pH value	Colour of Universal indicator
7 (neutral)	dark green
8	green-blue
9	blue-green
10	blue
11	blue-purple
12	purple
13	purple
14	purple

Many coloured plant materials can act as indicators, changing colour in the presence of an alkali. For example, red cabbage solution turns from purple to bright red in an acid and blue in an alkali. Many flower petals and vegetables can behave in a similar way (see indicators).

How alkaline?

Different alkalis can have different strengths. Some solutions may be described as strongly alkaline, others as weakly alkaline. The strength of an alkaline solution is described by its pH value. The pH scale ranges from 0 to 14. Alkaline solutions can take a range of values between 7 and 14. A value of 14 indicates a strongly alkaline solution while a pH value of 8 indicates a very weakly alkaline solution. Milk of Magnesia has a pH value of approximately 9 and is considered to be weakly alkaline. The pH value of an alkali can be determined using an indicator such as Universal indicator which gives a different colour for each pH value (*see* indicators and pH).

The pH scale:

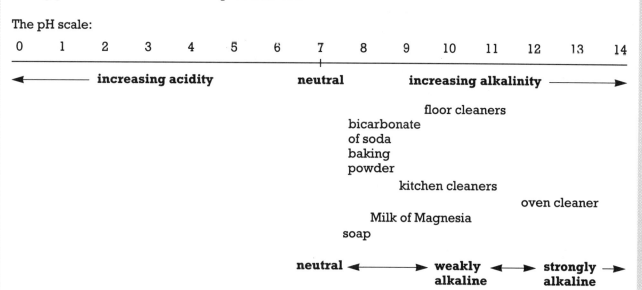

■ ANIMAL

Living organisms can be divided into two broad groups: animals and plants. Both animals and plants can range from simple, single-celled organisms to complex organisms such as trees and mammals. The distinction between plants and animals at the single cell or micro-organism level is not clear and often these single-celled organisms are placed in a separate group called protists. This group includes bacteria.

Both plants and animals have the same life processes which take place in different ways. The main difference between the two groups is how they obtain their nourishment. Animals feed on other living things (predators) whereas green plants make their own food from simple chemicals using the Sun's energy through photosynthesis (producers).

Animals can be divided into two subgroups:

- Vertebrates (backbone).
- Invertebrates (no backbone).

Invertebrates can be subdivided into further groups:

- Coelentera (jellyfish and anemones) – jelly-like bodies, tentacles, live in the sea.
- Molluscs (slugs and snails) – body not in segments, often have shells and single foot.
- Echinoderms (starfish and sea urchins) – spiny external skeleton, live in the sea.
- Segmented worms (earthworms) – long thin bodies, segmented.
- Flatworms (flukes) – flat body, no segments.
- Roundworms – long thin body, no segments.
- Crustacea (crabs and lobsters) – several pairs of legs, jointed skeleton.
- Arachnida (spiders) – 4 pairs of legs, 2 body segments.
- Millipedes and centipedes – many pairs of legs, long body divided into segments.
- Insects (beetle, fly, moth, butterfly) – 3 pairs of legs, 3 body parts, most adults have wings.

This is an incomplete list of invertebrate groups. There are many invertebrates in the world, the largest group being insects. It has been estimated that the total weight of insects in the world is greater than the weight of all the vertebrates.

Vertebrates can be subdivided into 5 further groups:

- Fish – cold blooded, scaly skins and fins, live in water only.
- Amphibians – cold blooded, moist soft skin, lay eggs in water.

- Reptiles – cold blooded, dry scaly skins, lay eggs with soft shells.
- Birds – warm blooded, wings and feathers, lay eggs with hard shells.
- Mammals – warm blooded, skin covered with hair or fur, give birth to live young and suckle their young.

A warm blooded animal maintains its internal environment at a constant temperature. The advantage to the animal is that it is able to move at any time of day or night and in quite cold conditions. The disadvantage is that the animal needs to feed regularly and often in order to generate and maintain its body heat.

Cold blooded animals do not maintain a constant body temperature: instead they are warmed by the Sun. This is why you often see lizards (reptiles) basking in the mid-day Sun. The disadvantage is that they are reliant on their surroundings for warmth, so cannot move very quickly until they have absorbed sufficient heat. The advantage is that they do not have to feed frequently or often, since the energy from the food is not used in maintaining a constant internal body temperature.

> At Key Stage 2 children will often only regard mammals as being 'animals'. Insects, spiders and worms are often not regarded as animals. Humans are also often regarded as being distinct from animals. Children need to be encouraged to think of animals in a wider context than just mammals.

■ AQUEOUS

An aqueous solution is formed when substances are dissolved in water as opposed to any other solvent. Solutions can be made with other solvents, for example alcohol, but these are not aqueous solutions. An aqueous solution of sugar is sugar dissolved in water and is neutral. An aqueous solution of sodium carbonate (washing soda) is alkaline, and an aqueous solution of citric acid is acidic.

■ BAKING POWDER

Baking powder is a 'raising' agent. It consists predominantly of bicarbonate of soda, an alkali, together with a small amount of an acid such as tartaric. Bicarbonate is present in a greater amount, so the powder produces an alkaline solution when dissolved in water. The baking powder acts as a 'raising' agent by producing carbon dioxide gas which bubbles through a cake mixture to produce a honeycombed texture. The carbon dioxide gas is released by two reactions:

When wet the bicarbonate and acid in the baking powder react to produce carbon dioxide gas:

$$\text{acid} + \text{bicarbonate} \rightarrow$$
$$\text{salt} + \text{water} + \text{carbon dioxide}$$

When heated the bicarbonate produces carbon dioxide gas as the bicarbonate changes into a carbonate:

$$\text{bicarbonate} \xrightarrow{\text{heat}} \text{carbonate} + \text{carbon dioxide}$$

Note: bicarbonate is a common name for a group of chemicals referred to as hydrogencarbonates. Hydrogencarbonate and bicarbonate are the same.

■ BALANCING SYSTEMS

Balancing systems such as see-saws and simple 'weighing' balances can be used to explore the effects of forces. Imagine two people, one adult and one child, sitting at either end of a see-saw. The adult's greater weight will force the see-saw down on their side. In order to make the see-saw balance the adult will need to move closer to the central pivot, so their weight will have less effect.

Whether a see-saw is in balance depends on two factors:

- Sizes of the forces (weights) on each side.
- Distance of the force (weight) from the central pivot.

For example, a see-saw will balance if:

- People of equal weight sit at an equal distance either side of a central pivot.

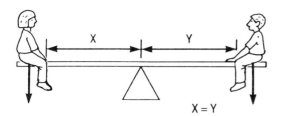

$$X = Y$$

- One person half the weight of another person sits at double the distance from a central pivot.

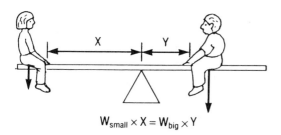

$$W_{small} \times X = W_{big} \times Y$$

The combined effect of force and distance on each side of a central pivot is called a 'moment':

moment = force × distance from a central pivot

For a person weighing 700 Newtons sitting at a distance 2 m from a central pivot the moment will be:

moment = 700 N × 2 m = 1400 Nm
(Nm = Newton metre, the unit of moment)

For a balancing system (for example, a see-saw) to balance, the moments acting clockwise must be equal to the moments acting anticlockwise.

Balanced see-saw

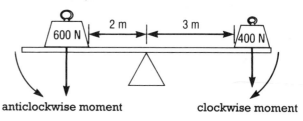

anticlockwise moment   clockwise moment

moments acting clockwise   = 400 N × 3 m
  = 1200 Nm
moments acting anticlockwise = 600 N × 2 m
  = 1200 Nm

Therefore moments acting clockwise = moments acting anticlockwise.

Unbalanced see-saw

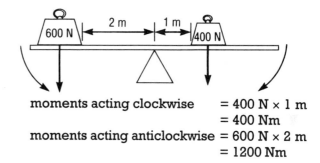

moments acting clockwise   = 400 N × 1 m
  = 400 Nm
moments acting anticlockwise = 600 N × 2 m
  = 1200 Nm

The moments acting clockwise are less than the moments acting anticlockwise, therefore the system will not be balanced and the left-hand side lowers because it is subject to greater turning moments.

This 'law of moments' is introduced at Key Stage 3, an understanding of which is required at Level 7. Experiences with balancing systems at Key Stage 2 should enable children to see the effects of opposing forces acting and how the relative size of a force affects movement. This could also enable them to appreciate that whether a system is balanced or unbalanced depends on not only the relative sizes of the forces but also their relative position from a central pivot or fulcrum.

Note: a mass of 70 kg will weigh 700 N on Earth.

A lever can be regarded as a type of balancing system (*see also* lever, force).

■ BASE

A base is a substance which neutralises an acid. Typically these bases are compounds such as metal oxides and metal hydroxides. Carbonates and hydrogencarbonates

(bicarbonates) can also be considered to be bases since they too neutralise acids to produce carbon dioxide gas as well as a salt and water. A list of common bases is:

- sodium oxide
- calcium oxide
- magnesium oxide
- zinc oxide
- iron oxide
- copper oxide
- sodium hydroxide
- calcium hydroxide
- magnesium hydroxide
- zinc hydroxide
- iron hydroxide

- copper hydroxide
- sodium carbonate
- calcium carbonate
- magnesium carbonate
- zinc carbonate
- iron carbonate
- copper carbonate.

Alkalis are those bases which are easily soluble in water, for example sodium hydroxide (*see* salts, alkalinity).

■ BATTERY

A battery provides energy to an electrical circuit. Chemical reactions take place inside the battery and it is these which supply electrical energy causing an electric current to flow round a circuit. Batteries are classified according to how much energy they supply, the amount of energy being measured in volts. Volts are units of energy (joules/coulomb).

  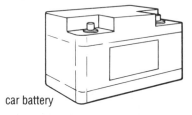

watch battery   1.5 V small batteries   9 V   6 V   car battery

Battery or cell?

In everyday language we use the word 'battery' to refer to electrical sources which may either be cells or batteries. A 1.5V torch battery, for instance, is more correctly referred to as a cell. A cell has only one positive pole and one negative pole. Outwardly batteries appear to have only one positive and negative pole but in reality consist of a number of cells connected together. A 4·5 V battery for instance consists of three 1·5 V cells connected together.

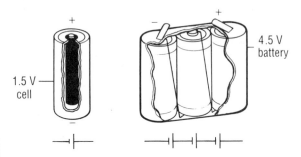

1.5 V cell   4.5 V battery

How does a battery work?

Electricity can be produced if strips of two different metals are placed close to each other in a solution of a salt or an acid. Such solutions

Hence a 6 V battery can supply four times as much energy as a 1·5 V cell.

Batteries come in many different shapes and sizes. However it is important to realise that a small 1·5 V cell provides the same energy as a large 1·5 V cell, although the large one will probably last longer.

react with the metals. This was first discovered approximately 180 years ago by Alessandro Volta. He wrote at the time:

> In order to experience the taste, one must place a clean smooth strip of tin against the tip of the tongue and press firmly. On some other part of the tongue a gold or silver coin is placed, then these two applied bodies are brought into contact with each other. It is worthy of note that this taste lasts as long as the tin and silver are in contact . . . the flow of electricity is continuing without interruption.

You may have experienced a similar 'taste' of electricity if you have a filled tooth and have inadvertently eaten some 'silver' paper from a chocolate wrapping. In both cases the reacting solution is the saliva (containing dissolved salts), and in the case of the filling the two metals are mercury in the filling and aluminium in the 'silver' paper.

Not every solution will behave in this way with metals. Those that do are called electrolytes and contain ions. An ion is a particle containing an electrical charge (either positive or negative). Substances such as salts (for example, table salt), alkalis and acids contain ions, whereas a substance such as sugar does not. Sugar consists of molecules.

A simple cell (battery) can be made using a strip of copper and a strip of zinc placed near to each other in an acidic or salt solution (the electrolyte). The subsequent chemical reaction supplies energy which produces an electric current, lighting the bulb. The cell (battery) will go 'flat' when the chemical reaction ceases.

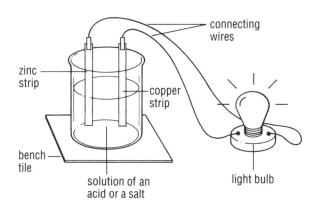

All substances are made up of particles; either atoms, ions or molecules. The atom (the fundamental particle from which ions and molecules can be formed) consists of a nucleus (positively charged) surrounded by electrons. Each electron carries one negative charge.

Any chemical reaction involves the transfer of electrons (negative charges) between reacting atoms to form ions. In a battery this produces a surplus of electrons at the negative terminal, which in turn causes the 'free' electrons which naturally exist in the metal wires of the circuit to move; thus producing an electric current. An electric current is a flow of electrons (*see* circuit).

What makes a good cell ('battery')?

Some metals are more reactive than others. They have a greater tendency or potential to lose their electrons during a chemical reaction. Metals can be placed in order of their reactivity. This order tends to be the same, no matter with what the metal reacts:

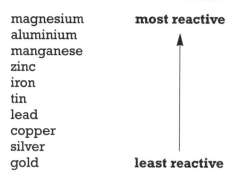

magnesium   **most reactive**
aluminium
manganese
zinc
iron
tin
lead
copper
silver
gold   **least reactive**

In a battery electrons will move around a circuit from one metal to the other. The amount of (electrical) potential energy produced by a cell (referred to as the potential difference and measured in volts) is dependent on the type of metals and the solution (electrolyte). A large potential difference will be produced by a pair of metals which are as far apart in the reactivity series list as possible (i.e. a very reactive metal which loses its electrons readily and one which is not very reactive). The further apart the metals are in the list, the more 'different' they are, and consequently the greater the 'potential difference' (volts) produced.

From the list above a magnesium/gold pair would produce the highest voltage. Unfortunately the reaction would be so fast that it would be over very quickly.

The solution (electrolyte) used could be a dilute acid (for example, vinegar or lemon juice), a dilute alkali (as in alkaline batteries) or a salt solution (for example, table salt, or Epsom salts).

■ BEHAVIOUR

Animal behaviour (including that of humans) can be explained in terms of the effect a type of behaviour has on survival. Certain behaviours are simple and easy to explain, others are more complex.

Some animal behaviours:

- Defending territory.
  Establishing and defending territory is common amongst mammals, birds and fish and even some insects. A territory can provide a steady food supply and a safe place for breeding.

- Aggression.
  Aggressive behaviour is advantageous in that it enables individuals to defend a territory and themselves, protect a source of food and offspring. However, disputes between animals rarely lead to fights which can prove harmful even for the victor, so threatening displays are more common.
- Protecting young.
  Protecting offspring is more likely to ensure the survival of a species.

(*list continues*)

- Social behaviour.
  There are many cases within the animal world where groups of animals co-operate to the benefit of all. Certain groups of animals share 'look-out duty' watching for predators; other animals co-operate in rearing young, for example bees. Many carnivores co-operate by hunting for food in packs to increase their success rate.

- Huddling.
  There are occasions when animals will group together or 'huddle' to keep warm or as a form of protection. Sheep and penguins do this, those on the outside exchanging places at intervals with others from within the group.
- Courtship.
  Courtship displays are designed to attract a mate and hence continue survival of a species.

BELTS

Belts can be used to transfer rotary movement, and hence energy, from one position to another, for example in traction engines.

Escalators and conveyor belts are also examples of belts in action. Thick, wide rubber bands make good belts to use in simple models.

BIODEGRADABLE

Waste products can be classified as biodegradable or non-biodegradable. Biodegradable materials break down naturally by the action of microbes such as bacteria and moulds. Materials which are biodegradable include wood, paper and cardboard. The majority of plastics and man-made fibres are non-biodegradable. However some plastics are now being manufactured so that they are biodegradable. Biodegradable waste materials are advantageous, since they can be disposed of in land-fill sites, without causing undue harm to the environment.

BIOMASS

The amount (mass) of living material within an ecosystem, i.e. a food chain or food web, is called the biomass. It is calculated by weighing all the living things at each feeding level, i.e. total mass of producers and total mass of primary consumers and secondary consumers. The term biomass is also used to describe fuels derived from once-living materials. Wood from trees is an example of a 'biomass' fuel.

BLOOD

Blood forms the transport system of the body. It delivers nutrients and oxygen to cells and removes wastes from cells (see circulation). Blood is composed of a straw-coloured liquid called plasma, red blood cells, white blood cells and platelets.

Blood function

- Plasma transports dissolved substances such as salts and sugars around the body.
- Red blood cells transport oxygen from the lungs to cells and carbon dioxide away from cells to the lungs. Blood is red because of the presence of an iron-containing pigment called haemoglobin.*
- White blood cells fight against disease and harmful bacteria entering the body.
- Platelets aid blood in the clotting process, so helping to seal a wound.

*If the body does not receive enough iron from the diet it is unable to make sufficient red blood cells. As a result an anaemic person feels tired and run-down. Medical advice in this instance is to take more iron. Red wine and liver are good supplies of readily available iron. A vitamin C-containing fruit, for example oranges and grapefruit, should be eaten at the same time as an iron-rich food because iron is only absorbed efficiently into the body in the presence of vitamin C. Blood cells are manufactured in bone marrow of the long bones, for example the femur.

BODY TEMPERATURE

Adult humans maintain a constant body temperature of around 37°C although this value does tend to drop slightly at night. Young children have slightly higher temperatures than adults.

This internal body temperature remains constant even when we exercise and 'feel hot' or when we 'feel cold'. The body is able to control its internal temperature in the following ways.

Excess heat is lost through the skin. The extra heat is brought to the surface by the blood which flows into tiny blood vessels (or capillaries) just below the skin's surface which widen to accommodate more blood. (This is why people often appear flushed after exercise.) The skin then loses this heat by radiation from its surface and, more effectively, by evaporation of water from the skin (sweating). Heat is also lost via warm water vapour when exhaling. Dogs lose most of their extra heat in this way, aiding the process by panting, which causes cooling by evaporation.

On a cold day heat can be generated by shivering. Shivering is a rapid continual contraction and relaxation of muscles to generate heat. 'Goose-pimples' and the raising of hairs on the skin are the body's attempt to retain heat by increasing the insulation at its surface. This is more effective with birds or cats, who 'fluff up' their feathers or fur to trap warmer air. This is why some birds may appear 'fatter' in winter. Humans tend to put on more clothes to produce the same effect. The body also reduces heat loss by narrowing the blood capillaries and vessels near to the surface of the skin to restrict blood flow to the surface, hence reducing heat loss by radiation. This can explain why faces and hands sometimes go 'blue' in the cold (less oxygenated, i.e. red blood getting near to the surface and a reduced rate of removal of carbon dioxide-rich (blue) blood away from the skin).

When a person is ill their body temperature changes (usually rising) as the immune system fights an infection. High temperatures (38°C or 39°C) are an indication of an infection.

At Key Stage 2 body temperatures can safely be taken using forehead thermometers or placing clinical thermometers under the arm. These methods are no good however for taking internal body temperatures after exercise when the surface temperature will rise. A clinical thermometer has to be placed under the tongue for this purpose. Great care needs to be exercised however since the thermometers will need to be sterilised. The school may have safety guidelines governing the use of thermometers which need to be checked before they are used.

BREATHING

Breathing is the process by which air is taken into the lungs (inhaled) and then passed out of the lungs (exhaled). The lungs are a site of gas exchange. Exhaled air is warmer, contains less oxygen, more carbon dioxide and more water vapour than normal or inhaled air. A 'normal' breathing rate for healthy adults is about 12–15 breaths per minute; during exercise this often doubles. The reason for an increased breathing rate is that more oxygen is needed by the muscle cells to release energy from chemicals originating in food, and more carbon dioxide, produced as the waste product of this process, has to be removed.

How do we breathe?

The movement of a large abdominal muscle called the diaphragm largely controls inhaling and exhaling. As the diaphragm moves it causes the lungs to inflate and deflate. The lungs are like two 'sponges' which occupy the body cavity within the rib cage, at the bottom of which is the diaphragm. As the rib cage moves up and out and the diaphragm moves down the volume of the lungs is increased. As a result, the air pressure within the lungs is now lower than the outside air pressure and the lungs inflate (air rushes in from the outside to fill up the space). As the rib cage and diaphragm move in the opposite direction to above then air is forced out of the lungs. The longer the air is inside the lungs the greater the extent of gas exchange that takes place.

At Key Stage 2 children can explore ideas about breathing rate, before, during and after exercise, look at pictures or models of the lungs and attempt to explain inhaling and exhaling as a result of movement of a large muscle (diaphragm) below the rib cage. They can feel their chest rise and fall as they inhale and exhale. They can consider ways in which exhaled air is different to inhaled air, by breathing onto mirrors and seeing the condensation.

Later in Key Stage 2 children could breathe into large glass jars and then light candles under jars in both exhaled and normal air. The candle in the exhaled air will be extinguished first, showing a difference between inhaled and exhaled air.

CARE OF LIVING THINGS

There are many issues concerning the handling and care of living things in schools: Local Education Authorities or governing bodies may well have health and safety guidelines relating in detail to this area which of course must be followed. Many plants and animals are protected and must not be taken from their habitat; details can be found in the *DES Administrative Memorandum No. 3/90* (31 August 1990) *Animals and Plants in Schools, Legal Aspects*, sent to all schools but now obtainable from the Department For Education (DFE). Teachers should also make themselves aware of those plants which are poisonous; there are various posters available listing these.

As far as possible it is better to study plants and animals in their natural habitats, but occasionally it may be desirable to collect animals to observe them for short periods of time. It is important to ensure that such animals are properly cared for and returned to their environment as quickly as possible. It is not appropriate to collect plants from habitats to study them.

Cultivating plants for use in investigations

Useful seeds to study germination in include:

- Various dried beans, for example, broad, runner, lima.
- Chick peaks (soaked overnight these will usually germinate within 1–2 days).
- Cress and mustard.
- Cabbage.

- Trees – acorns, horse chestnut, sweet chestnuts.
- Pips – try orange, lemon, lime. (These will take 2–3 weeks to germinate: place in moist soil in a plastic bag which is then placed in a warm cupboard. Check every few days after 2 weeks and as soon as the pips begin to germinate transfer them to individual pots. The trees produced usually take 7 years to flower.)

Useful plants to study plant growth in include:

- Runner bean, broad bean.
- Chick pea.
- Mustard.
- Cress.
- Sunflower.
- 'Fast plants' (fast growing brassicas available from specialist suppliers).

Care of animals

- Slugs, snails and caterpillars can be kept for short periods of time in plastic tanks with lids. These animals need fresh food every day. If sufficient sized tanks are used lettuces can be grown in the bottom of each tank. The tanks should not be placed on windowsills where they are at risk of overheating by the Sun.
- Woodlice can be kept in similar tanks in which old branches or pieces of bark have been placed.
- Earthworms can be kept in 'wormeries'; the soil must be kept moist and a supply of leaf litter placed on top.

CELL (LIVING)

Cells are the basic building blocks of living organisms (both plants and animals). It is the smallest unit capable of carrying out the essential life processes of producing energy and reproducing.

All cells have the same basic structure:

- Cell membrane, which acts as a boundary.
- Cytoplasm, a solution which contains

dissolved substances, such as salts and sugars.
- Nucleus in the cytoplasm which contains genetic material which regulates a cell (Note red blood cells do not have a nucleus.)

In addition to the above structures, plant cells have a thickened cell wall composed mainly of cellulose, which is dead.

Animal cell

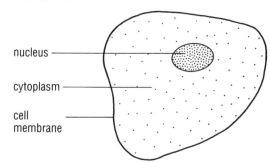

Plant cell

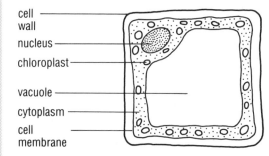

Nerve cell

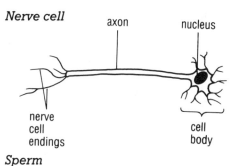

Sperm

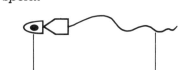

Muscle cell

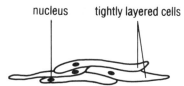

Cell structures can be seen in onion skin, or the leaf of a moss when a microscope at magnification ×20 is used.

Even though all cells have the same basic structure within the body of animals or plants certain cells are specialised (for example, a cell may have a particular shape) which help them perform specialised functions. For example there are nerve cells, sex cells (for example, sperm), and muscle cells each having a characteristic which helps it perform its specialised function.

Cells have only a limited life-span and are gradually replaced by new ones as old ones die. It has been estimated that we effectively have an entirely new body every 4 years! Within living organisms cells are organised into groups.

Structural organisation:

- Cell – the basic unit of all living organisms.
- Tissue – groups of the same type of cell (performing a specific function, for example muscle tissue or nerve tissue (*see* tissue)).
- Organ – layers of tissues collectively performing a specific function, for example the skin, made of different layers of tissue, or the heart, made of different layers of tissue, mainly muscle (*see* organ).

CHEMICAL CHANGE

There are many ways in which changes in materials can be effected, for example squashing, stretching, heating, burning. A chemical change is one in which a new substance is formed which has different properties to the starting substance(s). It is a permanent change which cannot easily be reversed. A physical change is one which can easily be reversed, and no new chemical substance is formed. Melting ice to form water is an example of a physical change since no new substance is formed chemically: the ice has only undergone a change of state and it can easily be returned to ice by cooling. However, when paper is heated it will catch fire and burn to leave ash. This is an example of a chemical change since a new substance is

formed (ash) and the change is permanent. The ash cannot be reconverted to paper.

Chemical changes always involve an exchange of energy with their surroundings. After initial heating, paper will burn. Combustion transfers energy to the surroundings by heating. Whilst there are many other chemical changes which transfer heat to the surroundings, many absorb heat during a course of a reaction.

A chemical change:

- Produces a new substance with different properties.
- Is a permanent change.
- Involves an energy transfer with the surroundings.

Examples of chemical changes

Heating food
When food is heated it changes permanently: the cooked food has different properties. For example the 'white' of a raw egg is a clear liquid, but when cooked the 'white' is white and solid. This change cannot be reversed, because the protein which forms egg-white has been 'denatured', it has undergone an irreversible and permanent chemical change.

Firing clay

wet clay

↓

the clay loses water and becomes hard but the change can be easily reversed by adding water

↓

dry clay

↓

the clay now loses mass by loss of some chemically-attached water molecules. The molecules rearrange, producing new compounds with different properties. These changes are irreversible.

↓

fired clay

Mixing plaster of Paris
When water is added to plaster of Paris (calcium sulphate) a chemical change takes place and the plaster sets. A new substance forms with new properties. Reaction between the dry plaster and water gives out heat energy. As the reaction proceeds the plaster gets warmer as it sets. Energy is transferred to the surroundings.

Mixing baking powder with vinegar
Baking powder contains mainly sodium bicarbonate and vinegar contains mainly acetic acid. An acid reacts with a carbonate (and a bicarbonate) to produce a carbon dioxide gas (*see* acidity). This will be seen as a 'fizz' when the two substances are mixed.

The reaction:

sodium bicarbonate + acetic acid → (in baking powder)   (vinegar)

sodium acetate + water + carbon dioxide (a salt dissolved   (the 'fizz')
in the solution)

If a few drops of some red cabbage solution (an indicator) are placed in a small container of vinegar it will turn red, because vinegar is acidic. Adding the baking powder a spoonful at a time will produce a reaction. After a time the reaction will stop when all the acid in the vinegar has been used up. At this time the acid will have been neutralised by the baking powder and the indicator will change colour to blue, indicating that the overall solution is now slightly alkaline. Careful addition of the bicarbonate a little at a time until the indicator changes to blue-green indicates a neutral solution, where the volume of acid exactly balances the volume of alkali added. In practice, however, using red cabbage solution it is difficult to arrive at an exact neutral point. The reaction can be speeded up if the solution is warmed, if the solution is stirred or if a more concentrated vinegar is used.

Rusting iron
Rust, which is a red-coloured chemical compound called iron oxide, is produced by the reaction between iron and oxygen in air. This reaction takes place in damp conditions:

iron + oxygen → iron oxide

The new substance, rust, has different properties to iron. For example it is not strong, neither is it magnetic. If iron nails are placed in each of the containers as shown in the diagram it is only the nail in container C which rusts – a demonstration of the necessary conditions for rusting to occur.

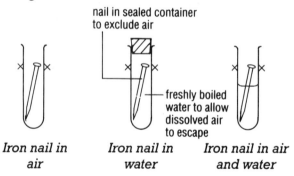

nail in sealed container to exclude air

freshly boiled water to allow dissolved air to escape

Iron nail in air   *Iron nail in water*   *Iron nail in air and water*

If the water is substituted by salt water, the nail will be found to rust much more quickly. This helps to explain why cars tend to rust more quickly near the seaside, and also underlines the importance of washing cars down which have been driven on salted roads in winter.

The rate of rusting can be increased by using iron filings rather than a single nail (an increase in surface area) or by warming the water or by adding salt. Rusting is an oxidation reaction and is similar to burning which is also an oxidation reaction. If iron is heated strongly enough it too will burn: the product is iron oxide. Steel wool will burn when held in a naked flame:

heat
iron + oxygen → iron oxide

CHEMICAL COMPOUNDS

Chemical compounds are pure substances with fixed compositions. Many materials such as wood and concrete are made of combinations or mixtures of chemical compounds, whereas some materials, such as glass and many plastics, consist predominantly of one chemical compound. There are many million different compounds known, so many that scientists have had to cope by finding systematic ways of grouping and naming these compounds. All these compounds, however, are derived from a relatively small set of chemical elements. Elements are substances which consist of only one type of atom. There are 109 different elements known to exist. The Periodic Table is a complete list of the different elements known to man. They can be divided into two groups: metals and non-metals.

All metals are elements; examples of metallic elements are aluminium, zinc, sodium and iron. (*Note:* steel is an alloy, a mixture of the element iron and a small amount of another element, typically carbon which is a non-metal.) Examples of non-metal elements include carbon, oxygen, sulphur and chlorine.

All the chemical compounds in the world are made of different combinations of these elements and are named accordingly. For example, a compound made by combining iron with oxygen is called iron oxide, another made by combining carbon and oxygen is called carbon dioxide.

Compounds can be grouped into two broad groups: organic and inorganic.

Organic compounds

These are compounds which make up all living organisms, plastics and many natural and man-made fibres. They all have the basic structure of a skeleton of carbon atoms, which are joined in chains or rings. Different organic compounds are formed by attaching different atoms to the chains. This group forms the largest group of known compounds. There are many millions of different organic compounds.

Inorganic compounds

These are compounds which are not based on carbon chains; they include such substances as mineral acids, alkalis and salts.

CHEMICAL REACTION

A chemical reaction is a chemical change and is the process by which a single substance or several new substances are formed.

All substances are made up of particles (atoms, ions or molecules) which are chemically joined together by chemical bonds. In any chemical reaction the bonds holding the particles together in the reactants (substances at the start of the reaction) must be broken and new bonds formed when the particles rearrange themselves to form the products.

- Energy is needed to break bonds.
- Energy is released when bonds are formed.

As a consequence of this all chemical reactions involve a transfer of energy. If the energy released when new bonds are formed in the products is greater than the energy required to break the bonds in the reactants then the reaction is exothermic and energy is released to the surroundings. If the reverse is true then the reaction is endothermic.

- A chemical reaction in which energy is transferred to the surroundings is called exothermic (the reaction generates heat).

The burning of fuels, respiration and neutralisation reactions are all examples of an exothermic reaction.

- A chemical reaction in which energy is taken in from the surroundings is called endothermic (the reaction takes in heat). Photosynthesis is an example of an endothermic reaction.

Since a chemical reaction is simply a rearrangement of particles which make up the substances no matter is lost or gained, therefore the total mass of reactants is always equal to the total mass of products.

Chemical equations are used to represent chemical reactions. The equations can give information about the reactants, new substances formed and the proportion of each material in a reaction. All equations follow the general pattern:

reactant(s) → product(s)

There may be one, two or more reactants and one, two or more products formed in a reaction. Word equations are introduced to pupils at Key Stage 3 and describe the reaction in words, for example:

$$\text{magnesium} + \text{oxygen} \xrightarrow{\text{heat}} \text{magnesium oxide}$$

The reaction can also be described in symbol terms which provides more information about the reactants and products, by telling you how much material reacts, and how much product is formed:

$$2Mg + O_2 \rightarrow 2\,MgO$$

This representation tells us that two particles of magnesium react with one particle of oxygen to form two particles of magnesium oxide.

■ CHROMATIC ABERRATION

When a beam of light passes through a lens it is refracted and in some circumstances this can lead to a separation of the colours making up white light. Looking through a lens (for example, on a camera) you can sometimes see these colours around the edges of images, producing a halo effect. This is due to light being dispersed (separated into different colours) by the lens and is called chromatic aberration. This is undesirable in photographic lenses and much effort is put into designing lenses and lens systems which will reduce this effect (*see* lens and prism).

■ CHROMATOGRAPHY

Chromatography is a technique for separating the components of gases, liquids and solutions, allowing the individual substances to be analysed. The technique involves passing the mixture through a 'medium' which, in simple terms, retards the movement of some components more than it does others.

Gas chromatography

In this process, the mixture is injected into a long, coiled tube packed with a solid adsorbent material. A gas at high temperature carries the mixture along the tube, where it begins to separate, the adsorbent material retarding some parts of the mixture more than others. Some substances adsorb onto the surface of the solid more readily than others. The operator knows how long it takes for certain substances to pass through the tube and hence can identify components in a mixture. This is a technique which can be used to detect and quantify the amount of alcohol in blood, for example.

Liquid chromatography

In this process the mixture is added to the top of a column (a glass tube packed with an adsorbent material, for example silica) and is then washed down by a liquid solvent. Once again the adsorbent material retards some components more than others and the mixture separates.

Paper chromatography

In this process the adsorbent material is a type of blotting paper called chromatography paper.

The mixture is applied to a marked 'spot' near to the bottom of a strip of the paper. The paper is then dipped into a solvent. As the solvent travels up through the paper it dissolves the components of the mixture and carries them along. The paper retards some substances more than others so the mixture separates.

At Key Stage 2 blotting paper can be used for the adsorbent material and water-based felt-tip pens can be used to provide a mixture. Black felt-tip pens are a good source.

Method:
A large dot can be placed in the centre of a square or circular piece of blotting paper of area 10–15 cm^2. The paper can then be placed so that its centre rests over the top of a glass. Water can then be dropped slowly onto the centre of the paper allowing it to soak in between each drop. This will gradually carry the components of the mixture outwards when they will begin to separate. Black felt-tip pen inks often contain blue, purple, red and sometimes green.

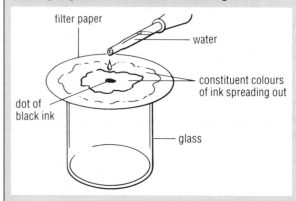

Other mixtures to try:
- Bottled blue or black inks (same technique as described above using water as the solvent).
- Chlorophyll (green) from grass. (Grind the grass thoroughly in a little water in a pestle and mortar. The solution is then dropped onto the paper as described above. One green colour will separate and at least two different 'chlorophylls' will be visible, a green and a yellow pigment. It may also be possible to see an orange pigment (carotene). Whilst this technique will work with grass, water is not the best solvent. Alcohol or nail varnish remover is much better although this introduces the risk of flammability and is not advisable for primary classrooms.)

■ CIRCUIT (ELECTRICAL)

An electrical circuit needs to be 'complete' before an electric current will flow. In making circuits using batteries, wires and an electrical component (for example, a bulb or a motor) wires must connect the component to the battery so that an electric charge can flow through the circuit. The wires must be made of a material which allows electricity to flow through it. Such materials are called conductors. Metals are good conductors of electricity, as is graphite (pencil leads), a form of carbon. When making electrical circuits it is a common mistake of young children to join the plastic coating of the wire to the battery terminals, not realising the significance of the metal acting as the conductor. This will often continue to happen even when children have investigated what makes a good conductor. To overcome this problem it is often helpful to provide children initially with bare wires when constructing circuits.

Electric current

In simple terms, when a metal wire is connected to a battery, the 'free' electrons in the metal pass from one atom to the next. Each electron carries a negative charge. This movement of electrons and hence electric charge is called an electric current. The size of an electric current is measured in amperes and is a measure of the amount of negative electric charge passing any point in the circuit per second.

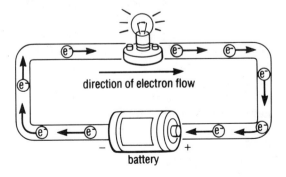

direction of electron flow

battery

Resistance

Materials differ in their ability to conduct electricity. Some materials, such as metals, have electrons which are 'free' to move so are good conductors; other materials such as plastics do not, so these materials offer a high resistance to the flow of electricity.

Wires which are thin offer a greater resistance to the flow of electricity than thick wires; also the longer the wire, the greater its resistance. Resistance is measured in units called ohms.

The wires carrying electricity around the home (the mains) also complete a circuit. The live wire carries the electric charge to the wall socket and hence a device (for example, a television), the neutral wire then carries the electric charge back to the supply box. Hence when the device is plugged in and switched on an electric current flows through the mains circuit. The Earth wire is there as a protective measure and does not normally carry electrical current and will only do so if a fault develops (see mains electricity).

Measuring electricity

There are two fundamental aspects of electricity that can be measured, the size of a current flowing through a circuit and the potential difference (often referred to as the voltage) across a circuit or component.

Two different electrical meters are used to measure these variables.

- *Ammeter*
This meter measures the quantity of electric charge flowing (size of current) in a circuit. The current flowing is the same at any point in a circuit. Therefore the ammeter can be connected anywhere within the circuit. The ammeter must, however, be connected in sequence with components, i.e. in series. Current is measured in amperes (A). Electric current is not 'used up' when it passes through a bulb or any other component.

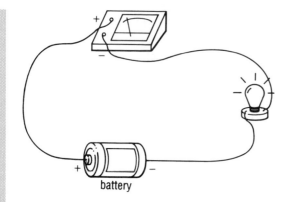

battery

■ *Voltmeter*

This meter measures the difference in electrical potential energy levels (potential difference) across a circuit or component. The voltmeter has to be connected 'across' a component, i.e. in parallel with it. Energy carried by a current is transferred in different ways as it passes through different components (for example, in a bulb electrical energy is transferred by heating and light). The quantity of energy transferred by a component is the potential difference between two points either side of a component and is different for different components. Potential difference is measured in volts (V). Potential difference is often referred to as the voltage.

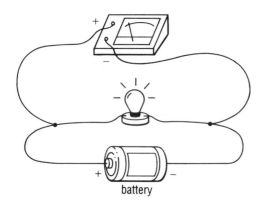

battery

Within a simple electrical circuit potential difference (voltage) and current are related. This connection is described by the relationship:

$$V = I \times R$$

This is known as Ohm's Law where V is the potential difference (voltage), I is the current and R is the resistance. This relationship is accurate for most metal conductors.

Connecting components to form a circuit

Components can be connected to form a circuit in two different ways. It is important to realise that components behave differently when connected in series and in parallel.

A circuit where components are connected in line with each other (the example has three

A series circuit

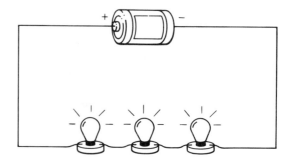

A parallel circuit

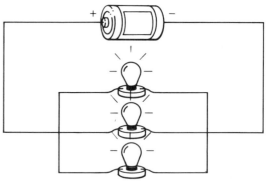

identical bulbs connected in series, forming a chain) is called a series circuit. Each bulb is one-third the brightness that a single bulb would be in the same circuit.

In a circuit where components are connected parallel to each other (see example), each component is in effect connected directly to the battery. In the example the circuit has three identical bulbs connected in parallel. Each bulb is as bright as a single bulb would be in the same circuit.

Choosing components

At Key Stage 2 the emphasis is on children continuing to gain experience of constructing circuits using a range of simple components. Suitable components are:

■ Switches – push switch, microswitch, reed switch, toggle switch and slide switch.
■ Bulbs – screw torch bulbs (1·25 V 0·12 A) are best to use with one 1·5 V battery but will be blown if two batteries are used. In this case 2·5 V 0·2 A bulbs are better. 6 V bulbs can also be purchased to use with 6 V batteries. Light emitting diodes (LED) can also be used.
■ Variable resistors – rotary type (dimmer switches and volume controls on HiFi are examples of variable resistors).
■ Motor – small electric motors which run off 6 V batteries.
■ Buzzer – 6 V or 9 V.
■ Bell – 6 V or 9 V.

CIRCUIT DIAGRAM

A circuit diagram is a stylised drawing of an electrical circuit. Standard symbols are used to represent the different components in a circuit.

Examples

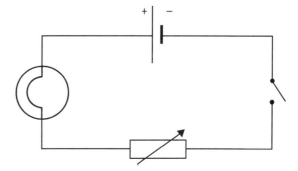

Component	*Symbol*
■ Battery or cell (the long line represents the positive terminal; the short line represents the negative terminal)	
■ Two cells connected	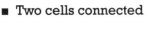
■ Bulb	
■ Switch	
■ Variable resistor	
■ Buzzer	
■ Ammeter	

Connecting wires in an electrical circuit are drawn by convention as four sides of a rectangle.

The circuit shows a battery connected to a bulb, switch and variable resistor (dimmer switch).

> At Key Stage 2 the Programme of Study requires children 'to plan and record construction details of a circuit using drawings and diagrams'. Not all children will be using this more formal and symbolic approach but it will be appropriate for some of the more mature and able children. Most children find it difficult to interpret circuit diagrams and at first they should be encouraged to plan and record by drawing circuits in a three-dimensional form as shown in the example.

light bulb   ammeter

CIRCULATION (BLOOD)

In the human the circulatory system connects the heart with the arteries, veins and capillaries of the body. It carries the blood to all cells, delivering oxygen and food, removing waste and distributing heat. The blood acts as a transport system.

The heart acts as a pump. It has four chambers, arranged in two pairs distinguished by the size of the chambers and thickness of its muscular wall. The two large chambers, called ventricles, pump the blood around the body (you can feel the effect of this pumping action

Diagram of circulatory system

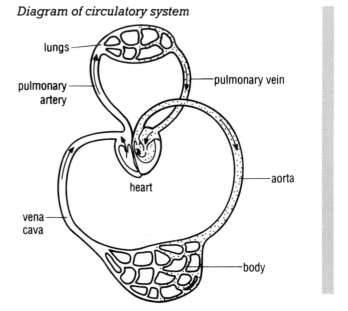

Key

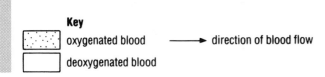

oxygenated blood   ⟶ direction of blood flow

deoxygenated blood

by 'taking your pulse'). The two small chambers are called auricles and receive blood from the body. Arteries carry blood away from the heart whilst veins take blood to the heart.

Deoxygenated blood from the body enters the right auricle via the main vein, the Vena Cava. The blood then passes through a one-way valve into the right ventricle, a pumping chamber with thick muscular walls, which pumps the blood to the lungs via the pulmonary artery.

In the lungs oxygen is absorbed by the blood and waste carbon dioxide (the waste product of respiration) passes out of the blood and is exhaled. The oxygenated blood returns to the left auricle via the pulmonary vein, passes through another one-way valve into the left ventricle and is then pumped to the rest of the body via the aorta, the main artery.

The left ventricle has a very thick muscular wall since it has to pump blood around the body (compared with the right ventricle pumping blood to the lungs only). The aorta branches into smaller arteries which eventually branch into capillaries. Capillaries are very thin-walled vessels which allow blood plasma to leach out and bathe individual cells, exchanging 'food' and 'waste' chemicals with each cell.

Blood returns to the heart via capillaries and veins.

Blood in the circulatory system is also delivered to other major organs, for example kidneys, liver, stomach where other chemicals are exchanged with the cells.

Diseases of the circulatory system

High blood pressure (hypertension) is caused by a narrowing of the arteries and veins which leads to a restriction of blood flow. It is often caused by a build up of deposits of cholesterol (a fatty substance) inside vessels.

A heart attack (myocardial infarction) is caused by an interruption in blood flow to the muscles of the heart. This can be caused by a blockage in the arteries supplying the blood.

At Key Stage 2 children should become aware that blood is circulated throughout the body in 'tubes' called arteries and veins . They can look at their own arms, legs and necks to distinguish the arteries and veins and they can feel their heart beating.

They can take pulse rates, as an indicator of how fast the heart is pumping. (The pulse rate in an adult is about 70 pulses per minute; in young children it is higher and more varied.) They can measure the increase in pulse rate after exercise and see that it does not take long to return to normal (a few minutes). In adults the speed at which the pulse rate returns to normal can be used as a measure of fitness.

They could also make simple models or posters of the circulatory system.

■ CLASSIFICATION OF MATERIALS

At Key Stage 2 pupils are asked to classify materials as solid, liquid or a gas according to properties:

Solids	Liquids	Gases
have a definite fixed shape	have no definite shape, but will take the shape of the container	have no definite shape, will fill completely any container
have a definite fixed volume	have a definite fixed volume	have no fixed volume, will occupy all available space
cannot easily be compressed	can be compressed a little	can be compressed easily
will not readily mix or diffuse into other solids	will mix or diffuse with other liquids	will diffuse or mix with other gases rapidly

Solid, liquid and gas are the terms used to describe the three states of matter. All materials can be assigned to one of these groups. It is possible to convert one state into another by either heating or cooling.

$$\text{ice} \underset{\text{cooling}}{\overset{\text{heating}}{\rightleftharpoons}} \text{water} \underset{\text{cooling}}{\overset{\text{heating}}{\rightleftharpoons}} \text{steam}$$

Change of state from a solid to a liquid is called melting, a change of state from a liquid to a gas is called evaporation or boiling. When substances are heated they also expand and in general the liquid state occupies a greater volume than the solid state of a substance; for example, when a metal is melted it takes up more space than when in its solid state. The exception to this is water. Ice (the solid state) occupies a greater volume than the liquid state (this is why frozen water can burst pipes in the winter).

At Key Stage 3 children are introduced to the kinetic theory which considers all materials to be made up of particles. These atoms, ions or molecules are constantly moving, and increasing the temperature by heating will make them move faster and further apart. Also smaller, lighter particles will move faster.

Solid	*Liquid*	*Gas*
	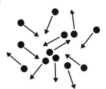	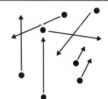

Solids contain particles which are close together and move slowly, vibrating about a fixed position. Solids keep their shape and volume and cannot be easily compressed since there are only small gaps between the particles. Heating increases the energy of the particles, making them vibrate faster. They are able to move further apart slightly, thus the material expands when it is heated. Further heating causes the particles to move further apart with more energy.

Liquids contain particles that are further apart than those in a solid and are moving more freely. This means that they still have a fixed volume but no definite shape. There are also larger gaps between the particles in a liquid which means that they can be compressed slightly. As the liquid is heated the particles gain more energy and move further apart so the liquid expands. Gradually the particles gain enough energy to escape the surface of the liquid and so become a gas.

Gases contain particles that are very fast moving and relatively very far apart. This is why gases have no fixed volume and can easily be compressed, because of the relatively large spaces between the particles. Gases easily mix with each other because of the free movement of their particles. This free, random movement of particles in a gas also explains why smells can spread quickly in a room. The more the gas is heated the faster the particles move and the harder they hit the walls of any container, hence the greater pressure the gas exerts on its container.

Other methods by which to classify materials

By type of material

A material can be classified according to its type, all those of a particular type having similar properties:

- Metal – copper, gold; iron; some metals are alloys, for example brass is a mixture of copper and zinc.
- Glass – glass is made by heating sand with limestone and sodium carbonate; other additives produce different glasses.
- Ceramic – made from clays (silicates), similar in many ways to glasses.
- Plastic – made by linking small molecules in long chains (poly-). All molecules contain carbon.
- Fibre – can be natural or synthetic. Natural fibres include cotton, wool, silk. Synthetic fibres include nylon, acrylic, carbon fibre.

These material groups have differences in their physical properties which determine their use.

Property	Material				
	Metal	Glass	Ceramic	Plastic	Fibre
strength	good, strong when stretched (can be drawn into wires) and strong when squeezed (compressed)	poor, cannot be stretched, but reasonably able to be compressed	cannot be stretched but good at carrying heavy loads (compressed)	reasonably good for stretching; ability to carry loads depends on plastic	high strength when stretched
flexibility	reasonably flexible	not very, brittle	not flexible, brittle	good to reasonable, depending on plastic	very flexible

table continues

Property	Metal	Glass	Material Ceramic	Plastic	Fibre
hardness	generally hard	hard	hard	depends on plastic: some hard, some not	not hard
conductor of heat	good conductor	conducts heat	conducts heat	insulator	insulator
conductor of electricity	good conductor	insulator	insulator	insulator	insulator

Uses of materials:

Metal	Glass	Ceramic	Plastic	Fibre
in building as beams, in car industry as moulded panels, wires for carrying electricity	as containers, windows	as containers, linings in industrial furnaces, building materials, on electricity pylons as insulators	building materials, making sheet materials, containers, as electrical insulation for wires	woven and knitted fabrics, cloth, ropes

By whether material is an element, a compound or a mixture

At Key Stage 3 children will be asked to classify materials according to whether they are elements, compounds or mixtures.

If an electric current passes through water two gases are evolved: oxygen and hydrogen. This is a result of water particles (molecules) being broken down into smaller units. If common table salt is added to the water, chlorine gas is also evolved; this too is a result of salt particles breaking down into simpler particles. If an electric current is passed through mercury (a liquid), it is not broken down into other substances, neither is graphite (a form of carbon). All of these individual substances can be regarded as being 'pure' (for example water only contains water particles), yet some break down whilst others do not.

■ *An element*
A substance which cannot be broken down into other substances by chemical means (for example, transferring energy by heating or electrical current) is an element. An element contains only one type of particle, called an atom. All atoms within an element are identical. Atoms within one element are different to atoms within another element. There are 109 different atoms which are known to exist. All other material in the world is made of different combinations of these atoms.

All metals are elements and some other substances called non-metals.

some metal elements	some non-metal elements
calcium	hydrogen
zinc	oxygen
iron	chlorine
gold	sulphur
mercury	carbon

The complete list of elements can be found in a table which scientists call the Periodic Table (*see* Periodic Table).

■ *A compound*
A substance which can be considered to be 'pure' but which can be broken down into simpler substances by chemical means is classified as a compound. Water is a compound, each water particle (molecule) containing three atoms chemically joined together.

Water, H_2O

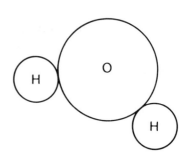

Some typical compounds:

Compound	Chemical formula	Atoms present
carbon dioxide	CO_2	carbon, oxygen
copper sulphate	$CuSO_4$	copper, sulphur, oxygen
hydrogen peroxide	H_2O_2	hydrogen, oxygen
sand (silicon dioxide)	SiO_2	silicon, oxygen

■ *A mixture*

A mixture is an impure substance which can often be separated easily by physical means. An example of a mixture is two compounds such as salt and water. Salt can be separated from water by evaporation. A salt residue remains in the container. A mixture can be a mixture of elements, for example carbon and iron filings. It can be separated by adding to a stirred jug of water. The carbon floats and the iron sinks. An alternative separation method is a magnet which attracts iron but not carbon. Mixtures can be of any substances that, when mixed, do not result in a chemical reaction.

■ CLIMATE

Climate is a description of the typical prevailing weather features in a defined region over a long period of time (35 years). Climate in Britain, for example, is characterised by warm, wet summers and mild, wet winters.

■ COLOUR

White light is a mixture of different coloured lights. If white light passes through a transparent object, for example a raindrop, lens, prism or thin film of oil, it can be split into a range of colours. We see these colours as the 'colours of the rainbow'.

Coloured surfaces

If white light strikes a coloured surface, the surface reflects a proportion of the light and absorbs some wavelengths and so an object appears to be a certain colour.

For example when light strikes a red surface all the colours which make up white light will be absorbed by the object except red light which is reflected back into the eyes so the object appears red.

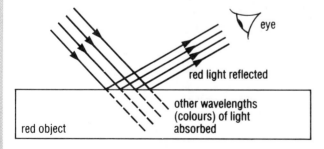

Coloured paints

If coloured paints are mixed, the mixture appears darker, because its surface now absorbs a greater proportion of different colours and less light is reflected. If the coloured paints are mixed further until, theoretically, no light is reflected but is totally absorbed, the mixture appears black.

Coloured lights

If coloured lights are mixed they behave differently to a mixture of coloured paints. In fact, effects are produced which might appear quite surprising at first. The primary colours of light (red, green and blue) when mixed on a screen produce white light.

Try shining torches covered with different coloured filters onto a white screen. Where the coloured light overlaps a region of white light is produced. (A murky grey colour is often seen if the filters used are of insufficient quality and do not produce pure colours.)

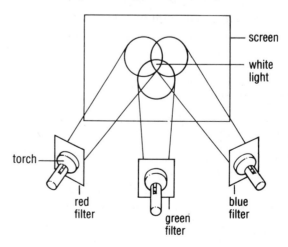

A combination of two primary coloured lights, for example red and green, produces secondary colours as shown.

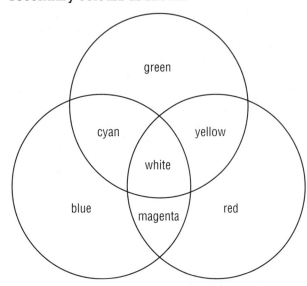

Television

A television sends a beam of electrons to a screen coated in chemicals which give off light when struck by electrons. The screen is made up of a series of dots each of which emits either red, green or blue light.

The circuitry inside the television controls the electron beam by altering its position or switching it on or off for a dot. The image and all the colours on the screen are therefore just different combinations of red, green and blue light of differing intensities. A corner of the screen viewed through a magnifying glass shows red, green and blue dots which together make up a 'unit' of a screen.

Monitors for computers are sometimes referred to as RGB ('red, green, blue') monitors.

Television

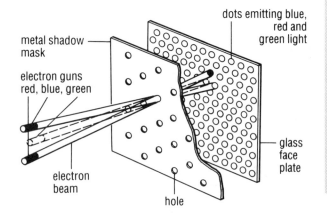

COLOUR FILTER

White light is a mixture of different colours (red, orange, yellow, green, blue, indigo and violet). Colour filters filter out certain colours in white light and transmit certain others. For instance a blue filter transmits (allows to pass through) blue light and absorbs all the other colours.

Some interesting effects can be observed by looking through coloured filters. Objects appear to be coloured because their surfaces only reflect certain colours (*see* colour). Looking through a blue filter at a red object will make the object appear black. This is because red objects reflect red light only and blue filters transmit blue light only so no 'colour' is observed and the object appears black.

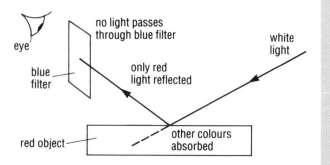

By shining light through coloured filters beams of light of single colours can be produced and these can then be mixed on a white screen. Using different combinations of coloured lights other colours can be made (*see* colour).

COMBUSTION

Combustion takes place when a substance burns in oxygen.

In order for fuels to burn they need heat and oxygen. Removal of any one of these three factors from the 'Fire triangle' prevents combustion from taking place.

Burning a fuel is an example of a combustion reaction in which oxygen from air reacts with

Fire triangle

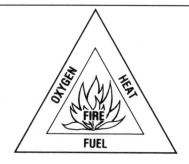

the fuel to form waste products with a transfer of energy by heating. A reaction which transfers energy to the surroundings is exothermic. Energy is released as new chemical bonds form between fuel atoms and atoms of oxygen. Most fuels contain carbon and hydrogen. During combustion oxides of carbon and an oxide of hydrogen (water) are formed:

carbon-based fuel + oxygen
→ carbon dioxide + water (hydrogen oxide) + heat

Combustion reactions

Coal is a carbon-rich fuel and burns in a plentiful supply of air to produce carbon dioxide:

$$\text{carbon} + \text{oxygen} \rightarrow \text{carbon dioxide} + \text{heat}$$
$$(C) \qquad (O_2) \qquad (CO_2)$$

Natural gas is methane-rich and burns in a plentiful supply of air to produce carbon dioxide and water:

$$\text{methane} + \text{oxygen} \rightarrow \text{carbon dioxide}$$
$$(CH_4) \qquad (O_2) \qquad (CO_2)$$
$$+ \text{water} + \text{heat}$$
$$(H_2O)$$

■ COMMUNITY

A community is a group of animals and plants which live and interact in a particular habitat.

A climax community, once established, is one in which the balance of organisms does not change over time: the community is stable. A climax community can develop over sometimes a long period of time. A community may change if its balance is disturbed, for example if man cuts down trees in a forest (*see* succession, human influences).

■ COMPETITION

In order to survive all living things need food, water, shelter and space in which to reproduce. Green plants also need light. As a result of this living things are in competition with each other for the resources available. Competition is often fiercest between individuals within a species.

Examples of competition:

Hens exhibit competitive behaviour by establishing a 'pecking order'. Birds such as robins establish territories large enough to support them and defend these areas vigorously against other members of their own species. Nesting birds will compete for space and defend their nest sites. Some animals co-operate in groups defending their territories against others. Plants, too, compete for scarce resources, some species being better at it than others, for example 'weeds'.

Mustard seeds if a large number (hundreds) are sown in the same area, those seeds that are close will be in strong competition. The plants will grow tall and spindly as they each compete for available light. Only a few flowers will be produced leading to only a few seeds developing on each plant. A plant grown on its own will be strong, healthy and produce many seeds because it has a plentiful supply of available resources.

A plant growing amongst other tall plants will itself have to grow tall to compete and survive.

A plant may grow larger leaves in areas with scarce light resources. Plantains growing in shady conditions, for example in woodland areas, may well have larger leaves than those in open sunny conditions since they have to compete for light.

Adaptations for successful competition

A species can establish a competitive edge over other species when competing for the same resource. For example, fast-growing plants and fast-germinating seeds.

The wild oat is an example of a very successful competitor, possessing the adaptations mentioned above in addition to one further feature which gives it a competitive edge over its competitors. Each oat seed has a twisted orme which slowly untwists when the seed is moistened by rainfall and drills the seed into the ground. To observe this, simply place an oat seed in the palm of the hand and wet the orme; it will untwist.

Examples of adaptation:

Plant	Characteristic	Competitive edge
dandelion, poppy, cow parsley, groundsel	produces a large number of seeds	increases chance of some seeds surviving to maturity
groundsel	short life-cycle, more than one generation per season	increases chance of some seeds surviving to maturity
dandelion (wind dispersal), rose bay willow herb (explosive pod), sycamore seed (wind), blackberries (eaten by animals)	good seed dispersal	increases chance of some seeds surviving to maturity
bindweed, ivy	rapid growth, means of attaching to other plants, structures	increases availability of light
dandelion, daisy	grows very close to the ground	less chance of being grazed or trampled
creeping buttercup	reproduces asexually, new plantlets produced on runners	increases number of offspring, spreading rapidly

COMPONENT (ELECTRICAL)

An electrical component is a device which once inserted into an electrical circuit performs a defined function:

Component		Function
bulb		energy transferred from current to bulb results in light and heat
capacitor		stores electrical charge
diode		allows electricity to flow in one direction but not the other
motor		energy transferred from current to motor results in movement
reed switch		a magnetic switch, activated by a magnet. Two types: normally open (switch off) and normally closed (switch on)
relay		a type of switch where a current in one circuit can open or close a switch in another circuit
resistor		controls the amount of electricity passing. (It resists the flow of electricity.) A high value (for example, 20 000 ohms) allows less current through than a low value (for example, 2000 ohms)
switch		controls electricity passing through a circuit: it is either on or off. There are different types: push, toggle, pressure, tilt and reed switches
variable resistor		controls the quantity of electricity passing through a circuit. A dimmer switch is a type of variable resistor

COMPOSTING

Well-rotted compost takes months to form. During composting the vegetation (in particular cellulose) is broken down by aerobic microbes. These are bacteria and fungi which require oxygen to live. These bacteria also need nitrogen to help them break down plant material. During this process heat is produced, the temperature inside compost heaps steadily rising throughout. The microbes which act in this way occur naturally in the soil and on plant material. The rate at which compost is produced is increased by keeping the heap moist, well aerated (providing oxygen) and supplied with nitrogen by adding nitrogen rich material such as manure, nitrate fertilizer, blood or fish meal. Compost provides a rich source of minerals needed for plant growth as well as improving the texture of any soil to which it is added.

DAILY CHANGES

See environmental conditions.

DAY AND NIGHT

The Earth takes 24 hours to rotate once on its axis. A location on the Earth will therefore be facing the Sun for part of the time (day) and away from the Sun for the rest of the 24 hours (night). The proportion of the time spent by any particular location depends on the distance from the equator and the season (*see* day length).

The Earth spins through 360° during 24 hours, therefore it spins through 15° every hour. The idea of day and night can be demonstrated by shining a torch onto one side of a globe and slowly rotating the globe. During the day the Sun seems to move across the sky; this apparent movement can be demonstrated by imagining you are standing on the globe. Try to describe the position of the torch as it would be seen by an ant placed on the area representing Britain as the globe spins.

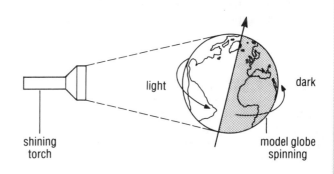

DAY LENGTH

The axis of spin of the Earth is tilted at 23.5°. This gives rise to the seasons which cause variation in day length, as well as the height of the Sun in the sky. During summer the northern hemisphere of the Earth is tilted towards the Sun so more time is spent in the light; during the winter months the northern hemisphere is tilted away from the Sun so the opposite is true.

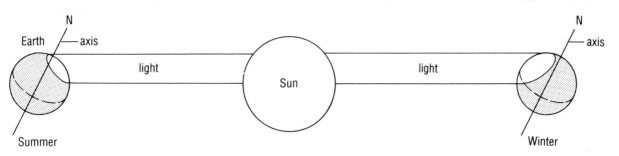

DECAY

Decay is the process by which micro-organisms such as bacteria, moulds, and fungi break down plant and animal materials. These microbes occur naturally in the soil and need moisture, warmth and air in which to multiply and feed on plant or animal material. Decay can be slowed or prevented by changing these conditions. For example, if plant or animal materials are sterilised (any microbes present killed by chemicals such as bleach or sulphur dioxide (released from sodium metabisulphite)) they will not rot. Another method of preventing decay is by excluding air: this is why animal (including human) bodies are preserved in boggy or peat areas. Yet another method of preventing decay is to exclude moisture which is vital for the function of micro-organisms. Well preserved plant and animal remains have been discovered in very dry areas such as deserts. Lowering the temperature, by placing material in a fridge or freezer, slows down decay by inhibiting the action of microbes. Raising the temperature significantly (for example, above 90°C) will prevent most decay by killing the micro-organisms which cause it.

When investigating the key factors in the process of decay (for example, finding out under what conditions bread goes mouldy the quickest) there are health risks involved. There is a legal requirement under the Control of Substances Hazardous to Health (COSHH) Regulations 1988 to carry out an assessment of these microbiological risks. Local Education Authorities or governing bodies as employers will be able to offer advice and will be able to supply codes of practice that must be followed at all times when dealing with microbes.

General guidelines for dealing with microbes

Work involving decay should not be carried out in any part of the room where food might be eaten or prepared.

Only vegetables, fruits and foods from non-animal sources should be allowed to decay. There are much greater risks associated with the decay of animal materials such as meat.

Any foodstuff allowed to decay should be sealed inside a container such as a transparent plastic box or bag preferably with adhesive tape. Once sealed these containers should never be opened and should be disposed of when finished with or when they begin to smell.

If possible children should not handle the containers but if they do they should always wash their hands afterwards.

Decaying material should not be kept in a fridge or freezer where food is stored.

DEFENCE SYSTEMS OF THE BODY

The body has its own natural defence mechanisms. It protects itself against harmful organisms or toxins and combats disease in a variety of ways:

Skin   forms a natural barrier to dirt, germs, etc.; the oil in skin helps to make the skin waterproof.

Nose   contains hairs which filter out particles of dust and other potentially harmful substances.

Vomiting   if contaminated food is eaten, the body may respond by vomiting to eject the harmful substance.

Blood clotting   if the skin surface is damaged, for example by a cut or graze, platelets and other substances in the blood cause it to clot thus sealing the wound and preventing entry from foreign bodies or micro-organisms.

White blood cells   blood also contains white blood cells which form the main defence system of the body. They fight disease caused by micro-organisms (bacteria and viruses). Certain types of white blood cell attack microbes and kill them. Pus is the result of dead microbes and dead white cells. Other white cells can produce antibodies, types of protein which help to destroy invading microbes.

High temperature   when disease is being fought the body temperature rises, causing a fever, and many scientists now believe that this too is a defence mechanism of the body; the higher temperature helps to speed up the production of white cells and also kills certain bacteria.

DENTAL CARE

Decay results when acids attack the enamel of teeth. After eating and drinking, sugary deposits are left behind which are digested by plaque-forming bacteria (amongst others) which convert sugars to acids.

Certain foods are also naturally acidic, such as Coca-Cola, and contain a high proportion of sugar.

In recent years tooth decay has declined considerably, mainly as a result of the introduction of fluoride into toothpastes, and drinking water in some parts of Britain. However, gum disease remains a problem. It is caused by a build up of plaque, which is a layer of bacteria. Unles removed the plaque can spread under the gums causing inflammation which if not treated can lead to the gums receding and eventually loss of teeth.

Checklist for care of teeth:

Avoid sugary foods and drinks especially between meals.
Brush teeth regularly at least twice a day with a good toothbrush and fluoride toothpaste (spend at least two minutes brushing).
Visit your dentist regularly.

At Key Stage 2 pupils can find out about the causes of tooth decay for themselves by collecting leaflets from dentists and health centres. 'Disclosing' tablets can be used to show the difference between well brushed and 'dirty' teeth. These are available from chemists, or through a local dentist.

■ DIET

Diet has a direct link to health. Scientists' views about diet have changed considerably over the last thirty years. In the late 1950s, for example, it was thought that in order to lose weight all that was needed was to reduce carbohydrate intake (the 'starchy foods which were bad for you') and to continue to eat as much fat as desired. New knowledge about foods, digestion and the connection between diet and health has led to different, often conflicting, views, but most scientists seem to agree it is the fat content of the diet which needs more careful control.

Food is eaten to provide energy for the body, raw materials for building new body tissues and the vitamins and minerals to ensure proper functioning of the body processes.

Constituent	Food	Use
carbohydrate (sugars, starch)	potatoes, wheat, bread, beans, peas, fruit	supply of energy
fats	oil, butter, cheese	high supply of energy (more energy than carbohydrate)
protein	meat, cheese, pulses	supply of building materials for the body, but can also be used to supply energy
fibre (roughage) (for example cellulose from cell walls)	vegetables, fruit	provides indigestible 'bulk' which aids digestion. Fibre 'bulks out' the intestine improving its absorption capability. Bulky foods are also satisfying

Healthy diet

A healthy diet is one in which the intake of different food types is properly balanced. No single food contains all the essential ingredients needed to maintain health and sustain growth. The following is a list of unbalanced diets and their possible effect on health:

High fat (particularly saturated fats) diets are linked to obesity, heart disease and cancer.
High salt intake is linked to circulatory problems and heart disease.
Low fibre intake is linked to digestive problems and intestinal cancers.
High sugar intake is linked to obesity, diabetes and tooth decay.

In the 1980s a number of reports were published (COMA 1984, 1989 and NACNE 1983) on healthy diets. The following were recommended:

Fat intake this should account for no more than 35% of the total calorie intake. In particular saturated fats (found mainly in red meats, dairy products and hard margarines) should account for no more than 15%. Unsaturated fats (found mainly in vegetable and fish oils) account for the rest. The number of calories available from fat can be found on food labels. In practice this means consuming no more than about 80 g of fat (from whatever source including meat) per day.
Fibre intake should be increased.
Salt intake should be reduced.
Sugar intake should be reduced.

An average active adult male needs approximately 1500 – 2000 kcal (6300 kJ – 8500 kJ) per day and an adult female needs approximately 1000 – 1500 kcal (4200 kJ – 6300 kJ).

kcal = kilocalories (1000 calories)
kJ = kilo joule (1000 joules)

Both calories and joules are units of energy measured on different scales. (An analogy is the measurement of length in units of centimetres or inches.)

DISPERSION

When white light passes through a prism it is refracted (changes direction) and is often separated into a range of colours. This separation effect is called dispersion. Dispersion of light can occur in other circumstances; for example, when sunlight passes through water, or through raindrops, a rainbow results.

The ease with which light is dispersed depends on a number of factors including the angle of the light beam, the material it passes through and the shape of the transmitting material. High quality glass 60° prisms cause marked light dispersion and for this reason are known as high dispersion prisms.

DISSOLVE

This term describes the 'disappearance' of a substance when it is stirred into a solvent, for example when sugar dissolves in water. Young children often confuse the terms melt and dissolve and sometimes talk about the sugar in water 'melting' or a block of ice 'dissolving'. They need to be encouraged to use these terms appropriately (see melt, solution, solubility).

An explanation of dissolving

The 'disappearance' of sugar in water can be explained at a simple level using the idea of particles. A substance is made up of tiny particles (atoms, molecules or ions) which are in constant motion. Water particles constantly bombard sugar causing small sugar particles to gradually move away and mix with the water. This concept can be demonstrated by placing a number of marbles in a small circle

and then constantly bombarding them with marbles from outside the circle (see particles).

Experiments can be carried out to find what factors affect how quickly a substance dissolves:

Heating   increases the rate at which solids dissolve in water.
Stirring   increases the rate at which solids dissolve in water.
Fine powders   dissolve more quickly than lumps of the same substance.

Examples of substances which can be used in such experiments are:

Table salt (sodium chloride)   large crystals (for example, sea salt) small crystals and crushed salt.
Sugar   lump, granulated and caster.
Epsom salts.
Bath salts.

DRUGS

Examples of drugs are:
- Nicotine (tobacco).
- Alcohol (beer, cider, wine, spirits).
- Caffeine (tea, coffee).
- Cocoa (chocolate).
- Solvents (glues, aerosols).
- Illegal drugs (cannabis, cocaine, heroin).
- Medicines (cough syrups, throat sweets, aspirin, paracetamol, etc.).

Drugs are substances which affect the functioning of living cells (body cells, bacteria and also viruses). All medicines are drugs. Drugs act as stimulants or depressants on the

nervous system, or as narcotics or hallucinogens. They are often addictive.

Many drugs come from plants and belong to a group of substances called alkaloids. Certain alkaloids are powerful painkillers such as morphine or cocaine whilst others such as caffeine and digitalis act as stimulants. Caffeine is the drug found in coffee and tea, and cocoa (in drinks and chocolate) contains theobromine, an alkaloid similar to caffeine which also acts as a stimulant. Tobacco made from dried and fermented leaves of the tobacco plant contains an alkaloid called nicotine which is poisonous but also very addictive and produces a relaxing effect on the nervous system. Smoking cigarettes, the normal way of taking in nicotine, causes many health problems such as high blood pressure, heart disease and lung cancer. Alcohol is also an addictive drug that can have serious side-effects as a result of long-term abuse such as increased risk from heart disease, kidney and liver damage.

■ EAR

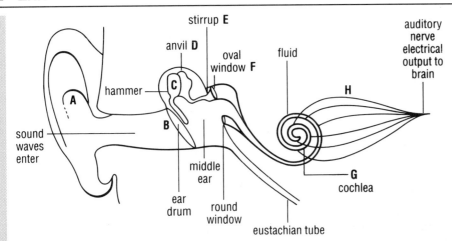

Key
A sound waves enter ear and,
B set the ear drum vibrating,
C, D, E vibrations transferred by three small bones,
F to the oval window,
G which sets the fluid in the cochlea vibrating,
H the nerve endings are stimulated and electrical impulses travel to the brain

The ear is an organ. It receives sound waves which it transmits to the inner part of the ear where they are converted into electrical impulses which then travel via the auditory nerve to the brain.

The external part of the ear is shaped (like an ear trumpet) so that it can channel the sound waves into the outer-ear canal. The canal is lined with hairs and wax in order to prevent entry by foreign bodies. If the amount of wax increases to the extent that sound waves are prevented from reaching the ear drum, a person's ears are normally 'syringed'.

When sound waves reach the ear drum (a tightly stretched membrane) it vibrates. Ear drums can become perforated or in the case of ear infections, inflamed. In both cases the ear drum is prevented from vibrating efficiently and so hearing is impaired.

The ear drum is connected to three pivoted bones which transmit sound waves by vibration across the middle-ear cavity. The bones are connected and pivoted in such a way that they act as tiny levers magnifying the vibration. Hearing can be lost if these bones (the smallest in the body) become dislodged. This can sometimes be rectified by an operation.

The vibrations are then transmitted to another tightly stretched membrane called the oval window. The vibrations set a fluid inside the middle-ear vibrating in a wave-like motion. These vibrations are detected by tiny hair-like structures which trigger electrical impulses to the brain via the auditory nerve.

■ EARTH

Earth is the fifth largest planet in the Solar System and orbits the Sun at a distance of approximately 150 million kilometres (93 million miles). Earth takes 365.25 days to orbit the Sun.

Earth is roughly spherical in shape with a slight 'bulge' at the equator and about 12 750 kilometres in diameter. It is surrounded by an atmosphere approximately 400 kilometres in depth.

Earth is not consistently solid, but instead consists of different layers. The outer layer, called the crust, is made up of solid rock arranged as large plates. These plates migrate extremely slowly as a result of currents flowing in the mantle. It is when these plates move against each other that geological events occur such as earthquakes, mountain formation and volcanoes (see geological events).

The mantle is a semi-molten mass of very hot rock. It is material from this layer that is ejected from erupting volcanoes.

The core is thought to consist of two major parts:

Outer core molten iron and nickel.

Inner core an estimated temperature of about 5000°C, mainly iron with some hydrogen, but exists as a solid due to very great pressures existing at its centre.

An appreciation of the proportions of the different layers can be gained by imagining the Earth as an apple with the depth of the peel representing the crust.

At Key Stage 2 children sometimes ask questions such as *How do they know that the Earth is hot and has liquid in the middle?* Such questions are not easy to answer to the full satisfaction of children but they do provide an opportunity to point out that scientists look for evidence to support their ideas or explanations of the way things are. An example is *I think volcanoes erupt hot, molten rock because deep below the Earth's surface all rock is hot and molten.* If this is true the deeper one digs into the Earth's crust the hotter it should get. In order to test this hypothesis scientists have drilled 'boreholes' (very deep holes a few kilometres in depth) and have indeed found this to be the case. The arguments to support the existence of the cores and their composition are more complex and involve indirect evidence such as the existence and measurement of the Earth's magnetic field, and a study of seismic waves (shock waves caused by earthquakes).

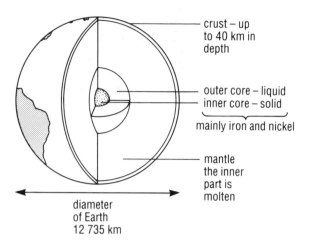

crust – up to 40 km in depth

outer core – liquid
inner core – solid

mainly iron and nickel

mantle the inner part is molten

diameter of Earth 12 735 km

Plates

The Earth's crust is believed to be in a state of constant motion. The crust is believed to be divided into a number of distinct plates. This idea forms the basis of the theory of plate tectonics. The boundaries of these plates coincide with earthquake zones and areas of volcanic activity; indeed this movement can explain the existence of earthquakes and volcanoes. A plate in the crust can be imagined to appear like an area of skin which sometimes forms on custard as it cools. If the custard was being stirred from below one could imagine the skin 'plate' moving around. One theory suggests that the convection currents in the molten rock of the mantle do just this to the plates on the Earth's crust. Sometimes plates are forced against each other when one plate dips underneath the other or buckles (mountains could be formed). Sometimes plates move apart from each other and new rock material comes to the surface, as in ocean trenches.

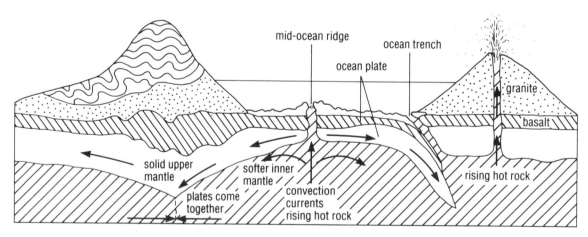

mid-ocean ridge
ocean trench
ocean plate
granite
basalt
solid upper mantle
softer inner mantle
rising hot rock
plates come together
convection currents rising hot rock

■ EARTHQUAKES

Earthquakes are trembling or shaking movements produced on the surface of the Earth. Their intensity can vary enormously. The energy released is measured on the Richter

scale (named after a Californian seismologist, Charles Richter, who invented it). The point on the Earth's surface directly above an Earthquake focus is called the epicentre. These epicentres are concentrated in areas on the Earth's crust which coincide with the boundaries of the Earth's plates.

An earthquake is caused by the stresses and strains resulting from the plates in the Earth's crust moving against each other. The effect can be experienced by pushing two books (or rulers) hard together and then sliding them in opposite directions. They will slide smoothly for the most part but will sometimes stick and produce juddering movements. This is exactly what happens with two plates.

epicentre – the area on the Earth's crust that is directly above the focus

a line connects the points of equal strength detected by a seismograph

focus

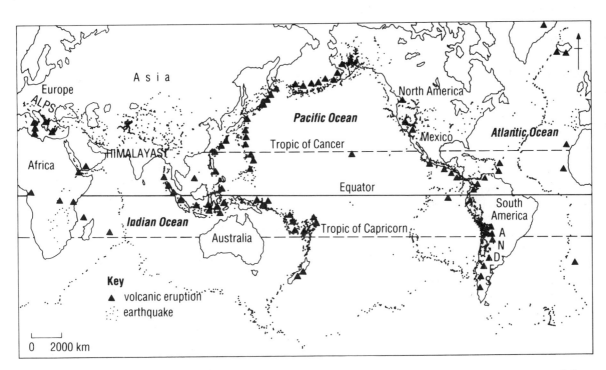

Key

▲ volcanic eruption

⠐ earthquake

0   2000 km

Earthquakes can produce three different kinds of shock wave: one which passes along the surface, called an L (long) wave, which causes damage and two which pass through the Earth.

These are called P (primary) waves and S (shear waves). Scientists can measure the time it takes for these waves to travel through different parts of the interior and emerge at the surface. They can be detected and recorded by seismographs. Interpretation of the evidence gathered yields information about the nature of the material through which the waves pass. Shear waves, for example, are not transmitted through liquids: they are cancelled if they pass through a liquid part of the Earth. Information derived from earthquakes shows that the Earth has three major layers: the crust, mantle and core.

Key

⌇ plate

⟷ pulling plate motion

⟞⟝ pushing plate motion

ECHO

Sound can be reflected from certain surfaces. The best reflectors are smooth, hard surfaces. Soft surfaces such as those provided by carpets, furnishings, fabrics and people absorb sound and prevent reflections. Sound takes time to travel (see speed of sound) and there is a slight delay between hearing an initial sound and its reflection. This results in the formation of an echo.

Echoes can be heard best in large, empty rooms such as school halls or dining areas, churches, pedestrian under-road passageways and from buildings in open spaces. Long curtains, a class of children or a carpet can reduce an echo in a room substantially.

ECLIPSE

An eclipse occurs when light from the Sun is obscured and is prevented from falling on the Earth or on the Moon.

Eclipse of the Moon

This occurs when the Earth lies in direct line between the Sun and the Moon so preventing the Sun's rays being reflected off the Moon to the Earth.

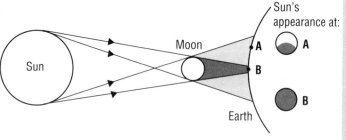

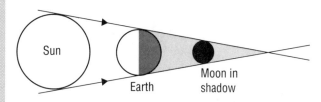

From Earth we see a dark disc moving across the Moon; this is the shadow of the Earth falling on the Moon. A total eclipse occurs when the Moon is in total shadow and cannot be seen. A partial eclipse occurs when the Moon is in partial shadow.

Eclipse of the Sun

An eclipse of the Sun occurs when the Moon moves directly between the Sun and the Earth, obscuring part or all of the Sun.

Eclipses can be illustrated by using a torch in a darkened room to represent the Sun and then using large circles of card to represent either the Earth or the Moon. Children can take up a position looking at the torch beam, and then the card can be 'walked across' the room between the torch and the children to illustrate the eclipse of the Sun. The torch positioned behind the children can illuminate a large white disc (representing the Moon) held up in front of the children. A large disc (representing the Earth) can then be 'walked across' the room behind the children but in front of the torch. This will illustrate an eclipse of the Moon as the 'Earth's' shadow falls on the 'Moon'. The phases of the Moon are sometimes confused with eclipses. Phases of the Moon occur because we see the Moon illuminated from different angles (see phases of the Moon).

ECOSYSTEM

All living things interact with each other and the habitat in which they live. The interdependence of living things can be shown using food chains which show how energy and material transfers from one organism to another. Nutrients are constantly being recycled. A system in which these cycles are balanced and self-contained is called an ecosystem.

An ecosystem may contain different habitats next to each other; for example, a deciduous woodland ecosystem contains a variety of different habitats such as the woodland floor, a leaf, the tree canopy, the trunk of a tree. Within

the ecosystem life is sustained because nutrients are constantly being recycled; for instance the insects on a leaf are eaten by birds whose waste fertilises the earth and provides nutrients for the tree.

A pond is another example of an ecosystem. Different habitats within the pond include the water surface, the water below the surface, the mud at the bottom of the pond and the pond edges. Each different habitat provides different conditions for life, yet material is constantly being recycled within the ecosystem, so that it can sustain itself.

EFFICIENT USE OF FUELS

The United Kingdom derives 93% of its energy by burning fossil fuels (35% oil, 33% coal, 25% natural gas). These fuels are either used directly (for example to provide heating in the home) or indirectly by first being used to generate electricity. Power stations consume one-third of the total fossil fuel supplied.

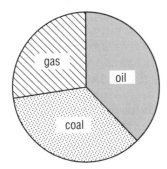

In a power station up to two-thirds of the energy released by the burning of fossil fuels is lost as heat escaping from cooling towers. This system is not very efficient. Power stations can be made more efficient if methods can be found to use this otherwise wasted heat productively.

In our homes too, much of the energy produced is wasted. In an average, poorly insulated house it has been calculated that 75% of the heat escapes:

- 20% heat loss through the roof.
- 25% heat loss through the walls.
- 10% heat loss through windows.
- 10% heat loss through draughts.
- 10% heat loss through the floor.

(*Source: Centre for Alternative Technology.*)

More efficient use of fuels can be ensured by employing higher levels of insulation. Ways of saving energy in the home include:

- Draughtproofing doors and windows.
- Insulating loft and roof spaces with 4" to 6" of insulating material.
- Insulating walls with cavity filler.
- Double glazing windows.
- Fitting heavy lined curtains.

Such measures can reduce the heat loss from houses by as much as 80%. Scandinavian countries have levels of insulation which reduce heat loss even further, to such an extent that in many cases the amount of fuel used to heat homes is less than in the United Kingdom.

The majority of the energy available from petrol used as a fuel in motor cars is wasted. The average car engine is only 15% efficient with much of the available energy in petrol being transferred to the surroundings by heating.

ELECTRICITY

The existence of electrical charge gives rise to the phenomenon of electricity. Atoms can be considered to consist of three fundamental particles, two of which possess electrical charges:

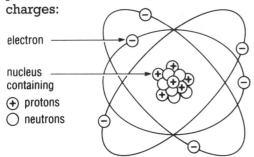

Neutrons found in the nucleus which have no charge, i.e. are neutral.

Protons also found in the nucleus which are positively charged.

Electrons found orbiting the nucleus which are negatively charged. The charge is opposite to, but equal in size to, the charge on a proton.

- Electrons and protons are present in equal numbers in an atom which is therefore electrically neutral.

- Like charges repel each other (i.e. two positive charges or two negative charges), unlike charges attract.

Charges at rest

Static electricity occurs when there is a build up of one type of charge on a material. Materials particularly susceptible to static are plastics or man-made fibres. This build-up can be achieved by rubbing one material against the other. The charge builds up as a result of 'rubbing-off' electrons from one of the materials. One material will end up positively charged whilst the other will become negatively charged.

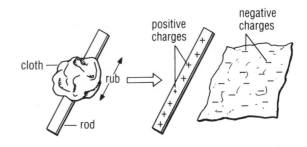

Moving charges

A current results if a negative electric charge (electrons) moves around an electric circuit. This flow of negative electric charge (or electrons) around a circuit is referred to as the electric current. The size of the electric current is measured in amperes, for example 1 amp (1 A) or 13 amp (13 A).

ELECTROMAGNETIC SPECTRUM

All visible light travels as waves. White light is a mixture of light of different colours each with its own characteristic wavelength. Red light, for example, has a comparatively long wavelength whereas violet light has a comparatively short wavelength. This mixture of colours forms what is referred to as the visible spectrum. Visible light, however, is not the only form of radiation which travels as waves: there are, for example, radio waves, microwaves, X-rays, ultra-violet waves and infra-red (heat) waves. All these different forms of radiation are related and are referred to as electro-magnetic radiation. Electromagnetic radiation travels as waves and is affected by electric and magnetic fields. A beam of light, for example, can be bent when it passes through a strong magnetic field. The difference between all these forms of radiation is their wavelength and together they make up the 'electromagnetic spectrum'.

Electromagnetic spectrum

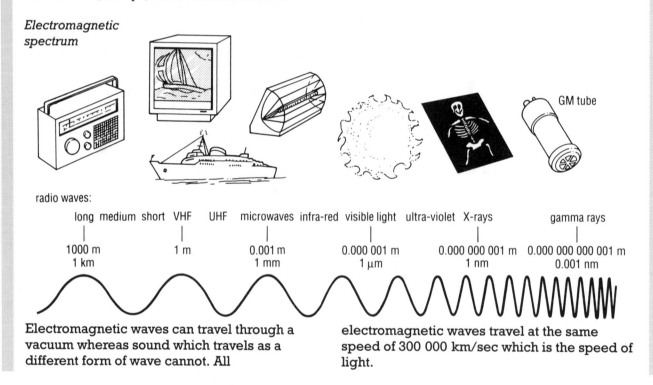

Electromagnetic waves can travel through a vacuum whereas sound which travels as a different form of wave cannot. All electromagnetic waves travel at the same speed of 300 000 km/sec which is the speed of light.

ENERGY

Energy is a useful idea or concept which helps science to explain and interpret different phenomena. Energy is needed to make things happen, and is often described as 'the ability to do work'. It is measured in joules (J). The concept of energy is treated in a consistent way throughout the Programmes of Study for Science in the National Curriculum across all key stages. Throughout, energy is discussed in terms of 'energy resources' (or 'energy sources') and 'energy transfers'. The approach suggests that:

Energy can neither be created nor destroyed.

Materials and objects have energy, and can be regarded as energy sources   It is often helpful to distinguish between energy which is 'stored' (potential energy) and energy associated with movement (kinetic energy). A moving car or kicked football has kinetic energy due to its movement. Potential energy includes the energy stored in fuels 'locked away' in the chemicals and is associated with the energy in the chemical bonds between atoms. Potential energy also includes the energy stored in a clockwork spring.

Materials and objects can transfer their energy to something else For example, when placed on a fire a lump of coal transfers its energy to the room by heating it. A ball moving through the air will transfer some of its energy to the air molecules and some to the ground when it eventually falls to Earth.

Energy transfers make things happen As a result of energy from coal being transferred to the room the temperature increases. When a moving car strikes a lamp-post the energy transferred bends the post.

Energy transfers are 'recognised' by the changes they bring about It is not always easy to 'recognise' energy but we can recognise energy transfers taking place. It is not easy to appreciate for example that a lump of coal has potential energy unless one experiences the energy transfers taking place when coal is burned, or that a ball has potential energy due to its position at the top of a slope until it is released and it starts to roll downwards.

When energy is transferred the total amount stays the same Most of the potential energy locked in the coal is transferred to the room by heating it. Some of the energy transfer however results in light (we see the coal burning) and some in the production of sound (we hear the fire crackling). The total amount of the energy after the event is the same as it was before. This theory is known as 'Conservation of Energy' and is introduced to pupils at Key Stage 3.

When energy is transferred it mostly becomes more spread out and less usable The energy transferred from the coal to a room by heating is more spread out, gradually warming the air, the walls and the floors in the room. It may pass through the walls and spread further in the atmosphere and perhaps eventually into Space. It has not been lost but it is no longer in a usable form.

Kinetic energy

Kinetic energy is energy associated with movement. Any object which is moving has kinetic energy. When energy is transferred from a moving body it slows down. The temperature of an object is dependent on the kinetic energy of its molecules. The hotter an object is the faster its particles vibrate or move (*see* classification of materials). When sound travels through air it is also a result of the vibrational kinetic energy of the air particles.

Potential energy

Potential energy is stored energy.

Examples of potential energy include:

The energy in chemicals There is stored energy in the chemical bonds between atoms.

The energy in batteries and electrical cells There is stored energy associated with the separation of positive and negative charges. Within an electric circuit the current carries the energy.

Examples of energy associated with position of objects:

Stored energy associated with an object raised above the Earth against the force of gravity A brick lifted above the ground has potential energy; the higher it is the more potential energy it has. The amount of potential energy possessed by an object also depends on its mass. The more 'massive' an object the greater its potential energy above the Earth.

Stored energy associated with changing the shape of an elastic object For example, squashing a spring, stretching a rubber band, or bending a ruler.

There are a number of different energy resources, some of which are called fuels. Energy resources include coal, oil, gas, wind, tidal and nuclear. There are also a number of different ways in which energy can be transferred. Energy transfers can be associated with electricity, sound, light, chemical changes, and heating. (*See also* energy sources and energy transfer.)

ENERGY SOURCES

There are two sorts of energy sources, renewable and non-renewable.

Non-renewable energy sources are those which include:

Fossil fuel coal, gas, oil.
Nuclear fuel these sources have the advantage that they are relatively easy to exploit and are reliable, the disadvantages being that they contribute to the world's pollution (*see* pollution) and that they will run out.

Renewable energy sources include:

Tide rise and fall of the tides is caused by the pull of the Moon's gravity on the surface waters of the Earth.
Wind caused by the uneven heating of the

Earth's land and seas by the Sun.

Waves   caused by the uneven heating of the Earth's land and seas by the Sun.

Solar   the Sun's radiant energy can be transferred to electricity by a solar panel and is transferred to green plants through the process of photosynthesis.

Geothermal   the energy from the hot rocks below the Earth's surface.

Biomass   living material (such as trees, plants, etc.) which can be used as a fuel. Green plants are able to photosynthesise.

These renewable energy sources have the advantage that they are relatively clean and non-polluting, and will not run out. The disadvantages are that they are not always easy to exploit on a large scale and they do not provide a consistent supply. (The Sun does not always shine when and where you want it to.)

Electricity is not an energy source (often regarded as such by children) but rather a means of transferring energy. At Key Stage 3 children are expected to 'understand that the Sun is ultimately the major energy source for the Earth' (Sc 4/6c). Directly or indirectly the Sun provides for the vast majority of our energy needs through winds, waves, solar energy, biomass (growth of plants) and the production of fossil fuels. Food is also an energy source, for ourselves and other living things. The energy of the Sun is used within the process of photosynthesis in green plants to produce carbohydrate from carbon dioxide in the air and water from within the plant. Energy from the tides and geothermal energy are not dependent on the Sun.

ENERGY TRANSFER

Energy transfers are needed to make things happen. Change occurs as a result of an energy transfer and can be recognised in a range of different processes or situations.

Energy transfers are associated with chemical change, electricity, heating, light, sound, and the position and movement of objects.

During chemical change energy is transferred to or from the surroundings. Most chemical changes result in a warming of the surroundings. Chemical reactions result in the rearrangement of the particles (molecules, atoms and ions) in substances resulting from the breaking and making of chemical bonds between atoms. Breaking chemical bonds requires energy whereas forming chemical bonds releases energy.

Electrical cells or batteries have potential energy due to the separation of positive and negative charge. Energy is transferred in an electrical circuit by the current.

Heating is an example of energy transfer always in the direction of a hot object to a cooler object. The particles which make up substances are in constant motion (*see* classification of materials): the hotter an object becomes the more kinetic energy its particles possess (the faster they are moving or vibrating). Heating is a common way by which energy is transferred, for example when a room is warmed by a fire, and an electric kettle transfers energy to the water by heating it, turning it into steam.

In many energy transfer situations some of the energy appears to be 'lost'. This can usually be accounted for by heating which accompanies many of these events. For example, when you transfer energy from yourself to a bicycle wheel by spinning it, the wheel will turn (having gained kinetic energy) but will eventually stop, the energy appearing to have been 'lost'. Much of this 'lost' energy has been transferred to the wheel and axle by heating it; this effect is caused by friction between the wheel and axle.

Light transfers energy from any light source to an object in its path.

Sound is caused by vibration and travels through the air (or any medium) by making the particles (atoms and molecules) vibrate. This vibration is kinetic energy, thus sound can transfer energy.

Energy can be transferred within mechanical systems; for example, one can follow the energy transfers from potential to kinetic energy when a clockwork toy car is wound. Winding the spring transfers energy to the spring as potential energy, releasing the spring transfers energy to the wheels of the car as kinetic energy.

Examples of energy transfer
Within any situation involving an energy transfer more than one is often taking place. For example when an electric drill is drilling a hole in a piece of wood, some of the energy is transferred to do something useful like making the drill bit move, whereas some is 'wasted' by heating the motor. This idea can be represented by 'arrow diagrams', for example:

Working a drill

electricity in drill → turning the drill bit → changing the shape of the wood

heating of the wood

sound of the motor

heating the motor

Burning a candle

energy in the wax → heating the air

light

Riding a bicycle up a hill

energy in person → kinetic energy in pedals → kinetic energy in wheels →

kinetic energy making the air move around cyclist

potential energy at the top of the hill

heating of axle and wheel due to friction

heating of pedal axle due to friction

heating of air from hot body

At Key Stage 2 pupils are introduced to the idea of energy transfer. This is best done by choosing familiar situations that perhaps involve movement of one kind or another. Children can be encouraged to identify where the energy is. *What makes it go? Where is the energy?* and then to attempt to identify where it goes. *Where is the energy now?* When introducing the idea of energy transfer it is appropriate to concentrate only on the main energy transfer. Examples are:

- Winding up cotton reel tank
  energy in person → energy stored (potential energy) in rubber band → movement (kinetic energy) in wheels.
- Ball at the top of a slope
  energy stored (potential energy) in ball → movement (kinetic energy) as the ball rolls down slope.

- Striking a match
  stored energy in chemicals in match (potential energy) → heat and light in burning match.
- Moving an electric toy car
  stored energy in battery (potential energy) → movement (kinetic energy) in the wheels.
- Ringing an electric bell
  stored energy in battery (potential energy) → movement (kinetic energy) in the clapper → sound travelling through air.
- Mixing plaster of Paris
  stored energy in chemicals (potential energy) → heating the chemicals and surroundings.
- Winding a clockwork toy
  energy in person → stored (potential) energy in spring → movement (kinetic energy) making toy move.

ENVIRONMENT

The surroundings and condition of those surroundings determine whether or not an organism can survive. Animals and plants are suited to the environment in which they live; this enables them to survive (*see* survival).

ENVIRONMENTAL CONDITIONS

Environmental conditions affect the survival and behaviour of animals and plants. Many changes in environmental conditions can be measured simply using home-made instruments or those purchased at garden centres. Many of these environmental conditions can also be measured using probes connected to a computer.

Environmental condition	Example of comparative study	Measuring instrument
temperature	plants growing in greenhouse/outside plants growing in north-facing/south-facing gardens	thermometer
humidity	plants growing in humid environment, for example bottle garden/plants growing in dry conditions	hygrometer (can be made from simple coils of thin card)
moisture	plants growing in moist soil/dry soil plants which grow in boggy conditions/dry conditions	moisture meter (available from garden centres)
rainfall	plants growing in areas of high rainfall/plants growing in areas of low rainfall	raingauge
light intensity	plants growing in shade/full Sun plants growing in north-facing/south-facing gardens	light meter
wind	trees growing in exposed areas/sheltered areas	anemometer
pH (acidity)	plants growing in acid/neutral or alkaline soil	pH meter (available at garden centre) or indicator made from plants or pH paper
salt	plants growing near sea/plants growing inland	–
mineral availability	plants growing in fertile soil/plants growing on barren soil plants grown with fertilizer/without fertilizer	soil test kits

Daily changes in environmental conditions

Light intensity

Many animals are more active in daylight because they use sight to help them search for food or because their prey is available during daylight. Some animals have adapted to being more active at night (i.e. nocturnal) when there may be less risk of predation or they may well be suited to hunting at night. For example, they may have good night vision and a keen sense of hearing such as owls, or have advantageous adaptations such as the radar in bats based on ultrasound. Green plants need light to photosynthesise and make their own food: some plants will twist and turn during the day so that they present themselves advantageously to the Sun. These can be seen to follow the path of the Sun across the sky (for example, daffodil and sunflower).

Temperature

The temperature can vary considerably within a day, particularly within certain environments such as deserts, which whilst being very hot during the day can become extremely cold at night. Animals in these environments often take advantage of the cool of the evening to hunt for food. Some moths, butterflies and those vertebrates which are cold-blooded such as reptiles, and amphibians need the warmth of the Sun to 'energise' them; they cannot become active until the Sun has warmed them. They are not so active early in the morning or during the night so are less able to hunt for food. On hot days many animals will seek shade whereas on cold days some will huddle (like sheep) to keep warm. On particularly cold days birds can be seen to 'fluff' their feathers; by trapping air they can increase their insulation. Photosynthesis is a chemical reaction and like many reactions will take place at a faster rate when in warm conditions. On hot days the leaves of plants can lose excessive amounts of water by evaporation (the process is called transpiration) so unless this water is being replaced by uptake through the roots, the plants will 'wilt' and eventually drop their leaves in order to protect themselves from excessive water loss. At night some plants such as clover are able to close their leaves.

Seasonal changes in environmental conditions

Light intensity and temperature

As the seasons change so the height of the Sun in the sky at midday changes. As summer changes to autumn and then to winter the Sun progressively appears lower on the horizon in the Northern hemisphere. The Sun's rays increasingly strike the Earth more obliquely, hence the light intensity and the warmth from the Sun reduces. The reduction in light levels and heat causes plants to photosynthesise much more slowly so the rate of growth decreases significantly. Many trees and shrubs (deciduous) drop their leaves during the winter months so losing their ability to photosynthesise. As a result of this reduction in the rate of plant growth the availability of plant food decreases. Animals prepare for winter either by developing extra thick fur coats or layers of feathers or by laying down extra layers of fat. Other animals hibernate, some birds migrate. Animals such as insects, beetles and spiders will overwinter in warm crevices well sheltered from the extremes of the cold.

Rainfall

Rainfall also changes from season to season, the more obvious effects occurring in the summer months, when a drought may threaten the survival of a number of organisms. Under dry conditions plants will attempt to reduce water loss by first closing the tiny pores in their leaves (stoma) and then by dropping their leaves.

■ EROSION

This is a general term which describes the wearing away of the Earth's surface. The first part of erosion is the fragmentation of rock into small loosened bits by weathering (the action of wind, rain, ice) or the action of plant roots or gravity. These loosened parts are then transported by wind, gravity, rivers, glaciers. These transported particles of rock produce abrasive effects which in turn cause further erosion (for example, rock fragments in moving glaciers produce a grinding action on the rocks which they pass over).

■ EVAPORATION

A puddle of water on the ground outside or a bowl of water left on a windowsill will eventually dry up. The water is said to have evaporated. The term evaporate applies to any liquid, not just water; for example a spillage of petrol at a garage will evaporate in the same way.

An explanation of evaporation

All substances can be considered to be made up of tiny particles (atoms, molecules or ions). This is described by the kinetic theory. Particles in a liquid move randomly with different energies and therefore different speeds; certain particles move fast and some move slowly. Other particles in a liquid have enough energy to leave the surface of a liquid and pass into the atmosphere, while others may leave the liquid, strike another particle from a liquid or air particle, and then fall back into the liquid. Increasing the temperature of the liquid provides more and more particles with sufficient energy to escape from the surface causing a liquid to evaporate. The process of evaporation is illustrated below, with increased energy coming from the Sun (*see also* classification of materials).

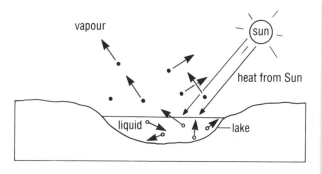

The rate of evaporation can be speeded up by:

Increasing the temperature of a liquid   if the liquid is heated sufficiently it will boil; boiling is rapid evaporation.

Increasing the surface area of a liquid   for example, putting a liquid in a shallow tray rather than a narrow-necked bottle.

Removing particles from above the surface of a liquid   to prevent them falling back into a liquid. This can be carried out by blowing on the surface (cooling a hot cup of tea). Puddles evaporate more rapidly on a windy day.

Reducing air pressure above a liquid   escaped particles are less likely to strike air particles and be forced back into the liquid.

Everyday examples of evaporation

Sweating   During hot weather a person sweats. This helps to control body temperature since heat is lost during evaporation of moisture from the skin.

Tap water   evaporates to leave a thin film of deposits in the container which are the dissolved substances in tap water. The solid deposits are salts, and are likely to contain salts of calcium and magnesium, for example, calcium carbonate, magnesium sulphate or calcium sulphate. 'Hard water' contains a lot of dissolved salts whereas 'soft water' contains very few.

Sea water   evaporates to leave a lot of salt deposits. These deposits contain salts such as sodium chloride (common salt or table salt), magnesium chloride, carbonates and iodides.

■ EVOLUTION

Evolution is the process by which various species have changed over long periods of time. For example, there is fossil evidence to support the theory that over millions of years, the horse has evolved from a small creature measuring only about 30 cm in height with three toes, to a creature of about 150 cm in height with single hooves.

The evidence for such changes has come from studying anatomy of existing horses and comparing this with that of extinct horses as revealed by fossil remains. The study of fossils shows that there are a series of extinct animals and plants, existing through time, each slightly different from the one before. Scientists believe that individual forms of life have, with time, gradually changed from one form into another, from one species into another, i.e. they have evolved.

This theory of evolution suggests that all living things have a common ancestor, one form gradually evolving into another. Charles Darwin and Alfred Wallace were the first people to suggest a credible mechanism for evolution, explaining why one form evolved into another. Darwin called this mechanism natural selection or survival of the fittest. Natural selection he said, 'almost inevitably causes much extinction of the less improved forms of life and leads to divergence of character'. These ideas were described by Darwin in his book *The Origin of Species*. The book, which sold out on the first day of its publication, 24 November 1859, is regarded by many as the most important book on biology ever published since his ideas are the foundation of modern biology. His observations can be summarised as:

Living things produce large numbers of offspring   For example frogs produce many hundreds of eggs at a time which are fertilised and develop into tadpoles.

The offspring within a species can vary considerably   Kittens with ginger, black, tortoiseshell and tabby markings may be born within one litter. It is this idea of the great variation of living things within one species that is key to the idea of natural selection.

> The theme of variation within species is developed at Key Stage 2, leading eventually to considering the evidence for evolution at Key Stage 4.

Many of these variations are inherited   The colouring of cats is inherited and passed on from one generation to the next. It is now known that the information is carried by genes which exist within the nucleus of all cells.

> At Key Stage 2 the idea that some characteristics are inherited is developed. Level 5 requires a knowledge of a gene as the means of passing on information.

Many offspring do not survive to breed   Of the hundreds of eggs laid by the frog only a few may survive to adulthood: some may be eaten, some tadpoles may starve, or suffer from injury or disease.

All of these observations led Darwin to conclude that in the struggle for survival those offspring with variations best suited to their environment are more likely to survive, breed and hence pass on their particular variation. If a species produces variations in colouring or marking, those individuals with markings that afford the best camouflage are more likely to survive where they are susceptible to predation. A good example is the peppered moth, common in the British Isles. In its silvery form it is well camouflaged against the lichens on trees. A black mutant form of the moth exists but not previously in very high numbers mainly because it was not well camouflaged and was easy prey for birds which fed on the moth. In 1849 the black variety was very rare (about 1% of the population). With the industrial revolution, however, came a rise in industrial pollution, which led to lichens on trees dying in areas around Manchester and Liverpool and trees becoming coated with soot. This afforded better camouflage for the black variety. The darker version was therefore more likely to breed and pass on its characteristics to the next generation hence its numbers rose significantly whilst the light coloured variety's population fell, suffering heavier predation due to lack of camouflage. By the end of the century the roles had reversed, with the light form becoming rare. As

industrial pollution lessens and the number of lichens in these areas increases then once again the light-coloured moth should regain its dominance, being once again better camouflaged. It is in this way that, as a variation or mutation, it is better suited to its environment and so is more likely to survive and its genes be passed on. Thus the characteristics of the species may gradually change. Over long periods of time these changes may be so numerous that they in effect give rise to a different species.

EYE

The eye is an organ.

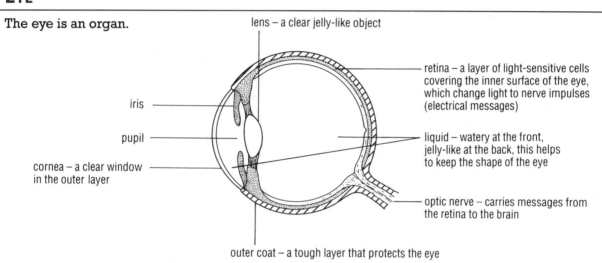

lens – a clear jelly-like object

retina – a layer of light-sensitive cells covering the inner surface of the eye, which change light to nerve impulses (electrical messages)

iris

pupil

cornea – a clear window in the outer layer

liquid – watery at the front, jelly-like at the back, this helps to keep the shape of the eye

optic nerve – carries messages from the retina to the brain

outer coat – a tough layer that protects the eye

Light enters the eye through the pupil, which appears as a dark circle in the centre of the eye. The size of the pupil is controlled by the iris, the coloured part of the eye which is a muscular ring. The pupil decreases in diameter in bright light conditions to prevent too much light from reaching the sensitive retina at the back of the eye causing damage. The pupil enlarges in a darkened room so as to allow more light to enter the eye. The change from a small to a large pupil is relatively slow as the eye adjusts to low levels of light. The change from a large to a small pupil is rapid to protect the eye.

Try sitting in a darkened room for several minutes in front of a mirror and then turning on the light: you will see the pupil in the eyes rapidly adjust to the light. Another interesting aspect of this change in pupil size is that pupils will dilate quite rapidly if the person is attracted by what they are looking at.

After travelling through the pupil light passes through a jelly-filled lens. Muscles hold the lens in place and also change its shape, either pulling it thin or allowing it to become fat. This change in shape enables a person to focus on objects near and far. Once the light has passed

through the lens, it passes through a liquid called the aqueous humour and falls on a light-sensitive 'screen' called the retina. The retina is lined with nerve endings. These generate electrical impulses which send messages to the brain.

Defects of the eye

Eye balls which are misshapen can give rise to either long or short sight, caused because the lens is no longer able to focus images onto the retina correctly.

Short sight

Long sight

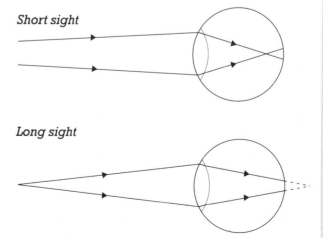

FEEDING

Feeding is the process by which a living organism obtains nourishment. Animals feed on other living things, either plants or other animals. Green plants obtain nourishment by making (synthesising) food in the cells in a process called photosynthesis. The plant produces simple carbohydrate foods (for example, sugars and starch) from basic chemicals such as carbon dioxide and water during this process, using energy from the Sun to power the process (*see* green plant).

Feeding in animals

Many animals have specially adapted mouth parts to help them to feed.

Mammal
A plant-eating mammal (herbivore, for example cow, elephant and deer) has large grinding teeth (molars) with which to grind plant material. A mammal which eats other animals (carnivore, for example tiger and dog) has sharp jagged and scissor-like teeth for tearing and ripping flesh. A mammal who eats both meat and plant (omnivore, for example human) has both grinding and tearing teeth.

Bird
Birds often have specially formed beaks suited to exploiting a specific food source. For example, a bird of prey often has a characteristic hook-shaped beak suited to tearing flesh, a humming bird has a long extended beak suited to extracting nectar from flowers, whereas a finch has a beak more suited to obtaining food such as nuts and grain.

Amphibian
A frog has a long tongue suitable for catching flies.

Insect
A caterpillar has strong jaws suitable for chewing through vegetation whereas a butterfly may have mouth parts adapted to feeding on nectar.

> At Key Stage 2 when exploring feeding, pupils could identify what different animals eat from reference books and consider how their mouthparts are adapted to help them feed. It is important for them to recognise that all animals, even a worm or a centipede, need to feed if they are to survive. There is no need to consider feeding of plants at Key Stage 2. Children often regard fertilizer and water as food for the plant, which is not correct. This view is reinforced by the common usage of the terms 'feeding plants' with fertilizer and water when gardening.

FILTRATION

Filtration is a technique for separating a solid or solids from a liquid in a mixture, for example muddy water. Filters work because the holes in the filter medium (paper or a loosely-packed solid material, for example sand) are large enough to allow tiny particles of a liquid and dissolved substances through but not the larger suspended material such as soil in water.

Suitable filters for use at Key Stage 2 include:

- Coffee filters.
- Filter papers (purchase from scientific equipment suppliers).
- Blotting paper (cut into circles 15 cm in diameter).
- Sand (different grades, for example coarse or fine).
- Cotton wool.

How to filter
Papers can be folded and placed in a small plastic funnel.

Folding a filter paper

Fold 1 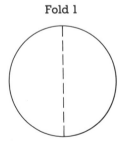   Fold 2 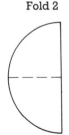   place in the funnel

Cotton wool and sand can be placed loosely in the funnel.

What to filter
Children can try filtering:

Salty water   filtering has no effect.
Muddy water   filtering removes the soil particles.
Ink   filtering has no effect.

FLEXIBILITY

The flexibility of a material describes the amount by which it will change shape when being pushed, pulled, squeezed or twisted by a force. A simple way of comparing materials is to fix strips of each material (for example, copper, iron, wood, paper and cardboard) to a table, so that they stick out over the edge parallel to the floor. Hang a weight on the end of each strip and measure the amount it bends. Materials that are not flexible (do not bend a lot) can be regarded as stiff.

FLOATING AND SINKING

When objects are placed in water (or any other liquid) they experience an upthrust produced by the water. When a tennis ball or plastic football is pushed under water its upthrust can be felt. A consequence of this upthrust is that objects weigh less in fluids such as water than they do in air.

It was Archimedes who first noticed that an object placed in a fluid loses as much weight as is equal to the weight of the displaced fluid. The volume of fluid displaced by an object depends on the object's size; the bigger the object the greater the upthrust it will experience when pushed under the fluid.

For example:

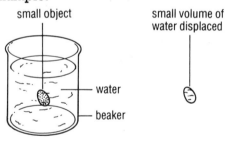

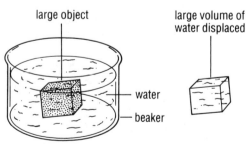

Whether an object floats or sinks in water depends on two factors:

■ Size (volume) of the object. This determines the maximum volume of water it is capable of displacing.
■ Weight of the object.

When an object is placed in water there are two forces acting in opposition to each other: the force of gravity which pushes an object downwards, and the upwards thrust acting on the object produced by the water.

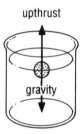

An object floats if it is large enough to produce sufficient upthrust to balance its weight. An object's size to weight ratio therefore determines whether or not it floats.
The size to weight ratio of an object is described by its density. Some objects are heavy for their size, and have a high density, for example an iron block, whilst others are light for their size and have a low density, for example a block of balsa wood.

The density of an object can be calculated using the following equation:

$$\text{density} = \frac{\text{mass}}{\text{volume}}$$

For example, the density of an iron block can be calculated as follows:

mass of iron block = 2370 g
volume of iron block = 300 cm³

$$\text{density of iron} = \frac{\text{mass}}{\text{volume}} = \frac{2379 \text{ g}}{300 \text{ cm}^3} = 7.9 \text{ g/cm}^3$$

The water that is displaced has a density and things will float provided they have a density less than that of the water. The density of water is 1 g/cm^3. Objects with a density of less than 1 g/cm^3 will float. Objects with a density of more than 1 g/cm^3 will sink.

The densities of some common substances are:

- Wood 0.4 g/cm^3
- Brick 2.5 g/cm^3
- Iron 7.9 g/cm^3
- Polystyrene 0.01 g/cm^3.

Why do ships float?

Iron blocks do not float, but ships are made of iron – why do they float? Consider the overall density of the ship. A ship is an object which is part air and part iron. The overall density of a ship is less than 1.0 g/cm^3, so it floats.

Changing the shape of a piece of Plasticine from flat to a boat shape will convert it from a 'sinker' to a 'floater'. By changing the shape, and effectively including air, the overall density has changed and hence the volume of the water displaced.

Why do objects float better in sea water than fresh water?

Sea water contains dissolved salts. Dissolving substances in water increases its density. Salt water produces a greater upthrust than fresh water, so objects float higher. Certain objects that sink in fresh water (for example, a bar of soap) can be made to float in salt water. The Dead Sea contains a high proportion of dissolved salts and is renowned for its ability to keep people afloat.

Ships also, of course, float higher in salt water than fresh water. In the past this caused problems with loading since when travelling from sea water into fresh water estuaries ships float lower so could run aground. Samuel Plimsoll solved the problem by painting on the side of ships the 'plimsoll line'. The line was really a series of lines indicating the maximum loading in different conditions: salt water, fresh water and in tropical waters, etc., since temperature also makes a difference. These differences can be readily seen by placing a fishing float or weighted cork in water under different conditions and marking its float level.

Why does temperature of the water affect how an object floats?

Another factor which has an effect on the density of water is its temperature. Above 4 °C the hotter the water the less its density, due to the expansion of water as it heats. Below 4 °C, water does something very odd that no other liquid does: it expands. This is referred to as the anomalous expansion of water. This explains why ice floats, since solids are normally more dense than their liquid form.

Other liquids

Since the determining factor for whether an object floats or not is its density, then the liquid in which an object floats is significant. Liquids such as cooking oils (various types), liquid paraffin and glycerin can be compared.

Factors that determine whether an object floats or sinks are:

- The shape of an object.
- The density of an object.
- The material from which the object is made (for example, whether it is absorbent or not and could become waterlogged).
- Whether the liquid contains dissolved substances (for example, sea water contains dissolved salts).
- The temperature of the liquid (although this is a minor factor in comparison to those above).
- The density of the liquid.

■ FLOWERING PLANT

Flowering plants are those plants which possess a flower and produce seeds. The flower contains the sex organs of the plant which are responsible for sexual reproduction.

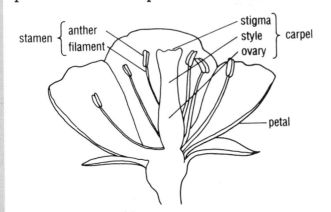

Plants which do not have flowers reproduce in other ways, for example fungi (including mushrooms and toadstools) produce spores from under the cap which are scattered on the ground and in the air. Mosses and ferns also produce spores.

FOOD

Food contains a number of substances essential for health and growth.

Carbohydrate (sugar and starch)

Provides energy this energy is released during the process of respiration, which takes place in all living cells (both animals and plants).

Manufactured during the process of photosynthesis a green plant makes use of the Sun's energy to combine carbon dioxide from the air with water, which enters the plant through the roots, to produce at first simple molecules of sugar which are built into complex sugars for growth and starch for storage.

Chemical compounds contain carbon, hydrogen and oxygen. Sugar molecules are relatively simple and are manufactured first during photosynthesis. Starch molecules are molecules of sugar joined.

Fat

Provides energy fats are a means by which living things can store energy, by converting unused carbohydrate into fat which the body is able to store.

High energy value when compared with carbohydrate.

Fat and oil molecules these are produced from carbohydrate in plants.

Contains carbon, hydrogen and oxygen.

Protein

Proteins are needed by living things for growth and repair. They contain the essential chemicals to help build cells and cell contents.

Protein can be used by living things to provide energy for example, where the body's energy requirements exceed the daily energy intake from food the body will first utilise fat reserves. Once these are depleted then protein is used to provide energy in order for the body to survive, thus resulting in muscle loss and weight reduction.

Plants can manufacture protein from carbohydrate and nitrogen obtained from minerals which enter the plant through the roots.

Protein molecules contain hydrogen, carbon, oxygen and nitrogen and sometimes other elements.

Vitamins and minerals

Supply essential chemicals to ensure healthy growth.

Ensure the functioning of many processes the absorption of minerals and the release of energy from foods.

Plants obtain minerals through the roots they manufacture the vitamins; animals obtain vitamins and minerals from plants.

Contain a wide range of different atoms.

Those essential to healthy plant growth nitrogen, phosphorous, sulphur potassium, magnesium and iron. These are found naturally in the soil and may be added in the form of fertilizers.

FOOD CHAIN

A food chain represents the transfer of material and energy from one organism (living thing) to another within a habitat or ecosystem.

A simple food chain is:

grass → rabbit → fox

By convention the arrows point in the direction of the energy and material flow. Plants are always at the start of every food chain.

The green plant is known as a producer. A producer manufactures complex chemicals such as carbohydrates and proteins from simple substances such as carbon dioxide, water and mineral salts starting with the process of photosynthesis using energy from the Sun.

A consumer is an organism that obtains all the chemicals it needs from the food it eats. Such organisms can be animals, fungi or bacteria. There are different levels of consumer.

A primary consumer feeds directly on producers. Animals which are primary consumers are known as herbivores (plant eaters).

A secondary consumer feeds on primary consumers; these are carnivores (meat eaters).

Tertiary consumers are those who eat the secondary consumer, but may also eat the primary consumer (*see also* food pyramid, food web).

leaf → caterpillar → shrew → owl
producer   primary   secondary   tertiary
            consumer   consumer   consumer

FOOD PYRAMID

Within any sustainable community there needs to be a sufficient number of producers and primary consumers present to sustain the predators higher up the food chain. For example, consider the simple food chain:

grass → rabbit → fox

There will need to be sufficient grass to sustain a rabbit population and there will need to be a sufficient number of rabbits to provide food for one family of foxes. This idea is represented in a food pyramid:

The length of the bar provides an indication of the number of each organism at each feeding level.

These food pyramids can be calculated from population studies within a measured area of habitat and show the total amount of food available at each level by the number of organisms present.

A pyramid of mass shows the total amount of food available within a given area by estimating the mass of organisms at each level.

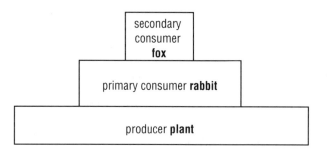

FOOD WEB

Within a community the transfer of energy and material from one organism to another can be shown using a food chain. However, food chains are often over-simplifications. Several food chains will coexist within one community and an animal can appear in more than one food chain, so the food chains are linked. The inter-relationships between food chains are shown as food webs. The direction of the arrows shows the direction of energy flow within the web.

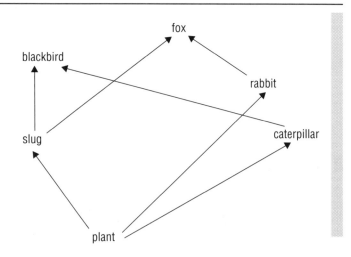

FORCE

A force is a push or a pull. Forces can make an object move, speed up, slow down, stop, hold an object in place and change the shape of an object. The effects produced by forces are the only evidence there is of their existence as they are obviously not visible. Sometimes even their effects are not obvious.

Describing forces

In everyday speech the terms force, pressure, energy and power are often used interchangeably. Science has specific meanings for each of these terms and it is therefore important to encourage children to describe forces in terms of pushes and pulls, dissuading them from using these other words. An example is that a child will often say *This force is the most powerful*. It is better to encourage the child to say *This force has the most push*.

Measuring forces

Forces (pushes and pulls) are measured in units called newtons (named after Isaac Newton). Bathroom scales and forcemeters (spring balances) can be purchased which are calibrated in newtons.

The weight of someone who is 10 stone is approximately 650 newtons

An apple weighs about 1.5 newtons and a 1 kg bag of sugar weighs about 10 newtons

Representing forces

It is conventional to use arrows in drawings to represent forces. The direction of the arrow indicates the direction of the force and the length of the arrow indicates the size of the force. Forces are vector quantities, having both size and direction.

For example:

Hammering a nail into a post

Action and reaction

Forces come in pairs. If you push something you will experience a push backwards on you. Imagine you are on roller skates and you push against a wall. You will experience a push back from the wall causing you to move backwards. The recoil from a gun is another example of this idea. Rockets move forward as a reaction to the force produced by the ejection of burned gases at the rear. This idea of pushing back is an important idea and is expressed within Newton's third law of motion, which says that every action has an equal and opposite reaction.

Skater and wall   *Rocket*

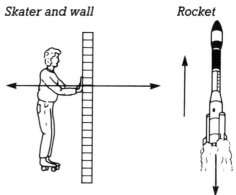

A book resting on a table appears to have no forces acting on it. In fact two forces are acting: gravity which is pulling it down (as can be experienced by holding the book) and that of the table pushing back with an equal and opposite force so as to keep the book in place. Even stationary objects have forces acting on them.

Book and table

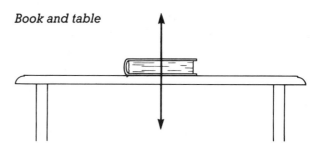

Forces and movement

Newton produced three laws which describe the connections between forces and movement. The first of these laws states that:

> An object will stay at rest or continue to move in a straight line at a uniform speed unless acted upon by some external force.

It is not difficult to imagine that an object will stay at rest unless a force pushes it. It is however more difficult to imagine that an object that is already in motion will continue for ever in a straight line since our experience on Earth tells us that after a time moving objects stop. The reason for this is that there are forces acting on objects which slow them up, for example a pushed toy car will eventually stop because of the friction forces acting on the wheels, and air resistance. In Space away from the influence of gravitational fields an object will continue moving in a straight line unless a force affects it.

The rockets which were sent to the Moon did not have to continually fire their engines throughout their journey. The engines were fired initially producing sufficient force to help them move far enough away from the Earth. Further away the Earth's gravitational field has less effect so the engines could be turned off, the rocket continuing to move on its selected path. A small boost could either increase or decrease the rocket's speed according to the direction in which the rocket engine nozzle was pointing.

Combinations of forces

The effects of different sized forces all acting in different directions will affect the movement of an object. Imagine a child in a playground being pulled in several directions by a group of friends. The eventual direction in which the child is pulled will depend on the direction and strength of the forces from the other children. This situation can be modelled by placing a lemonade bottle inside a circle of nails and

attaching different rubber bands between the nails and the bottle causing it to move.

Bottle and nails

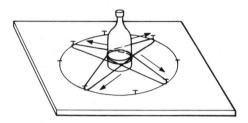

The resultant force will determine the eventual direction of movement (*see also* resultant force).

■ FOSSIL

Fossils are the remains or outline impressions of animals and plants preserved in rocks. It is unusual to find complete organisms preserved; fossils usually represent the hard 'parts' of an organism such as skeletons or shells of animals and the hard 'parts' of leaves, seeds or woody parts of plants. The soft tissue will have gradually decayed. Fossils also exist of footprint impressions left in rock by animals.

Fossils are formed when animals and plants die and fall into sediments (for example, mud or sand); the sediment then slowly builds up layer upon layer preserving the outline of the organism compressed below. Organisms may be petrified by the slow depositing of minerals within their bodies as they decay. These sediments over millions of years harden and as a result of pressure from layers above form sedimentary rocks. These sedimentary rocks may be brought to the surface as a result of Earth movements such as earthquakes, folding or faulting. Erosion by wind, rivers and rain will also expose different parts of sedimentary rock.

Impression of a fern sometimes found in coal

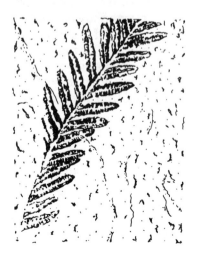

Sedimentary rocks where fossils are often found include limestones, shales (hardened muds), chalks and sandstones.

Fossils can also be found in some metamorphic rocks, i.e. rocks which started out as sediments but have been changed by the action of heat or pressure, such as slate or in layers of volcanic ash. Normally the body of any organism which dies is broken down by action of a combination of scavenging animals, bacteria and weather. For the organism to be fossilised it means that it must be rapidly buried after death to prevent such actions.

Some of the fossils found have been preserved in special circumstances, for instance insects preserved in amber (which is a fossilised form of tree resin), or complete mammoths in the frozen ground in Siberia. In both these cases the normal processes of decay by bacteria were prevented.

At Key Stage 2 children can model their own fossils.

Fossils in sediments or mud:

- Make a footprint in sand, pour on runny clay, let it dry so that it hardens and then remove it.
- Make imprints of leaves in mud and let them dry (mixing the mud with some plaster of Paris beforehand will help the mud dry more quickly).
- Pour some plaster of Paris into a tray, place on this a layer of leaves coated in Vaseline (or similar) then cover with another layer and allow to dry and harden. Once set the plaster of Paris can be split to simulate splitting a sedimentary rock.

Fossils in ice:

■ Place small pieces of fresh fruit in water in compartments of an ice tray to show how an 'animal fossil' is embedded and that it does not decay when the conditions are unfavourable for bacterial growth and hence decay.

Fossils in amber:

■ Try placing objects in resin used for model making and let it harden, or use gelatin as the embedding resin. Children must not handle resin.

FRICTION

Friction is a force which opposes movement. It is caused by the action of one surface on another. When pushing a table across the floor the force of friction acts in an opposite direction to the push.

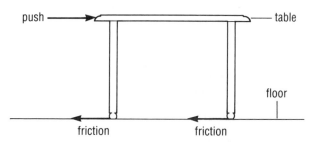

Frictional forces can produce heat, for example when the hands are rubbed together heat is produced. The re-entry of a space-shuttle into the Earth's atmosphere results in an extreme temperature rise of the hull caused by the friction of the air (also called air resistance) on the surface of the falling shuttle.

Frictional forces acting within bearings in wheels will eventually slow down and stop the wheels from turning. Internal friction within a car engine is responsible for wasting approximately 20% of the energy stored in fuel. Friction can be a hindrance to efficiency, but can also be a help. Cars are able to move because of friction forces between the tyres and the road. Animals, including humans, are able to move because of the friction forces between their feet and the ground.

At Key Stage 2 children can explore and investigate friction forces by sliding blocks or toys down slopes. They could try different surfaces. Rough surfaces can be made by sticking sandpaper to the slopes, using different grade sandpapers . Smooth surfaces can be made by waxing and polishing wooden slopes, or by using thick glass. A measurement of the height the slope is raised before an object starts to slide provides a simple and quick comparison of the size of frictional forces. Alternatively a forcemeter can be attached to a block and the block pulled. The force required to keep the block moving is a measure of the friction. A rubber band could also be used for this purpose, the length of the band indicating the size of the force required to overcome friction.

Children could also try:

■ The effect of surface area (a rectangular block can be tried on its side and back).
■ The effect of blocks of different masses but the same surface area (one block can be placed on top of another.
■ The effect of shape (triangles, squares and circles with equal surface can be cut).

The value of the force of friction depends on the nature of the surface (rough, smooth, etc.) and the force pressing the surfaces together (for example, weight of object on a slope), but not on the surface area of each surface. This independence of surface area is quite surprising since intuitively people often think the converse should be true.

FUELS

Fuels are concentrated sources of energy, which release their energy relatively easily. A chemical fuel is a substance which burns in the presence of oxygen with the release of heat. Many fuels are hydrocarbons indicating that they contain carbon and hydrogen only. Such hydrocarbons are also referred to as fossil fuels. When these fuels burn, the products of combustion are carbon dioxide and water.

Examples of fossil fuels are:

- Gas.
- Coal.
- Oil.

What makes a good fuel?

A good fuel would be one which produced a lot of heat for very little waste, was cheap to produce and easy to transport.

Fuel	Advantages	Disadvantages
North Sea gas	produces good level of heat produces little waste except carbon dioxide which increases greenhouse effect easy to light, burns well transported through pipelines	costly to produce difficult to store risk of explosion
Calor gas	produces high level of heat produces little waste except carbon dioxide (which increases greenhouse effect) easy to light burns well	costly to produce (from oil) difficult to store transported in cylinders, costly risk of explosion
coal	relatively cheap to produce produces a lot of heat burns well	heavy, bulky, costly to transport produces a lot of waste (ash, soot as well as waste gases). A lot of coal contains sulphur as an impurity which burns to produce sulphur dioxide gas, a major pollutant
heavy fuel oil	produces a lot of heat only waste gases produced	transport and storage difficult pollution from impurities in the oil (for example, sulphur)

GALAXY

A galaxy is an enormous cluster of dust, gases and thousands of millions of stars (and their planets). Galaxies are of different shapes: there are for example spiral galaxies and disc-shaped galaxies. The stars within a galaxy are rotating about its centre and are held together by gravity.

A typical spiral galaxy is a flat (in one plane) disc with spiral arms of dust, gas and young stars. Our Sun is one star within a spiral galaxy, the Milky Way. In the night sky the Milky Way seen spreading across the sky as a wisp of

smoke is but one arm of our spiral galaxy. A typical galaxy can be 100 000 light years across. There are many million galaxies within the Universe, separated by vast distances. Our nearest galaxy is the Andromeda galaxy, which is another spiral galaxy similar to our own. It is 2.2 million light years away and about 130 000 light years across. It is the only Galaxy visible to the naked eye. It appears as a faint 'fuzzy' patch beyond the stars which form the constellation Andromeda.

GAS

Gases are substances with no fixed shape or volume that fill the space available to them. They are easy to compress and mix readily with other gases. Certain gases, such as oxygen and carbon dioxide, can dissolve in water.

Air

Air is a mixture of gases: nitrogen (78%), oxygen (21%), carbon dioxide (0.03%), and argon and other gases (<1%).

At Key Stage 2 children can feel that air is compressible by pumping a bicycle pump or plastic syringe.

Carbon dioxide
Samples of carbon dioxide can be obtained by placing a balloon over the mouth of a bottle of any fizzy drink such as lemonade or Coca-Cola and gently shaking. The escaping carbon dioxide will partially fill

the balloon. Securing the neck of the balloon will provide you with a sample of carbon dioxide. Carbon dioxide is a gas that is heavier than air. This can be demonstrated by allowing the balloon to fall. It drops quickly to the ground. This can be compared with a balloon of the same capacity filled with ordinary air. Carbon dioxide will also extinguish fires. Gently 'pour' carbon dioxide gas from the balloon onto a lighted candle to demonstrate this property.

▮ GEARS

Gears in toys and models transfer energy by transmitting motion, by changing the direction of motion, or by changing the speed at which gears rotate. The maximum efficiency of a pair of gears is about 95%, 5% of transmitted power being lost due to the friction in bearings. Lower quality bearings are much less efficient.

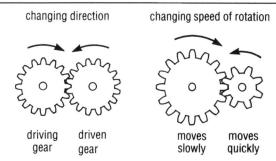

changing direction

driving gear   driven gear

changing speed of rotation

moves slowly   moves quickly

▮ GENE

Every inherited trait of an animal or plant is controlled by at least one gene. A gene is a length of nucleic acid called DNA, which contains a code or instructions for the development of a particular aspect of the organism.

All living cells contain a supply of this genetic material organised as strands called chromosomes within their nucleus. Along the length of these chromosomes are the many genes arranged like beads on a necklace. Except in the sex cells the chromosome strands always appear in pairs. Each of these pairs of chromosomes carries a corresponding set of genes.

Each individual thus has at least two genes governing any one characteristic. There will be for instance a pair of genes governing skin colour or type of hair. Sometimes a particular characteristic is governed by more than one gene, as with eye colour.

One gene is inherited governing a particular characteristic from each parent. For example, a gene instructing for straight or curly hair from one parent and a gene instructing for straight or curly hair from the other parent. This information is used to determine the individual characteristics of the offspring.

Recently, scientists have been able to identify and isolate a few individual genes responsible for particular characteristics. They have also discovered that a specific gene is responsible for the illness cystic fibrosis. The study and manipulation of genes within organisms is called genetics or genetic engineering.

Inheriting blue or brown eyes

The male sex cell and female sex cell (sperm and egg) each contain a gene which is responsible for a particular characteristic. The sex cell has half the normal complement of an ordinary cell in the body. Sexual reproduction brings these two 'half cells' together to make a whole new cell from which the new individual will grow. Growth occurs by this cell copying itself becoming two, these two copying themselves becoming four, eight, sixteen and so on many times over.

Information about the individual's eye colour comes from both parents. What will determine the eventual colour (blue or brown)? It is not simply a combination of the two inherited

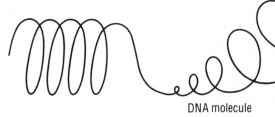

a chromosome

DNA molecule

a gene is a short section of a chromosome

types although this can happen, with some characteristics such as skin colour in humans, or the tortoiseshell colouring in cats which is a result of a combination of a ginger colour gene and a black or tabby colour gene.

Suppose both parents pass on the blue colour gene: the resulting eye colour would be blue. If, however, one parent passes on a brown gene and the other passes on a blue gene, the eyes of the offspring will be brown, the reason for this being that the brown gene is dominant whereas the blue gene is recessive, i.e. brown eyes take precedence. There are many instances of inherited characteristics which involve dominant and recessive genes, for example hair type where curly hair is dominant and straight hair is recessive; hair colour is another.

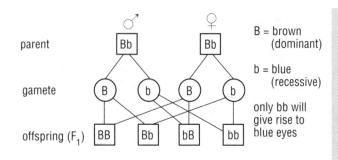

B = brown (dominant)

b = blue (recessive)

only bb will give rise to blue eyes

At Key Stage 2 children are not expected to be taught about genetics. However the Level 5 statement does require them to know that information is passed on from one generation to the next in the form of genes. This statement is more closely associated with the Programme of Study for Key Stage 3.

■ GENERATION

A generation is regarded as a group of living things in existence between birth and death, i.e. one whole life-cycle. A generation of peas, for example, could be regarded as those emanating from one set of seeds. These plants would flower and set seed of their own: this new seed would be regarded as the next generation. In the study of genetics, different generations are often labelled, for example, first generation, second generation, or as:

F_1 generation   first generation
F_2 generation   second generation
F_3 generation   third generation

Within the human population a generation is taken to be thirty years.

■ GEOLOGICAL EVENT

Geological events are those which change the surface of the Earth through the production of new rock material. These include mountain formation, faulting and folding of rocks, sedimentation, volcanoes and earthquakes. Whilst not being 'geological events' glaciation and water flow (rivers) also shape the land. Glaciers produce U-shaped valleys whilst rivers produce V-shaped valleys.

Earthquakes occur at the boundaries of crustal plates and result from stress when plates move against each other (*see* earthquakes).

Folding occurs when two plates moving towards each other push rocks upward, buckling them.

Faults occur when the plates slide past each other.

Both faulting and folding provide evidence for the movement of the Earth's crust and support the theory of plate tectonics.

Sedimentation over long periods of time can lay down successive layers of rock material, one layer upon another. The weight of upper layers can exert large pressures on those below resulting in the formation of sedimentary rock.

Folding

Faulting

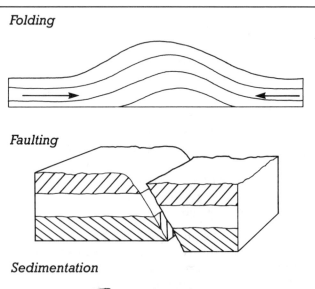

Sedimentation

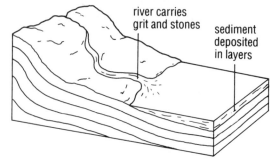

river carries grit and stones

sediment deposited in layers

Evidence for this process is present through observation of many rocks which are banded showing a layer-type structure.

Volcanoes occur at the boundaries between crustal plates where the crust is very thin and erupt new rock material called lava. Rocks

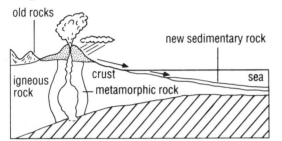

which have been produced in this way belong to the igneous group and are often glassy in appearance, contain small crystals (a result of rapid cooling), and are hard.

> At Key Stage 2 earthquakes and volcanoes provide evidence that the Earth's crust is not stable. Through a study of and comparison of different rocks children should begin to appreciate that rocks can be produced in different ways which in turn give rise to rocks with different characteristics. How this is achieved is dealt with more fully at KS3 (*see* rock cycle).

GLOBAL ENERGY RESOURCE

Directly or indirectly the Sun provides energy for all our needs. It provides energy for growth of plants (biomass), for solar power, for winds, waves and direct heating (radiant heat). The energy stored in fossil fuels originated from the Sun. Coal, oil and gas are formed from the remains of living organisms. On a global scale fossil fuels meet 77% of the world's energy demands. Fossil fuels are non-renewable resources and the world's supply is being used at a high rate. At present usage levels available United Kingdom coal supplies may last another 300–400 years, whereas North Sea gas has a predicted lifetime of only another 30 years.

The use of energy sources worldwide is shown below:

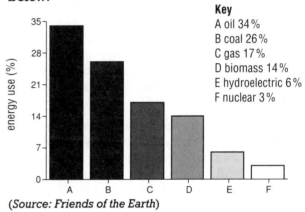

Key
A oil 34%
B coal 26%
C gas 17%
D biomass 14%
E hydroelectric 6%
F nuclear 3%

(*Source: Friends of the Earth*)

GRAVITY

Newton's explanation of gravity states that everything in the Universe attracts everything else and that the force of attraction between objects depends on their masses. The greater the mass of an object the greater the force of attraction.

Forces of attraction exist between a pen and a rubber on a desk and between the objects and the desk. However, the forces are so insignificant compared with the force of attraction between the objects and the much more massive Earth that they cannot be perceived. The pull of the Earth is, however, evident. The small forces which exist between objects have, however, been measured.

It is the pull of gravity which provides humans with a sense of 'up' and 'down', whether a person stands in Britain or in Australia. 'Down' means towards the centre of the Earth. Gravity also gives a measure of weight. If a person stood on the Moon, although they would be the same mass they would weigh less because the

Moon is less massive than the Earth so its gravity is less. The opposite would be true if a person journeyed to and stood on the surface of the Sun. A person weighing 700 N on Earth would weigh approximately 20 000 N on the Sun and 120 N on the Moon.

The further away from the Earth the less the pull of gravity becomes. It is however, the pull of the Earth's gravity which keeps the Moon in orbit around the Earth and the pull of the Sun's gravity which keeps the Earth in orbit around the Sun.

Rate of fall

The force of gravity on Earth is 10 N/kg of mass, so the more massive the object the greater the pull downwards it experiences. The result of this is that all objects fall at the same rate on Earth. If for example, you dropped a heavy object and a light object from a tall building they would hit the ground at the same time. In reality this does not always happen because if the objects are of different shapes and sizes then they will be affected differently by the air resistance acting on them. A bulky object would be more affected by air resistance than a more compact object and so would be slowed.

> At Key Stage 2 children often believe that heaviest objects fall fastest and that gravity has something to do with the air. For example, they often say *The Moon has no gravity because there is no air there.*

■ GREEN PLANTS

Green plants are capable of producing complex substances such as carbohydrates, fats and proteins needed by living organisms from simple substances such as carbon dioxide, water and mineral salts using energy from the Sun. Green plants are said to 'make their own food'. This synthesis begins with the process of photosynthesis. Only green plants are capable of photosynthesising. It is the green pigment in certain plant cells, called chlorophyll, that absorbs energy from the Sun which 'fuels' the process.

The green leaf of a plant is like a factory, taking in raw materials and with energy from the Sun (in the form of light) synthesising, or making, more complex substances, hence the term 'photo' (light) 'synthesis' (to make).

The first step in the process is the manufacture of simple sugars from the raw materials of carbon dioxide and water. A sugar molecule is manufactured by combining six carbon dioxide molecules and six water molecules.

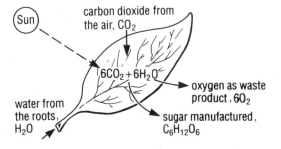

$$\text{carbon dioxide} + \text{water} \xrightarrow[\text{chlorophyll}]{\text{sunlight}} \text{sugar} + \text{oxygen}$$

Once simple sugars have been manufactured more complex carbohydrates, proteins and fats can be assembled by the plant.

During the process of photosynthesis carbon dioxide is absorbed from the air and oxygen is released into the atmosphere as a by-product. This reaction acts to maintain the balance of gases in air since during the respiration of both animals and plants oxygen is used to 'burn' food; carbon dioxide is released into the atmosphere as a waste product. Approximately 21% of air is oxygen, whereas less than 0.05% is carbon dioxide.

> At Key Stage 2 it is not expected that children should be taught about photosynthesis although they should be introduced to the idea that green plants use energy from the Sun to produce 'food'. Many children may, however, have come across the term 'photosynthesis' or be aware that plants produce oxygen as a by-product of this process. It is important to establish that plants both photosynthesise and respire since children may believe that only plants photosynthesise and only animals respire.

■ GREENHOUSE EFFECT

The greenhouse effect is the name given to phenomena which are thought to contribute to global warming. The Earth is surrounded by an atmosphere which acts as a 'blanket' keeping the Earth warm and at a reasonably constant temperature (average surface temperature = 20 °C). On the Moon, however, which has no atmosphere the surface temperature can vary greatly from well below freezing to well above. The average surface temperature is –18 °C. Almost a century ago scientists were aware that the burning of coal was releasing carbon dioxide into the atmosphere which could have the effect of increasing the 'blanket' effect of the

atmosphere and cause the surface temperature to rise. This is called the greenhouse effect.

When energy from the Sun in the form of light strikes glass greenhouses, energy passes through the glass and is absorbed by the contents of the greenhouse. This absorbed energy is re-emitted as infra-red radiation (heat). This infra-red cannot pass back through the glass easily so the energy levels within the greenhouse build up resulting in an internal temperature increase. The carbon dioxide and water vapour in the Earth's atmosphere have a similar effect to greenhouse glass, so as the amount of carbon dioxide in the atmosphere increases the temperature will rise. The greenhouse effect on Venus, which has a very 'thick' atmosphere of mainly carbon dioxide, is very high. The surface temperature on Venus is 460 °C.

On Earth only a small rise in the Earth's surface temperature will have enormous consequences on the Earth's climate, melting the polar ice caps, raising sea levels, creating areas of drought and subjecting new areas of land to flooding.

■ GROWTH

Growth is a life process, and in general living organisms grow until they reach an optimum size (maturity). The size of an organism at maturity can vary from one species to another and within a species; in addition the rate of growth can vary between and within species. Both size at maturity and rate of growth can be affected by environmental conditions, for example the consistency and quality of the food supply, whether the environment is warm or cold, and how well an organism is suited to environmental conditions. Plant growth is affected by such factors as water, mineral supply, light intensity and temperature. Animal growth is affected by factors such as food availability (including availability of protein, carbohydrate, fats, vitamins and minerals), water supply and shelter.

The size of an organism at maturity is also affected by heredity. For example, it is likely that parents who are small will produce offspring who are also small, independently of food supply. These inherited traits (small, large, heavy, light, quick-growing, etc.) are passed on from one generation to the next by the genes held within the nucleus of every cell (*see* gene). This is true for both plants and animals.

Selective breeding is a process which takes account of the parents' inherited characteristics and seeks to encourage certain characteristics by breeding from parents both of whom show desired traits.

Growth patterns

If a living organism is measured as it grows and the results plotted on a graph they tend to fit a general pattern for growth.

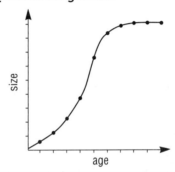

At Key Stage 2 size can be measured using a convenient dimension such as height, length or weight. Suitable organisms to measure regularly over a period of time include: sunflowers, wheat, barley, beans, pet mice, hamsters, kittens, and humans of different ages within a family. It might be interesting to collect data for girls and boys at different ages separately throughout the school and plot the average heights or weights, since girls and boys develop at different rates.

■ HABITAT

A habitat is where an organism lives, and provides a particular set of conditions for life. A habitat may be large, such as a field, or it may be small, such as a leaf or a moss. A habitat may support a community of living organisms (*see also* survival, environmental conditions).

Habitat	Typical community	Suitability of each member to its habitat
playing field	daisy, clover, grass, beetle, earthworm, snail, small birds, hedgehog	daisy and clover plants grow close to the ground so are well suited to open ground such as fields because they can resist trampling. A grass plant grows from its base rather than its tip as is normal in most plants, so is not damaged by grazing and continues to grow. The shape of an earthworm makes it suitable for burrowing through soil. Snails and slugs are small enough to travel through grass for the most part undetected
woodland	earthworm, caterpillar, hedgehog, bark beetle, small	caterpillars and other small organisms are usually well camouflaged; certain moths, for

table continues

Habitat	Typical community	Suitability of each member to its habitat
	birds (for example blackbird), sparrow hawk, mouse, squirrel, tawny owl, oak and beech trees	example, are camouflaged against the bark of trees. A squirrel has sharp claws and a long balancing tail which helps it to move easily between trees. Sharp teeth also help it eat through the tough outer layer of nuts. Birds of prey have good eyesight and are powerful flyers so are able to move across woodland with ease searching for food. Plants which grow on the floor of the woodland can tolerate low levels of light.
pond	fish, water snail, microscopic algae, mayfly, dragonfly (adult and nymph), water flea (daphnia), water louse, bloodworm, fish (for example carp, minnows), pond skater, pond weed, reeds	fish have fins and a body shape which enables them to move easily through water. They also have gills which enable them to extract oxygen from water. Other aquatic organisms also have body shapes and parts adapted to life in the water; the webbed feet of frogs for example, or the small mass and long legs of a pond skater. A consequence of a plant growing in water is that it will often have a limp stem, being able to bend easily with the movement of the water. A stiff stem is not needed since the water acts as a support.
brick wall	spider, beetle, moss, lichen, ant, ivy, wall barley, ragwort	ivy plants are climbers and have tendrils which cling. Mosses do not have long roots and are able to trap moisture in the dense foliage so maintaining their environment under potentially dry conditions. Other plants which grow in crevices in walls often have comparatively short roots and are able to retain moisture. The size of organisms also means that many are suited to this habitat.

■ HANDLING OF FOOD

All foods naturally contain microbes (bacteria, moulds and yeasts). These microbes multiply rapidly under favourable conditions, i.e. warmth, moisture, low acidity. Air is usually also necessary.

Food decay is caused by the activity of micro-organisms and natural enzymes. Food poisoning results from the contamination of food by certain bacteria (for example, salmonella) which increase in number to a point where they become toxic if ingested. Raw meats and poultry are often contaminated by such bacteria.

Food should be handled in such a way to ensure that microbes (for example, bacteria) are prevented from multiplying to a dangerous level:

Food stored needs to be kept cool to prevent rapid growth of bacteria. (Freezing does not kill bacteria but does prevent them multiplying.)

Raw meats and poultry are particularly susceptible to contamination and should be thoroughly cooked to kill bacteria (Approximately 70% of poultry are contaminated with salmonella.)

Wash hands before handling any foodstuff to prevent transfer of bacteria to the foods; this is particularly important after going to the toilet or handling soil.

Wash hands after handling raw, uncooked meats and poultry before handling other foods or eating, once again to prevent transfer of bacteria.

Prevent cross-contamination of uncooked meats and poultry by storing them away from cooked foods.

Different chopping boards and knives should be used for uncooked meats and poultry and other foods.

Change dishcloths and tea towels daily.

■ HARDNESS

The hardness of materials can be compared by a simple 'scratch test'. An iron nail or other suitable sharp instrument can be used to attempt to scratch the material. The size and depth of scratches are then compared and the materials placed in order of hardness. Another method is to discover which materials will scratch others and place them in order.

This is in essence a simplification of the system invented by F. Mohs in 1812 to test and compare the hardness of minerals, which is still used today. He arranged ten minerals in order of hardness so that each scratches those lower in the scale.

The hardness of an unknown mineral can be determined by finding out which of the above minerals it will scratch and which it will not. On this scale a finger-nail has a hardness of about 2.5 and a knife blade approximately 5.5. The hardness of glass has a value below 6.

Mohs' scale

1	Talc	softest
2	Gypsum	
3	Calcite	
4	Fluorite	
5	Apatite	
6	Orthoclase	
7	Quartz	
8	Topaz	
9	Corundum	
10	Diamond	hardest

■ HEALTH

Health can be affected by lifestyle or the presence of microbes.

Lifestyle and health

Health can be affected by the use of drugs (for example, solvents, alcohol, tobacco), sexual behaviour, relationships between family and friends, attitude towards safety, amount of exercise, diet, personal hygiene, and the attitude of others towards the environment (for example, health hazards produced by discarding rubbish, or smoking).

Microbes and health

Microbes such as bacteria, viruses and fungi can affect health. Many can affect health adversely but a number of microbes (certain fungi, bacteria and moulds) are beneficial since they naturally produce a group of chemicals which can be used as antibiotics. Antibiotics are widely used in medicine to treat bacterial infections: they either kill bacteria or inhibit their growth. Many harmful microbes enter the body through unhygienic practices such as poor food preparation, or poor personal hygiene (*see* microbes, personal hygiene and handling of food).

■ HEATING

Heating is a means by which energy can be transferred. Energy passes from hot objects to cold objects by heating. Energy can be transferred by heating in three ways: conduction, convection and radiation.

Conduction

Conduction is a method by which energy is transferred through a solid. Energy can be transferred in any direction through a material. A liquid and a gas also conduct heat but not as well as a solid. This is because energy transfer relies on the vibration of particles passing on energy to neighbouring particles, and particles in a liquid and a gas are more spread out than those in a solid (*see* solid, liquid, gas). As an object is heated its particles gain kinetic energy and vibrate more rapidly. This vibrational energy is gradually passed on from neighbour to neighbour and so heat energy is conducted in the object.

Convection

Convection is the means by which energy is transferred upwards through gases (for example, air) and liquids (for example, water). It occurs because as the particles in a gas or liquid are heated they become more energetic, they gain more kinetic energy, move more rapidly and become more spread out. The heated volume of gas or liquid (for example, air or water) is less dense than the cooler gas or liquid surrounding it, and it rises up, carrying the energy with it.

Radiation

Radiation is a method by which energy is transferred through a space (a vacuum) and a gas (for example, air) as an energy-carrying wave, sometimes referred to as infra-red radiation.

■ HEATING EFFECT (OF ELECTRIC CURRENT)

When an electric current passes through a wire or a component a proportion of the electrical energy is transferred to the surroundings as heat (the component warms up). This is commonly referred to as the 'heating effect of an electric current'. This effect can be very useful, but can also be a nuisance.

The heating effect can be of benefit:

Electric fires   use a coil of a high melting point alloy wire such as nichrome (an alloy of nickel and chromium). The resistance offered by the wire ensures that the wire will glow red hot thus heating the room.

Light bulb filament   is a very thin wire with a high resistance to electric current. This causes the wire to glow white hot so producing light as well as heat.

Fuse   relies on the heating effect of an electric current. Larger electric currents produce greater heating effects. A fuse is a strip of metal or wire of a certain thickness which is designed to heat up and melt when a current above a certain limit passes through it. Melting will produce a break in the circuit so the current can no longer flow.

The heating effect can be a disadvantage. If electrical equipment such as a television, a video or Hi-Fi equipment is operated it too becomes hot as a result of current passing through the many components in the circuits. This heat causes the resistance of the circuits to change so the device does not function as it should. Special care is taken to reduce this heating effect either by using low-power circuits, providing cooling fans (as with many computers) or by using black fins called 'heat sinks' which radiate excess heat to the room.

> At Key Stage 2 children can easily experience the heat given out from a torch bulb connected to a battery and by even sometimes feeling the wires in a circuit containing two batteries. Care is needed as when batteries are short circuited they can occasionally cause the wires to become very hot and to even melt. This could cause burns to the skin.

■ HEAT ON EVERYDAY MATERIALS

The action of heat on substances can result in no apparent change, a temporary change or a permanent change. A permanent change, one in which new substances are formed, is known as a chemical change. Examples of changes when different substances are heated are:

NB If sand is heated very strongly then it too will change; it will melt, forming glass.

No change on heating	Temporary change on heating	Permanent change on heating
sand	ice water	egg (cooking) wood (burning) gas (burning)

■ HOT AND COLD

A child describes an object as hot or cold depending on how it feels in relation to their own body temperature. The skin contains a number of receptors sensitive to changes in temperature.

> Early in Key Stage 2 children should be encouraged (as in Key Stage 1) to link sensations of hot and cold with temperature readings. Provided there are no draughts all the objects within a room should be at the same temperature; this can be checked using a thermometer. However, when objects are touched they may 'feel' to be at different temperatures. The reason for this is quite straightforward. Some materials are good conductors of heat so conduct the heat away from the hand making them feel quite cold (for example, metals and glass). Certain objects, however, may feel warm to the touch because they are good insulators (do not allow heat to pass through them), thus the heat generated in your hand is prevented from escaping into the air as it normally does. Good examples are wool and polystyrene.

The connection between heat and temperature

Heating is a way by which energy is transferred; for example, the chemical energy stored in coal can be transferred to a room in the form of heat by burning the coal. As a result the room becomes warmer (it has a higher temperature).

Heat and temperature are not the same. For example, an object can contain a lot of heat energy yet still not be as hot as another object. Equally, more heating is needed to make larger objects reach the same temperature as smaller objects. Suppose that two saucepans,

one large, one small, each full of water, were heated on two identical cooker rings: it would take longer to boil the larger saucepan of water than it would the smaller one.

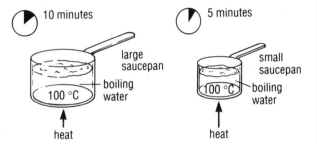

■ HUMAN INFLUENCES

There are many ways in which a local environment can be changed by human activity.

Activity	Changes	Benefits	Detrimental effects
farming	woodland cleared, ploughed fields created	increased area for growing crops	destroys habitat for wildlife, upsets balance of ecosystem
	hedgerows cleared	increased area for planting increased ease of access	destroys habitat for wildlife
	ploughed fields left bare over winter	reduced cost	allows natural nitrates in the soil to leach out, polluting water courses
	fertilizers used	increased yield	excess amounts can produce rapid growth of plants in nearby water courses causing a build up of water weed that clogs streams
	pesticides used	increased yield by killing pests	may also kill harmless insects and other animals, upsetting balance of ecosystem
mining open-cast (for example, coal, china clay)	pits and spoil heaps created	useful mineral or fuel extracted open-cast mines less costly and safer	spoils landscape damages habitat creates a waste problem (spoil heaps) pit covers large areas
mining underground	mine created	useful mineral or fuel extracted mining underground hidden from sight	produces waste, spoil heap dangerous to miners
industry	siting factory	materials manufactured jobs created	creates pollution destroys habitat
quarrying	creating pit	useful material extracted mainly for building purposes	destroys habitat spoils landscape

■ HYPOTHESIS

An hypothesis is a prediction about some event or property qualified by a tentative explanation. At Key Stage 2 this will often appear as an *I think…, because…* type response.

A statement *I think this ball will bounce higher* can be considered to be a prediction or guess. However the statement *I think this ball will bounce higher because it is made of rubber* (i.e. rubber balls bounce higher) can be considered to be an hypothesis because the prediction is qualified with the tentative explanation that balls made of rubber bounce higher than those which are not.

Hypothesis formation can be encouraged with appropriate effective questions, for example:

What do think will happen?   *Why?*
What do think causes...?   *Why?*
What affects...?   *Why?*
What factors affect...?   *Why?*

■ INDICATOR

An indicator is a solution of a dye which changes colour in the presence of an acid and to a different colour in the presence of an alkali. The indicator may be used as a solution or as strips of absorbent paper carrying dye, which must be wetted before use.

Many coloured plant materials act as indicators. Indeed many standard indicators were originally obtained from plants.

Litmus is a standard indicator which turns bright red in acidic conditions and deep blue in alkaline conditions. It was originally obtained from lichens. Some indicators that are in use today are more sophisticated in that not only can they indicate the presence of an acid or an alkali but can also indicate how acidic or alkaline the substance is.

Universal indicator changes through a range of colours from red, orange, yellow, green, blue and violet indicating increasingly more alkaline conditions (*see also* pH).

Typical colour range of a Universal indicator:

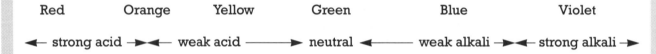

| Red | Orange | Yellow | Green | Blue | Violet |

← strong acid →←— weak acid ——→ neutral ←——— weak alkali →←— strong alkali →

Strips of litmus paper and Universal indicator paper, sometimes referred to as pH paper, can be purchased at home-brew shops and chemists, as well as education equipment suppliers.

At Key Stage 2 children are introduced to acidity and alkalinity by encouraging them to make their own indicators. This can be achieved by taking some plant material and cutting it into small pieces using scissors and then grinding it in water. The mixture then needs to be filtered to obtain a good clear solution. This indicator solution can then be used by adding small amounts to a suspected acidic or alkaline solution or by first soaking absorbent paper in the solution, allowing it to dry, cutting into strips and using the strips to test the acidic or alkaline solutions.

Suitable plant materials for making indicators

Plant	Colour in acidic solutions	Colour in neutral solutions	Colour in alkaline solutions
red cabbage	red	green	blue
onion skins*	pale yellow	–	bright orange
onion flesh*	colourless	pale yellow	green
red rose	red	purple	deep blue
pink geraniums	red	green/blue	blue
fuchsia (red)	red	–	blue
blackcurrant	red	–	blue/black

*Onion indicators can be made by boiling some onion in a pan with a little water for approximately one minute.

Once children have tried one indicator to identify everyday acidic and alkaline solutions they can be challenged to find their own indicators. Flower petals, coloured leaves and vegetables are worth trying. Almost any coloured plant material may provide suitable sources, especially those containing reds (for example, red cabbage), blues or purples (for example, aubergine). Exceptions include yellow flowers such as dandelions and daffodils, green plants and beetroot.

INHERITANCE, MECHANISM OF

See gene.

IRON

Iron is a metal element. It has the typical properties of a metal – it is shiny, strong, conducts heat and electricity well, and is ductile (can be drawn into wires). Iron is also magnetic.

Iron is found in rocks called iron ores. These ores contain iron chemically joined to other elements.

Ore	Chemical name	Elements present
haematite	iron oxide	iron, oxygen
kidney ore	iron oxide	iron, oxygen
fool's gold (pyrites)	iron sulphide	iron, sulphur

Iron is extracted from its ore in a blast furnace. A mixture of coke (carbon), limestone and iron ore are heated in the furnace. A reaction occurs under extreme heat which reduces the iron ore to iron. This can be represented in simple terms:

iron oxide + carbon → iron + carbon dioxide

Many of the iron ores are red in colour, as are many other compounds of iron. Soils and clays are often coloured red because of a high level of iron compounds (for example, soils in Devon). Blood is red due to the presence of an iron compound, haemoglobin. Haemoglobin carries oxygen. It is often recommended that people take 'iron' tablets when they are anaemic or always feel tired, as iron is needed to make more haemoglobin. Red wine is a good source of iron, containing iron in a form which the body can easily absorb, the red colour being due to another iron compound.

Rusting and burning

The reactions resulting in iron rusting and iron burning are similar. Both involve the reaction of oxygen from air on iron; burning simply proceeds at a more rapid rate. In both cases iron is oxidised, the product being iron oxide (a red colour):

Rusting

iron + oxygen $\xrightarrow{\text{moist conditions}}$ iron oxide

(slow oxidation)

Burning

iron + oxygen $\xrightarrow{\text{heat}}$ iron oxide

(rapid oxidation)

Iron needs to be heated very strongly before it will burn, but an appreciation of the effect can be gained by heating a small amount of iron-wool in a flame when the iron will spark and discolour as it forms the oxide.

Alloys of iron

An alloy is a mixture of melted metals. An alloy has properties which are different to the original metals. Iron can be mixed with a small quantity of carbon (less than 1.7%) to produce an alloy of iron called steel. Steel is much stronger than iron and can be treated to make it more resistant to rusting. Different steels can be produced by varying the quantity of carbon added, or by introducing small quantities of other metals, for example spring steels for making springs (carbon is added), stainless steel (carbon and chromium are added) and high speed steels used for drills and cutting machines (tungsten is added).

The magnetic properties of iron are not so pronounced in many steels: some stainless steels for example will not be attracted to a magnet.

JOULE

The joule (symbol J) is a unit of energy and is the amount of work that is done when a force of 1 N moves an object through a distance of 1 m. 4.2 J of energy are needed to raise the temperature of 1 g of water by 1 °C. The unit joule is named after the English physicist James Prescott Joule (1818–1889) who was the first to establish the relationship between mechanical energy (work) and heat. Food packets contain information about the amount of energy available from different foods. This information is quoted in kilojoules (1000 J).

Foods	Energy value (kJ)
can of baked beans	1500
bowl of cereal	750
chocolate biscuit	350
slice of bread	300

About 100 kJ of energy is expended in each of the following activities:

10 minutes light work, for example teaching
2 minutes brisk walk up a steep hill
15 minutes watching television
3 times 100 metre sprint

■ KEY

A key is information arranged in such a way that an unknown species can be identified

At Key Stage 2, keys can be made or used to identify trees (using differences in twigs or leaves), common hedgerow or meadow plants, pond animals, animals in leaf litter and soil, as well as vertebrate animals. Most keys work by asking questions or matching pictures to which the response is either 'yes' or 'no' which allows the organism to be identified or continually narrows down the choice through a branching key. Computer database keys are also constructed on this principle. Examples of two basic types of keys are shown below.

Simple yes/no key for identifying trees (looking at twigs).

Are the buds sticky? ——► yes ——► Horse chestnut

↓ no

Are the buds black? ——► yes ——► Ash

↓ no

Is there a collection ——► yes ——► Oak
of brown buds at the tip?

↓ no

Are the buds long ——► yes ——► Beech
and thin?

Simple branching key for identifying trees from twigs:

Do buds grow in opposite pairs?

yes ╱ ╲ no

Are the buds sticky? Are the twigs smooth?

yes ╱ no   yes ╱ no

Horse   Ash   Oak   Ash
chestnut

■ LENS

Lenses form images of objects by refracting (bending) light. The image that is formed depends on the size and shape of the lens. Lenses can be found in spectacles, binoculars, telescopes, slide projectors, magnifying glasses, magnispectors and midispectors. A plastic bag filled with water can also act as a lens. Lenses can also be purchased separately from science education suppliers. Lenses can be different shapes:

Biconvex   A lens which has sides which curve outwards and are thicker at the centre than the rim. They are sometimes called converging lenses since they make light bend inwards.

Planoconvex   A lens which has one flat side and one outward curved side.

Fresnel or 'Flat' lenses.   A lens that appears flat on both sides, but actually consists of concentric rings of 'lens sections', and behave in the same way as more traditional convex lenses.

Biconcave   A lens which curves inwards and is thinner at its centre than at its rim. Sometimes referred to as a diverging lens since it makes light bend outwards.

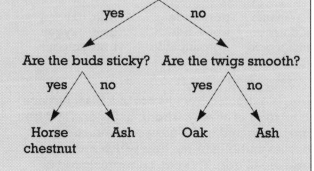

Biconvex

light rays

lens

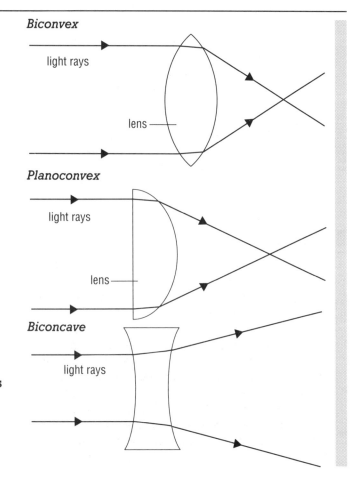

Planoconvex

light rays

lens

Biconcave

light rays

Forming images through convex lenses

Convex lenses can act as magnifying glasses. To what degree they magnify depends on their curvature (how thick they are at the middle). Thicker lenses make better magnifiers. Stronger magnifiers can be made by placing one lens on top of the other, effectively making the 'lens' thicker. Conversely, thinner lenses are weaker magnifiers. For a single lens to act as a magnifier it must be used close to the object it is magnifying. A plastic bag filled with water placed on a newspaper will magnify the text; filling the bag with more water will make it into a 'thicker' lens so magnifying the text more.

A magnifying glass can be used to obtain other images. Try placing a magnifying glass on a page of writing and then gradually lifting it from the page. A magnified image of

A convex lens being used as a magnifying glass

convex lens close to page

the writing forms, then, as the magnifying glass is continually lifted away, the image at first blurs and then another, much smaller, inverted image forms. These two sorts of images formed by the lens depend on how far away the lens is from the writing paper (the object). Each of these types of image has a name. The magnified image is called a virtual image, whereas the smaller inverted image is called a real image.

The lens is close to the object and a magnified (virtual) image is formed. A virtual image cannot be formed on a screen.

The lens is a relatively long way away from the object. A real image is 'real' because it can be formed on a screen.

A convex lens being used to produce a 'real' image

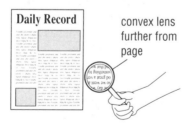

convex lens further from page

Hold the lens so that light from a nearby window can pass through it and fall onto a piece of white paper acting as a screen. If the piece of paper is moved slowly backwards and then towards the lens a point should be reached when a small, sharp, inverted image of the window is observed. This is the real image being formed on the screen instead of in your eye. The distance between the lens and this sharp image is called the focusing distance or 'focal length'. Thicker lenses have shorter focal lenses; they form sharper smaller brighter images.

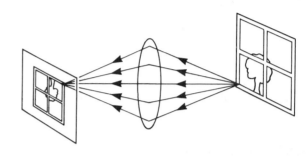

Concave lenses form only virtual images. Images formed by concave lenses cannot be formed on a screen. When looking through a concave lens you will see an upright image of the surroundings; shapes might appear distorted, however, since the images formed cover a wide field of view (see biconcave lens above).

Describing lenses

Lenses are described either in terms of the focal lengths (focusing distances) measured in centimetres or more often in terms of their power in units of dioptres.

Thicker convex lenses are more powerful and have shorter focal lengths. Suitable lenses for use in classrooms have powers of +5 D to +20 D.

▌ LEVER

Levers are considered to be simple machines because they can make work 'easier'. A lever allows a force to be applied at a distance from a pivot:

Any job requires a certain amount of energy to do it (the amount of work done). The amount of energy you have to expend depends on:

Crow bar acting as a lever

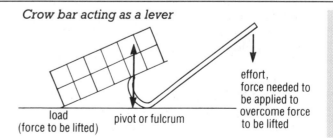

load
(force to be lifted)

pivot or fulcrum

effort, force needed to be applied to overcome force to be lifted

- How much force is needed to move an object.
- The distance through which you have to move the force.

For example, it is much harder work and requires much more energy to push a large, heavy car than to push a small, light car the same distance because you have to exert more force. It is also much harder work to push the same car 100 metres than it is to push it 1 metre.

Work done can be calculated by multiplying the force used by the distance covered:

> work done (joules) = force applied (newtons) × distance moved (metres)

Levers allow you to move heavy objects using less force than you would normally need. This makes the task easier. The job still needs the same amount of energy, however, so in order to compensate for this smaller force applied it has to be moved through a larger distance.

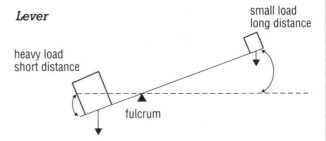

Lever

small load
long distance

heavy load
short distance

fulcrum

The same amount of work is done when a large force moves through a short distance as a small force through a large distance.

Levers can also be called energy transfer devices, the energy transfer being movement.

LIFE PROCESSES

A number of processes common to living organisms are described below.

Feeding and digestion
Animals have a different variety of mouth parts adapted to feeding on different foods. Digestion is the process of breaking down food to molecules small enough to be absorbed through the gut wall. The nutrients are delivered by the blood to all cells in the body. Green plants produce their own food by the very important life process of photosynthesis. Minerals are absorbed by the soil to enable more complex substances such as proteins to be made from the simple products of photosynthesis.

Breathing and respiration
All living organisms (plants and animals) respire – they use oxygen to burn up food to provide energy for cells of the organism. Green plants absorb oxygen through their leaves, whereas animals either breathe air into lungs or gills, or absorb it directly through the skin, exchanging oxygen in the air for carbon dioxide, a waste product of respiration.

Transport within the organism
Multicellular organisms have a transport system for distributing nutrients and oxygen to cells and removing waste products. In large animals this is the blood circulatory system whereas in plants material is transported through phloem and xylem vessels.

Reproduction and growth
Sexual reproduction involves the fertilization of a female egg cell by a male sex cell (sperm) to produce a new individual, different from either parent but similar to both. Most animals and flowering plants reproduce in this way. Plants and some small animals (for example, aphids) can reproduce asexually.

Asexual reproduction is a process of reproduction in which only one parent is involved, the offspring being genetically identical to the parent.

Removal of waste
Excretion is the process by which organisms rid themselves of the waste products of metabolism. Many animals including mammals have excretory systems involving kidneys, and carbon dioxide (a waste product of respiration) is expelled through lungs, gills or skin, etc. Plants exchange gases through the leaves. Oxygen, a waste product of photosynthesis, is disposed of through the leaf. Plants can also store certain wastes in a harmless insoluble form as tannins.

Movement and support
Larger animals are supported by internal skeletons, smaller animals are sometimes supported by external skeletons, and plants are supported by tough, fibrous materials called cellulose and lignin. Plant cells containing sufficient water will also add rigidity to a plant, thus supporting it (plants wilt when dehydrated). Water-plants do not need the same rigidity of land plants since the buoyancy of the water will support them. Some plants move in response to light; others, such as the Venus fly trap, can also move in response to the stimuli of touch; animals will move in search of food, to avoid danger, or to reproduce.

Sensitivity

Animals and plants are sensitive to a variety of stimuli which may include light, sound or vibration, touch, smell, gravity or taste.

Plants are sensitive to light – plant shoots grow towards light sources; they can also respond to gravity – plant roots grow downwards. Certain plants are sensitive to touch, for example the mimosa (sensitive plant) which closes its leaves when touched, or climbing plants which curl tendrils around objects they touch. Animals such as fish are sensitive to light (they have eyes), smell and vibrations in water.

LIGHT

Vision is dependent on light. Light from the Sun or alternative source is reflected off objects into the eyes.

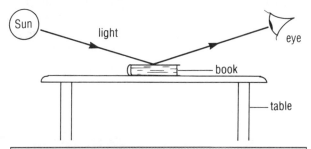

> At Key Stage 2 a common misconception amongst children is that vision is possible because light somehow comes from the eyes and strikes an object. Other misconceptions are that objects 'give off' light.

Light travels in straight lines

The formation of shadows, the fact that vision does not extend round corners and that straight torch beams are visible provides evidence that light waves travel in straight lines.

Light waves can be made to change direction by reflecting them from mirrors or by passing them through different transparent materials. When passing through materials the straight beam of light waves changes direction at the interface between the two media (for example, air and glass). It is said to be refracted (*see* reflection and refraction).

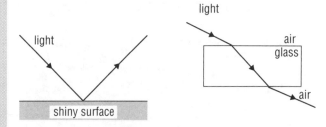

Light transfers energy

Light waves possess energy. There are two models which scientists have developed to explain the way in which transfer of this energy occurs. One model treats light as a wave, the other treats light as a particle (called a photon). Some of the behaviour of light is best accounted for by treating light as a wave and some by treating light as a particle.

Light as a wave

Light can be thought of as travelling in the form of a wave (the waves travel in straight lines). The way light waves travel outwards from a light source is similar to the ripples spreading out from a stone thrown into a pond. The wave carries energy outwards from a source.

Waves in a pond are caused by a series of vertical vibrations, the waves travelling at right angles to the vibrations. Light waves can be regarded in a similar way and are called transverse waves.

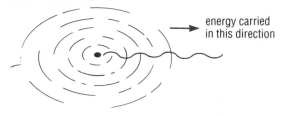

Any wave can be characterised by its wavelength, frequency and amplitude:

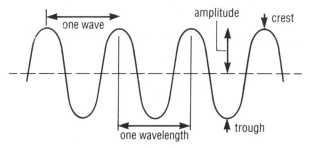

wavelength =	distance from one point on a wave to the next similar point, for example crest to crest or trough to trough, measured in metres;
frequency =	number of waves passing every second, measured in hertz (Hz) which is the number of waves or vibrations per second;
amplitude =	the distance a wave rises and falls; a wave with greater amplitude carries more energy and so will be a brighter light.

All light waves travel at the same speed; it follows, therefore, that a long wavelength will have a lower frequency. White light is a mixture of different colours; the colours of the spectrum. Each colour is characterised by its wavelength. Red light has a relatively long wavelength, whereas violet light has a relatively short wavelength.

LIQUID

Liquids do not keep their shape: they will take the shape of any container they are poured into. Their volume remains constant irrespective of the shape they take up (provided the temperature remains constant).

At Key Stage 3 children can explore liquids such as water, glycerol, liquid paraffin, various oils (for example sewing machine oil and 3-in-One). The children can compare how fluid a liquid is (or how viscous (sticky)) by dropping a marble through it and timing how long it takes to pass through. They can also shine a torch through a liquid to see how light travels through a liquid. Children can try to dissolve substances such as sugar and salt in a liquid.

The particles (atoms and molecules) which make up a liquid are relatively close together, but further apart than particles in a solid and have sufficient energy to move about and slide over and around each other (see classification of materials).

LOGIC GATES

A logic gate is an electrical component or device the electrical output of which 'logically' depends on the electrical input into the component. It acts as a gate, allowing electric current to pass or not. There are three common gates:

AND gate

This gate produces an output only when the first input AND the second input are carrying electric current.

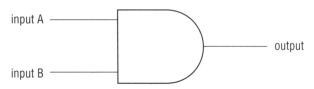

input A
input B
output

NOT gate

This gate produces an output when there is NOT an input of electric current.

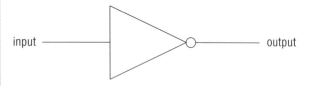

input
output

OR gate

This gate produces an output when there is either an electric current flowing at input 1 OR at input 2. (OR both inputs 1 and 2.)

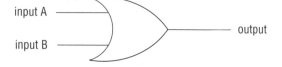

input A
input B
output

These three components can be used in a circuit to solve problems. For example, for a light to switch on automatically in darkness a light sensor (light dependent resistor) can be connected as the input to a NOT gate.

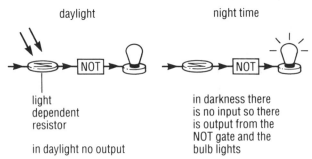

daylight   night time

light dependent resistor

in daylight no output

in darkness there is no input so there is output from the NOT gate and the bulb lights

At Key Stage 2 a convenient way of exploring the use of a logic gates in a circuit and solving problems is to purchase the *Microelectronics For All* (MFA) decisions boards manufactured and sold by Unilab Ltd. The NOT, AND and OR gates shown below are in complete circuits.

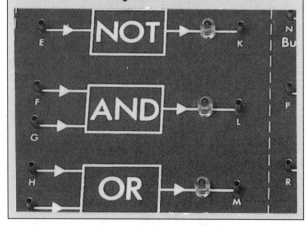

■ 'LOUDNESS'

A loud sound is produced by an object that possesses a large amplitude of vibration, which in turn produces large displacements of air (*see* sound).

Vibrating string

large amplitude
loud sound

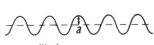

small amplitude
soft sound

a : amplitude

The loudness (amplitude) of a sound produced by a vibrating object can be affected by the following:

How hard an object is struck   The skin on a drum vibrates a large distance about its middle point when struck. The amplitude of the displacement is great. Striking a drum skin softly will cause a small displacement. The speed of the vibration is not affected by striking the drum skin hard or softly, but by the tightness of the drum skin.

The size of a vibrating object   A large drum produces a louder sound than a smaller one. A guitar with a larger 'body' produces a louder sound.

The material that vibrates   A steel guitar string sounds louder than a nylon string when plucked. Also the material the guitar 'body' is made of affects the loudness of the sound.

■ MAGNET

Magnetism is a force of attraction or repulsion between certain substances. A magnet produces a magnetic field around itself; the 'lines of magnetic force' in this field can be seen if iron filings are sprinkled around the magnet. The lines of force are concentrated at the poles (ends of a magnet). These are called the North (North-seeking) pole and the South (South-seeking) pole because if left to swing freely the magnet will orientate itself along the North-South lines of the Earth's magnetic field.

If a bar magnet is suspended from a string, and left to swing, eventually it comes to rest pointing North-South.

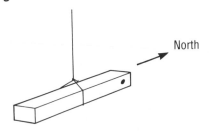

North

A compass is a free-swinging magnet.

The North-seeking pole of a magnet is often indicated by either an 'N' or a small dot, or indentation, at one of its ends.

Magnetic field around a bar magnet

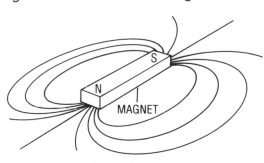

Magnets either attract or repel each other. Like poles repel each other whereas unlike poles attract. The magnetic field produced by two magnets close-by can be shown by sprinkling iron filings around the magnets.

Attracting magnets   *Repelling magnets*

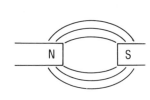 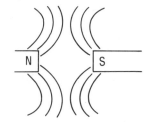

Magnets are made in a variety of shapes and sizes:

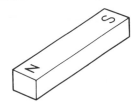 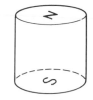

Bar-shaped   *Cylindrical-shaped*

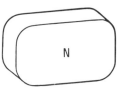 

Slab-shaped   *Horseshoe-shaped*

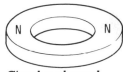

Circular-shaped

At Key Stage 2 it is important that children experience and use a variety of magnets and are able to feel the magnetic forces exerted by strong magnets. The magnets available in school are often too weak and lose their magnetism quickly. The purchase of good quality, strong magnets is recommended. Magnets lose their magnetism through physical shock, for example when hammered, dropped or heated. Magnetism can be retained by always storing a magnet with a 'keeper', and in the case of a bar magnet, in a pair with keepers. Keepers are simply pieces of iron or steel which fit across the poles.

Theory of magnetism

The magnetism exhibited by certain materials is due to the behaviour of electrons (negative electric charges) within the atoms. In a material such as iron small groups of atoms behave as if they were miniature magnets. This group of atoms is referred to as a 'domain'. A piece of iron can be considered to be made up of a whole series of these tiny magnetic domains which all point in different directions and cancel each other out to produce no overall effect.

When such a piece of iron is placed in a strong magnetic field the domains are forced to line up, converting the piece of iron into a magnet.

A permanent magnet can be created by 'stroking' a piece of iron in the same direction a number of times with a strong magnet or by placing the iron in a magnetic field created by an electric coil. This latter method is one used to manufacture many magnets.

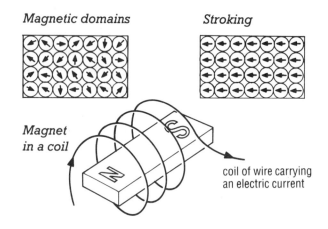

Magnetic domains　　　*Stroking*

Magnet in a coil

coil of wire carrying an electric current

MAGNETIC EFFECT (OF AN ELECTRIC CURRENT)

An electric current passing through a wire creates a magnetic field around the wire. The wire acts like a magnet (albeit a very weak magnet). This effect can be seen by placing a small compass near a wire and then connecting the wire to a battery. You should see the compass move slightly when the current is switched on or off. (Remember to include a bulb or some other device so that you do not short-circuit the battery.)

Electric current passing through a coil of wire makes the coil act like a bar magnet, the coil having a North and a South pole. Inserting a piece of soft iron into the hollow coil, for example a 6" nail, can help to concentrate the lines of magnetic force. The nail will then act like a magnet only when the current is turned on. This is the principle of an electromagnet. A simple electromagnet can be made stronger by:

■ Using more batteries.
■ Increasing the number of turns on the coil.

The wire used in the coil must be insulated: a coil of bare wire will merely allow the electric current to short-circuit the coil.

At Key Stage 2 challenging children with the question: *How can you make the electro-magnet stronger?* can provide an excellent opportunity for them to investigate Sc1.

The magnetic effect produced by an electric current is extremely useful to man:

Basis of the electric motor electrical (potential) energy is transferred to movement (kinetic) energy.
A means of generating electricity when a wire (or coil of wire) is moved in a strong magnetic field an electric current flows in the wire, the means by which movement (kinetic) energy is transferred to electrical (potential) energy. A generator is simply an electric motor 'used in reverse'. If you connect a bulb to an electric motor and spin the motor very fast the bulb will light; the faster you spin, the brighter the bulb.

An understanding of this electromagnetic effect has led to the development of a range of useful devices such as motors, generators, loudspeakers, microphones, tape recorders, and cartridges (pick-ups) on record players. The working of these devices can be readily explained and understood through the magnetic effect of an electric current.

■ MAGNETIC MATERIALS

Most materials in themselves are non-magnetic, the exceptions being the 'ferromagnetic' metals such as

- Iron (or steel which is an alloy of iron).
- Nickel.
- Cobalt.

Lodestone, the rock which acts as a natural magnet and was known in ancient times, is actually iron oxide which has been magnetised by the Earth's magnetic field.

Years ago magnets were made almost exclusively from iron; much more powerful permanent magnets are made today from combinations of materials, often alloys of iron, cobalt and nickel.

> At Key Stage 2 it is important to remember that it is a popular misconception amongst many children that all metals are magnetic.

■ MAINS ELECTRICITY

Mains electricity is different from electricity flowing in a circuit that contains batteries in two main ways:

Energy carried by the mains is large certainly sufficient to pass a fatal current through a person. It is important to realise that it is 'Current that kills', only a quite small current passing through the body can be fatal. A high voltage on its own is nearly always not fatal, for example a static discharge from a nylon carpet can produce several thousand volts, but an almost negligible current (*see* electricity). An electric shock can be received simply by touching the live wire from the mains. A person doing this will complete a circuit with the ground which forms a connection back to the supply, thus allowing the current to pass through them. In order to prevent this happening by accident all appliances are insulated and/or are protected by an 'earth' wire. The 'earth' provides an easier pathway for the electric current to flow to ground rather than through the person. For example, if a 'live' wire came loose inside a toaster and was in contact with the outer metal casing anyone touching it would receive a potentially lethal shock. The earth wire in a toaster is connected to the casing or any conducting (metal) part likely to be touched by a person so that in the event of this happening the earth will provide a route which will conduct the current away from the person, the electrical 'earth' wire providing a better alternative route. Metallic wires conduct electricity

better than people do (*see* electrical conductors).

Mains electricity provides a supply of alternating current' different to the 'direct current' from a battery. In the mains the alternating current reverses its direction 50 times per second. The supply is referred to as 50 hertz, hertz being a measure of frequency or cycles per second. The advantage of an alternating supply (AC) is that unlike direct current (DC) its voltage can be increased for transmission over long distances, then reduced to suit local voltages in towns and homes. This does, however, mean that devices designed to work from the mains will not necessarily work with batteries. Motors, for example, have to be designed differently, so that if a motor is rated at 12 volts and designed to run on mains electricity it will not work when connected to a 12 volt battery.

The wires in electrical appliances are colour coded. The diagram shows their connection to an electrical plug.

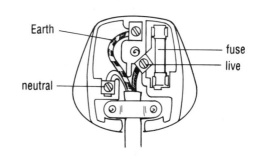

■ MAJOR GROUPS (PLANT AND ANIMAL)

Plants and animals can be sorted into groups according to features which they have in common. Sorting depends on a range of different features, for example the appearance

of a plant or animal, a skeleton of an animal, how an animal reproduces, the flowering parts of plants and how it develops, i.e. whether it produces seeds.

The living world can be divided into two main groups: animals and plants. A third group is the protists consisting of bacteria, viruses and single-celled organisms, although these too could be included in either of the main animal or plant groups. Each of these can be subdivided again into subgroups which can be regarded as the major groups of animals and plants.

Some simple groups are:

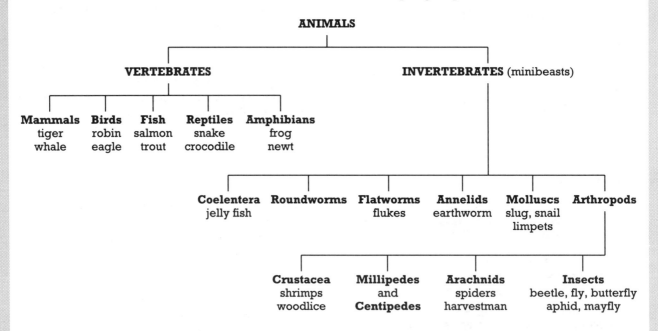

Group	Simple characteristics	Examples
mammal	warm blooded, hair or fur, suckles young, live young	cat, sheep, humans, whale
bird	warm blooded, feathers, lays eggs with hard shell	magpie, seagull, ostrich
reptile	cold blooded, scaly skin, lays eggs with soft shell	lizard, crocodile, snake
amphibian	cold blooded, moist skin, lays eggs in water	frog, toad, newt
fish	cold blooded, scales, fins, lays eggs, lives in water only	cod, plaice, goldfish
insect	3 pairs of legs, three body parts, most adults have wings	moth, butterfly, springtail, flea
crustacean	outer skeleton with joints, several pairs of legs	lobster, prawn, crab
arachnid	8 legs, two main body parts	spider
millipede } centipede }	many pairs of legs, segmented bodies	millipede centipede
segmented worm	long, thin body segments	earthworm
flatworm	flat bodies, no segments	fluke
roundworm	long thin body, no segments	threadworm
mollusc	body not in segments, one foot, many have shells	snail, slug, mussel, oyster
echinoderm	spiny hard exterior, lives in water	starfish, sea urchin, sea cucumber

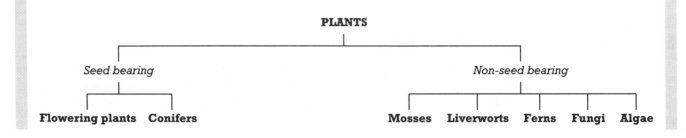

Group	Simple characteristics	Examples
flowering plant	flower, seed bearing	rose, oak tree, pineapple
moss and liverwort	produce spores, small	sphagnum moss
ferns	spores, often frond-like appearance	royal ferns, tree ferns
fungi	spores, body made of fine threads, feed on dead matter, often mushroom-like appearance	mushroom, toadstool
algae	no roots, stem, etc., photosynthesise, many live in water	spirogyra

■ MAMMAL

A mammal is a warm blooded animal possessing a backbone, a covering of hair or fur, and which produces live young (rather than laying eggs), and suckles their young. The duck-billed platypus and spiny anteater are, however, egg-laying exceptions.

■ MASS

To a scientist it is important to make the distinction between mass and weight. In everyday language the term weight is used to describe both mass and weight. Mass describes the amount of matter in an object, whilst the weight describes the pull of gravity on an object (a person weighs less in Space although they have the same mass).

> At Key Stage 2, it would appear from the Programme of Study ('. . . properties such as . . . mass (weight)') that no distinction is to be made between the two.

Mass and weight

The mass of an object, the amount of matter in an object, is measured in units of grammes (g), kilogrammes (kg) or tonnes. A large mass would weigh a great deal on Earth, but if this were taken to the Moon it would weigh much less (about 1/6th of the weight on Earth) although the mass would be the same, the amount of matter would not change. The mass of an object is not really a description of how heavy an object is but more to do with how difficult an object is to start moving. Imagine a person 'floating' in Space with a small and a large rock 'floating' in front of them. The small rock has a mass of 100 g whereas the larger rock has a mass of 100 tonnes. If the person pushed both of them, they would find that the 100-tonne rock was much harder to start moving.

The weight of an object is a pull of gravity on an object and is therefore a force and is measured in units of newtons. The weight of an object would therefore depend on the force of the gravity. The pull of gravity on the Moon is much less than on Earth so the object would weigh less on the Moon.

If a person weighed themselves on bathroom scales on Earth and then took the same scales to the Moon and re-weighed themselves, they would obtain a lower reading.

The main confusion about mass and weight arises because although we do weigh ourselves when we stand on the bathroom scales, the scales are calibrated in units of mass (i.e. kilogrammes, kg). This is acceptable provided the scales are only used on Earth. However a problem arises because 'I weigh 50 kg (about 8 stone)' really means 'my mass is 50 kg'. On Earth, gravity pulls on a 1 kg mass with a force of 10 newtons so if someone had a mass of 50 kg their weight would be 500 newtons.

> As children mature throughout Key Stage 2 it would be appropriate to introduce them to the term mass (without attempting an explanation of the difference between mass and weight). They could, for instance, after 'weighing' objects, be encouraged to make statements such as *The mass of the wood block was* . . . when recording their results.

It is not until Key Stage 4 that children will be expected to distinguish between mass and weight.

MATERIALS

See use of materials.

MEDICINES

All medicines are drugs which can have a beneficial effect on the body. Medicines can be classified according to their effects, for example, pain reliever (aspirin, paracetamol, etc.) or antibiotics which can kill bacteria or inhibit their growth (*see* drugs).

Drugs prescribed frequently are:

Medicine	Use
Paracetamol	mild pain
Amoxycillin	bacterial infection
Salbutomol	asthma
Atenol	angina and high blood pressure
Frusemide	fluid retention

MELT

Solids melt when they are heated. Melting and freezing are words which describe a change of state between a solid and a liquid phase.

$$\text{solid} \underset{\text{freezing}}{\overset{\text{melting}}{\rightleftharpoons}} \text{liquid}$$

At Key Stage 2 young children will often use the words melt and dissolve interchangeably. They need to be encouraged to use these words correctly. Melting applies to one substance whereas dissolving applies to two or more substances. Children can explore melting with ice, wax, butter, chocolate (when cooking), and with solder when using soldering irons, and with glue when using glue guns.

MICROBE

Examples of microbes (micro-organisms) include microscopic algae, fungi (including moulds and yeasts), bacteria and viruses. Microbes exist in a very wide range of different habitats. Most are free-living although some need a host in which or on which to live.

Common microbes are: the fungi that cause athletes' foot; yeast used in baking and brewing; penicillium used to produce penicillin; antibiotics; and the moulds used to produce blue cheeses.

Certain bacteria aid the recycling of nutrients through their role in decay, and others are used in industrial processes such as the production of cheeses, yoghurts, vinegar or even the extraction of copper from low-grade copper ore.

Examples of diseases caused by microbes:

Disease	Microbe type	Method of disease transmission
athletes' foot	fungus	by contact
ringworm	fungus	by contact
influenza	virus	in inhaled air
German measles	virus	in inhaled air
whooping cough	bacteria	in inhaled air
food poisoning (*Salmonella*)	bacteria	in contaminated food
typhoid	bacteria	in contaminated food and water
tetanus	bacteria	by entry to body through cuts, grazes, etc.

Many microbes cause disease in humans, and because of this teachers at Key Stage 2 need to take care when dealing with microbes to reduce the health risks to children and themselves. This is especially true when observing decay. It is important that teachers make themselves aware of any potential risks when handling microbes and abide by any Local Education Authority guidelines or safety information issued by the Department for Education.

At Key Stage 2 the main purpose for teaching about microbes is to introduce the children to the activity of organisms they cannot see with the naked eye, making them aware of how the microbes can affect health, and their role in decay (*see also* decay).

■ MINERALS

The word mineral can appear to be somewhat ambiguous, since it has different meanings – for example, there are minerals in foods, minerals in rocks, minerals are needed by plants, and even crude oil can be called a mineral. In general the term mineral refers to a naturally occurring substance which has a definite chemical composition.

> At Key Stage 2 the word mineral in the Programme of Study is concerned with minerals found in rocks.

Minerals in rocks

Some rocks contain only one mineral whilst others may contain many. For example, granite contains minerals such as feldspar and quartz whilst kidney ore, named after its shape, consists largely of one mineral – a form of iron oxide.

Certain minerals can be mined as elements, for example gold, silver, copper, sulphur or carbon (mined as diamond or graphite), whilst others are chemical compounds found in rocks. They often have common names as well as chemical names which describe their composition. The minerals found in rocks are often crystalline in nature and result from the cooling of molten rock. There are about 3000 different chemical substances making up the rocks on the Earth's surface.

Some common minerals are:

Mineral	Chemical name	Appearance	Occurrence (rocks)	Uses
quartz	silicon dioxide	transparent, crystalline, colourless in pure form, often tinged with impurities	igneous, sedimentary, metamorphic (and sands)	abrasives, glass, cement, electronic equipment, gemstones, for example amethyst (purple)
feldspar	silicates of aluminium, potassium, sodium, calcium	crystalline, white or coloured red, black, green-black	in most igneous, sedimentary, metamorphic rocks	paint, glass, china
gypsum	calcium sulphate	in beds as an evaporite	colourless or white, crystalline	plaster of Paris, cement, paint, school 'chalk'
calcite	calcium carbonate	colourless or white, crystalline	sedimentary, or metamorphic, main constituent of limestone	cement, plaster, paint, glass, fertilizer
dolomite	calcium magnesium carbonate	white	sedimentary and veins	building stone, cement
halite	sodium chloride (salt)	white/colourless crystalline	in beds as an evaporite	manufacture of chlorine for PVC manufacture, water purifying, dry-cleaning solvents, soap manufacture, manufacture of dyes, glass, fats, waxes, food, drink

It is the minerals in rocks which provide us with useful raw materials. Rocks containing minerals from which we can obtain metals are called ores:

Mineral	Chemical substance	Appearance	Raw material	Uses
bauxite	aluminium oxide	non-crystalline, white when pure, often coloured red by iron oxide impurity	aluminium	metal fabrication, aircraft, car body, saucepans, etc.
copper (native)	copper	copper-coloured lump	copper	electrical wires (good conductor), plating on cookware, alloys
galena	lead sulphide	grey, metallic lustre, crystalline	lead	electronic devices, semi-conductors, lead metal
haematite	iron oxide		iron	metal in car industry, buildings, manufacturing
malachite	copper carbonate		malachite	as semi-precious stone, facing stone for buildings, etc.
			copper	as above

Minerals in foods

Minerals are required by the human body: the word here has a similar meaning but is taken to mean the element (metal or non-metal) present in food, for example magnesium, iron, calcium, copper, phosphorus, etc.

The term mineral is also used to refer to anything extracted by mining. Hence coal, oil and even gas can appear under this definition as well as rocks containing useful elements, for example iron, copper, gold, etc.

■ MIRROR

Reflections or images can be seen in plane (flat) mirrors that appear to be the same distance behind the mirror as the object is in front. The reflection is also observed to be the same size as the object but is reversed.

The standard way of representing mirrors in diagrams is shown below together with the lines representing rays of light bouncing off an object, in this case a candle, and being reflected. The eyes perceive the rays to be spread out from the position behind the mirror.

The angle at which light beams are reflected from a mirror is the same as the angle at which the beams enter. This can be shown by using a torch. Bouncing a ball off a flat surface will produce the same effect (see reflection).

Curved mirror

The curved surfaces of mirrors produce different images.

Convex mirrors produce reflections from the outward curve of a shiny surface, for example the back of a spoon. Here the image produced

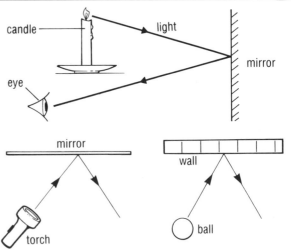

is upright and shows a wide angle; this is useful for a rear-view mirror in a car.

Concave mirrors produce reflections from the inner shiny surfaces of a curve, for example the inside of a spoon. Close up these can produce upright, magnified images, useful for a make-up, shaving or dentist's mirror. When looking from further away the image produced is smaller and upside down.

■ MOON

The Moon is the Earth's natural satellite (a satellite is a body which orbits a planet); the Moon is not regarded as a planet itself. It takes about 28 days for the Moon to orbit the Earth. The Moon is much smaller than the Earth, approximately 3500 km in diameter (the Earth is 12 756 km in diameter) and is about 400 000 km from the Earth. It shines because it reflects the Sun's light back to Earth. The apparent motion of the Moon across the sky is caused by the spin of the Earth on its axis. The Moon is held tightly by the Earth's gravitational field and turns only once on its own axis in the same time that it orbits the Earth (every 28 days). This means that the Moon keeps one face permanently towards the Earth. The 'dark' side of the Moon has only been seen by orbiting (and landing) spacecraft.

The Moon can be observed using binoculars or telescopes; with these aids features such as craters can be readily seen. (*See also* phases of the Moon.)

■ MOTOR

Electric motor

When an electric current flows through a wire it creates a magnetic field around it. If the wire is made into a tightly wound coil this field is intensified and the coil can behave as a magnet. This effect can be observed by connecting a coil of insulated wire to a battery and then sprinkling iron filings around the coil. A pattern will be produced similar to that around a bar magnet. If no pattern is observed more turns can be made in the coil or a battery of a higher voltage should be used.

Electric motor

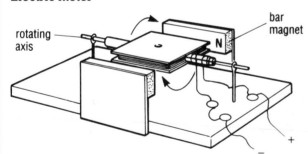

If a coil carrying an electric current is placed between two magnets it can be made to spin, because the coil acting as a magnet is itself repelled first by one magnet and then the next, causing it to continue to spin. With the coil spinning, the wires carrying the electric current from the battery cannot be connected directly to the coil. Rather they are connected via a set of contacts or brushes which are able to brush against a commutator (split metal ring).

The electric motor transfers the potential energy in the electrical source (e.g. battery) that the motor is connected to as movement (kinetic) energy. As the motor turns however other energy transfers are taking place. For instance some of the potential (electrical) energy is transferred to the surroundings by heating the motor and the air. The motor becomes hot. Thus some of the potential energy is wasted.

Clockwork motor

A clockwork motor stores energy in a spring, which is wound. This is called potential energy. This potential (stored) energy is transferred as movement (kinetic energy) as the spring unwinds.

Clockwork motor

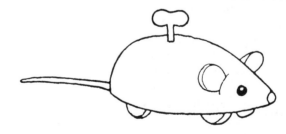

■ MOVEMENT

Movement in humans and other vertebrate animals is caused by the action of contraction and relaxation of muscles on a skeletal framework. The human skeleton consists of a number of bones connected together via a series of joints, for example hinge joints or ball and socket joints. A muscle is attached to a bone by a tendon. (A bone is attached to bone by a ligament.) Muscle tissue consists of a number of muscle cells which are capable of contracting or relaxing quickly in response to electrical signals from nerves. When these muscles contract they pull on the limb thus changing its position.

There are two main muscles in the upper arm acting in opposition to each other (an antagonistic pair):

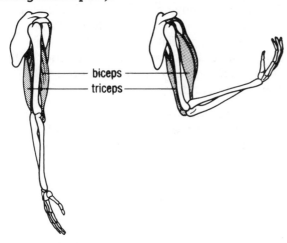

biceps
triceps

All movement is caused by the contraction of muscles. Contraction is fuelled by the 'burning of food' with oxygen (oxidation) in the muscle cells, thus releasing energy. When muscles are working hard (for example, when a person runs) then the demand for oxygen is increased so we breathe more rapidly. The structure of muscle can be seen by looking at meat. Most children do not relate muscle to meat. Children should not be allowed to touch raw meat.

◼ NATURAL MATERIAL

A natural material is one which can be found on or in the Earth's surface or in the atmosphere. Natural materials can be in any form – a solid, a liquid or a gas. The majority of natural materials are chemical compounds although a few are elements.

Naturally occurring elements:

- Gold.
- Silver.
- Carbon (found as diamond or graphite).
- Copper.
- Oxygen (in air).
- Nitrogen (in air).

Naturally occurring compounds:

- Metal ores.
- Aluminium oxide (in bauxite).
- Iron oxide (in haematite, magnetite).
- Iron sulphide (in pyrite).
- Zinc sulphide (in zinc blende).
- Lead sulphide (in galena).

Other naturally occurring rocks and minerals:

- Chalk.
- Sandstone.
- Basalt.
- Quartz.
- Salt in sea water or in halite (rock salt).
- Water.
- Carbon dioxide.
- Gypsum.
- Slate.
- Marble.
- Amethyst.
- Granite.
- Flint.
- Sand.
- Limestone.
- Chert.
- Calcite.

◼ NATURALLY OCCURRING

Many naturally occurring materials are used in their natural state, whilst others are used as raw materials in industrial processes. Some naturally occurring materials can be used as both; they can be found on land, in the sea or in air.

Material	Use in natural state
limestone	roadstone, iron and steel production, cement
clay	pottery production
gravel	concrete, road building
wood	building, furniture making
wool	knitwear and cloth
peat	soil conditioner
salt	manufacture of alkalis, glass and culinary use
water	irrigation, solvent

NEUTRAL

Neutral substances are those which have a pH of 7 and are neither acidic nor alkaline. Neutral substances can be detected using certain indicators. For instance with neutral substances Universal indicator will turn green.

Some common neutral substances are:

Water (pure) natural rain water is weakly acidic due to dissolved carbon dioxide from the atmosphere. Tap water may also be weakly acidic depending on the part of the country.
Sugar.
Salt (table salt).
Plaster of Paris (calcium sulphate).

NEUTRALIZATION

Neutralization is the result of a reaction between an alkali and an acid. The effects of an acid can be neutralised by adding an alkali. The amount of alkali needed will depend on the relevant strengths and concentrations of both the acid and the alkali.

Acidity is due to the presence of hydrogen ions (an ion is a type of particle (*see* particle)), whereas alkalinity is due to the presence of hydroxide ions.

During neutralization water is produced by the reaction between hydrogen ions from the acid and hydroxide ions from the alkali (*see* acidity, alkalinity).

$$2H^+ + 2OH^- \rightarrow 2H_2O$$
acid   alkali   water

NEWTON

The newton is the unit of force. The symbol for newton is N (*see* force):

10 N is the pull of gravity on a mass of 1 kg.

Forces are measured using forcemeters (spring balances, bathroom scales or dynamometers). They rely on springs being stretched or compressed to provide a reading. Force meters calibrated in newtons are sometimes called newton meters.

NIGHT

Night is caused by the rotation of the Earth (*see* day and night).

NIGHT SKY

A number of objects are visible in the night sky with the naked eye. Here is a check-list to help identify the objects:

Star or galaxy Does it twinkle? Stars seem to twinkle, because their light is bounced around by the surrounding air. Stars are also quite faint and can appear in any part of the sky, facing North, South, East or West. Stars also appear to remain in the same position from night to night.

Planet Does it move its position from night to night? The best way to identify a planet is to see if it moves. When checked at the same time every night a planet changes its position in the night sky relative to the star. It appears to move across the sky. Planets nearer the Sun change position from night to

Earth once every 90 minutes. Those which orbit the sky from West to East are probably American satellites and those orbiting from North to South are probably Russian.

Some satellites, however, do not move and are called geostationary and orbit the Earth at the same speed that the Earth spins. These are communication satellites. It is important for these to remain above a particular area of ground. Those satellites which appear to flash on and off will be tumbling in space, the flashing being caused by their different surfaces reflecting the light from the Sun.

Aircraft   Aircraft can be confused with satellites, but will move across the sky much more rapidly and will often show green or red blinking lights.

Meteorite   Meteorites or 'shooting stars' can occasionally be seen to cross the sky very rapidly, the light being caused by them burning up as they enter the atmosphere. Enormous amounts of heat are generated by air friction as the meteorites travel through the atmosphere. Very few survive to fall on Earth.

night faster than others (i.e. Mercury and Venus). Five planets are visible to the naked eye at certain times and these are: Mercury, Venus, Mars, Jupiter, Saturn. Jupiter and Saturn may take many weeks to move their position. These planets will move across the sky from West to East, due to their orbit around the Sun.

On some occasions the planets appear to go backwards. This is called retrograde motion and is caused by the Earth passing them on its own orbit. It is similar to being a passenger in a faster car which passes another: the slower car appears to go backward for an instant.

In the Northern hemisphere (e.g. in Britain) planets will not be seen in the northern sky (when looking North). Planets can also be spotted because they often appear quite large and bright (reflecting the Sun's light and do not 'twinkle' in same way that stars do.

Satellite   A satellite looks similar to a star in the night sky, except that it will be seen to drift across the sky. Many satellites orbit the

Moon   The appearance of the Moon goes through a cycle every 28 days from new to full Moon (*see* phases of the Moon).

Star tracks

During the time of one night, stars appear to rotate from East to West around Polaris the Pole Star. If a camera is left pointing upwards into the night sky for a long exposure time (about 2 hours) then the film will show a series of circular streaks around the central Pole Star which does not appear to move. The stars in fact do not move, but it is the Earth rotating that causes this apparent motion.

Constellations and star maps

Trying to identify stars or planets in the night sky can appear confusing. Looking for well-known constellations such as the 'big dipper' and using this to find other stars is one method. For example, Polaris the Pole Star can always be found from following a line from the 'pointer' stars in the constellation of the big dipper.

Star charts are also invaluable. Planets can be spotted because they appear to move their relative position from night to night, are relatively bright, do not twinkle and tend to be found in the southern sky.

NON-RENEWABLE ENERGY SOURCES

Non-renewable energy sources are those such as fossil fuels (gas, coal, oil) and nuclear fuels (*see* energy sources).

ORGAN

An organ is a collection of different tissues which together perform a specific function.

Major organs of mammals:

Organ	Main function
heart	pumps blood around the body
eye	detection of light to give sense of sight
ear	detection of sound to give sense of hearing
nose	detection of smells
brain	interpretation of messages, decision making, thinking, memory
skin	protective barrier against infection, touch, temperature, sensitive to pressure
stomach	aids digestion of food
intestine (large and small)	digestion of majority of food
liver	break-down and removal of harmful substances in the blood, storage of vitamins
kidney	removal of waste products from the blood
lung	oxygen, carbon dioxide exchange in the blood
male reproductive organ (testis)	production of sperm
female reproductive organ (ovary)	production of egg

Major organs of a flowering plant:

Organ	Main function
anther (male) ⎤	production of pollen
ovary (female) ⎟ flower	contains ovule
petal ⎟	attracts pollinators, for example insects
sepal ⎦	protects developing bud
stem	supports leaf, flower, transport of materials and water
leaf	photosynthesis, manufacture of food
root	anchors plant to ground, absorption of water and minerals

ORGAN SYSTEM

An organ system is a group of organs and tissues which collectively perform a function.

Organ system in human	Contains
digestive system	mouth, oesophagus, stomach, intestines
excretory system	liver, kidneys, bladder
transport system (or blood system)	blood, heart, arteries, veins
respiratory system	lungs, heart
reproductive system	male or female reproductive organs

In a flowering plant the flower is the reproductive system and contains the stamen (anther and filament), carpel (stigma, style and ovary), and petal.

The green leaf contains chlorophyll, and its main function is manufacture of food by photosynthesis.

The stem contains phloem and xylem vessels, and its main function is transport of fluids around the plant.

The main function of the root is absorption of water and minerals.

PARTICLE

All substances are made up of particles which cannot be seen through a microscope. There are three different types: atom, molecule and ion.

Atom

The most fundamental of these particles is the atom. There are 109 different known atoms. Substances which consist of only one type of atom are called elements, the element having the same name as the atom. Gold for instance is comprised of gold atoms. Atoms are so small that they cannot be seen even with the most powerful microscope. There are millions of atoms present in a pinhead.

The element copper consists of just copper atoms:

Atom   *Element*

An atom consists of electrons, protons and neutrons, sometimes referred to as sub-atomic particles. Protons carry a positive electrical charge and together with neutrons form the nucleus. Each electron carries a negative electrical charge and orbits the nucleus. Every atom contains an equal number of electrons as protons and hence an equal number of negative and positive charges; each atom is electrically neutral.

All atoms in an element carry the same number of electrons and protons, for example all carbon atoms contain 6 electrons and 6 protons. Atoms of one element differ from those in another element by the numbers of electrons, protons and neutrons they contain, for example magnesium contains 12 electrons and 12 protons.

A complete list of different elements is found in the Periodic Table (*see* Periodic Table).

Molecule

A molecule is a particle which consists of different combinations of atoms.

Examples of molecules:

Oxygen gas (as present in the air)   molecules of oxygen, each molecule consisting of a pair of oxygen atoms chemically joined.
Carbon dioxide gas   molecules of carbon dioxide, each molecule consisting of one carbon atom chemically joined to two oxygen atoms.
Water   molecules of water, each molecule consisting of one oxygen atom chemically joined to two hydrogen atoms.

There are rules which govern the ways in which atoms can combine to form molecules; these rules are determined by the number of electrons in an atom and the way in which they are arranged.

Ion

Ions are electrically charged particles. They may be electrically charged atoms or groups of atoms. The charge may be positive or negative. The charge is derived from the movement of electrons (carrying negative charge from one atom to another, or a group of atoms when substances react). The resulting compound contains positively and negatively charged ions. Table salt (sodium chloride) is a substance which contains positive and negative ions. Sodium chloride contains positive sodium ions and negative chloride ions:

sodium ion Na$^+$
chloride ion Cl$^-$

All acids in solutions contain positive hydrogen ions H$^+$ (*see* acids).

Salts are substances which contain positive and negative ions (*see* salts).

PERIODIC TABLE

The Periodic Table is a list of 109 known chemical elements. They are arranged in a pattern, in order of their atomic number. The atomic number relates to the number of protons the atoms of each element contain. Hydrogen (atomic number 1) is at the top of the table. Each hydrogen atom contains one proton (and hence one electron since atoms always contain the same number of electrons as protons) (*see* particles).

Second in the list is helium (atomic number 2), third in the list is lithium (atomic number 3), and so on.

As a consequence of this atoms at the bottom of the table are heavier than those at the top. The

Periodic Table is more than a simple list, however. Elements are carefully arranged in rows and columns in such a way that they form groups or 'families'. Each column of elements forms a group. The elements in any one column form a family of elements all having similar properties. These groups or families are often given names, for example the halogen group (comprising elements such as chlorine, bromine and iodine) or the alkali metals (sodium, potassium, etc.), named because these metals react readily with water to form alkalis. Knowing the position of an element in the Periodic Table can help predict its properties and how it will behave during chemical reactions.

PERSONAL HYGIENE

The skin is an organ that covers the body and acts as a barrier, protecting against infection. A dirty skin is likely to harbour disease-causing bacteria and other microbes. Skin should be washed regularly and thoroughly.

Hair should also be washed regularly (weekly), as it too is an ideal place for bacteria to grow.

Teeth need brushing twice a day to prevent a build up of plaque (containing bacteria) and tooth decay. The use of disclosing tablets can show up how effective brushing is.

The body, including face and underarms, needs washing regularly with a soap, to prevent build up of harmful bacteria.

Hands should be washed thoroughly before meals (to prevent transfer of harmful microbes from hand to mouth) and always after using the toilet.

The spaces between toes should be washed daily as the warm, moist conditions provide excellent breeding grounds for microbes (for example, athletes' foot).

pH

pH is a scale of acidity and alkalinity and runs from 0 to 14. The lower the number the stronger the acidity of the solution.

0	1	2	3	4	5	6	7	8	9	10	11	12	13	14

strongly acidic   **weakly acidic**   **neutral**   **weakly alkaline**   **strongly alkaline**

household
ammonia

floor
cleaners

milk

orange juice

vinegar

ordinary rain   sodium
bicarbonate

lemon juice

Coca-Cola

apple juice

yoghurt

battery acid   kitchen   oven
cleaners   cleaner

stomach
fluid

wine and   Milk of
beer   Magnesia

acid rain   soap

All acids contain hydrogen ions, the acidity of a solution depending on the concentration of hydrogen ions present. pH is a symbol invented by the scientist Sorensen in 1909 as a convenient expression for the concentration of hydrogen ions in solution.

The exact derivation of 'pH' is not clear. In French, the 'power' (or 'potential') of hydrogen is 'α'-Hydrogen although it is thought by many authorities that the 'p' is derived from the German 'potenz' meaning potential.

All acids contain hydrogen ions (an ion is a type of particle, like an atom, with a small electric charge on it, in this case a positive electric charge (*see* particle)). It is symbolised in the following way:

H^+ = hydrogen ion

Acids behave like acids, because of these hydrogen ions. The stronger the acid the greater the number of hydrogen ions formed in solution. The pH scale is derived from the concentration of hydrogen ions, but not in a straightforward way. It is a negative logarithmic scale:

pH = 1/log of hydrogen ion concentration

The consequence is the greater the hydrogen ion concentration (the greater the acidity) the lower the number on the scale, hence a solution of pH 1 is more acid than one of pH 2.

PHASES OF THE MOON

The Moon takes 28 days to orbit the Earth and as it does so it appears as different shapes according to how much of the illuminated Moon is visible to us from our position on Earth.

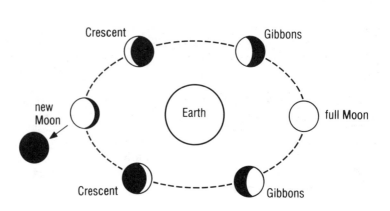

PHOTOSYNTHESIS

Photosynthesis is the process by which green plants manufacture their own food from the simple chemicals carbon dioxide and water, using the Sun's energy (*see* green plant).

PHYSICAL PROCESSES (FOR SEPARATING MIXTURES)

Mixtures can be separated by a variety of means according to differences in the components' physical properties:

Adsorption in paper chromatography some substances adhere to the surface of the paper fibres more readily than others so mixtures of coloured inks can be separated (*see* chromatography).

Fractional distillation when a mixture of liquids with different boiling points is heated, the liquid with a lower boiling point will vaporize first, effecting a separation. For example, when a mixture of alcohol (b.pt. 80°C) and water (b.pt. 100°C) is heated gently alcohol vaporizes first leaving water. If the vapour is passed through a cold tube it can be condensed and collected. This is called distillation. Distillation is introduced at Key Stage 3.

Filtering muddy water can be filtered using coffee filters or blotting paper (*see* filter paper) inserted into funnels. Alternatively, try plugs of cotton wool or passing the muddy water through sand and gravel, which is effectively what happens at filter beds in sewage plants.

Size soil is a mixture and if it is sieved it can be separated into different sized soil particles. With care and different sized sieves one can separate dry soil into a variety of components, for example stones, gravel, sand and clay.

Evaporation rock salt is the name given to an impure mixture of salt, sand and gravel that is mined and is a source of table salt. Rock salt is placed on roads in winter and is often available at garden centres. A mixture of sand and salt can be separated by stirring the mixture in water. The salt is soluble and the sand is not, so filtering will produce sand and salty water. The salt can then be extracted from the solution by allowing the solution to evaporate on a window ledge.

Density gold can be found in river beds mixed with gravel and sand. It is separated from the sand and gravel by 'panning', a process which involves swirling a pan (shallow bowl) which contains the gravel mixture, with a little water. Gradually the much heavier (albeit smaller) gold particles separate out in the bottom of the bowl.

> At Key Stage 2 'panning for gold' can be a stimulating activity for children. The gold can be simulated by brass filings which can be mixed with sand and a little gravel. Any round bottomed bowl can be used as the pan. With only a little practice children can become very proficient at separating the 'gold'.

PITCH

Sound is caused by vibrations, the pitch of the sound produced (highness or lowness of a note) being determined by the number of vibrations per second. If something vibrates very quickly a high note is produced, conversely a low, deep sound is produced by slow vibrations.

tightly-stretched objects vibrate quickly to produce high notes	high notes can be produced by tightening a guitar string, tightening a drum skin, tightening a rubber band
short objects vibrate quickly to produce high notes	high notes can be produced by shortening a guitar string (pressing fingers on a fret), short column of air in a recorder (only covering one or two holes), shorter tuning forks produce higher notes
thin strings vibrate quickly	high notes can be produced by thin strings on a guitar (thicker strings produce lower notes)

PLANET

A planet is a large body which orbits a star. There are nine planets in the Solar System all of which orbit the Sun (a star) in approximately elliptical orbits. The orbits lie in the same plane except for that of Pluto (*see* Solar System). The larger planets lie towards the outer edges of the Solar System. Planets shine because they reflect sunlight.

	Planet	Size (Earth diameters)	Average distance from Sun (millions of km)	Time to orbit Sun	Surface temperature (°C average)	Satellites (number of)
INNER PLANETS	Mercury	0.4	58	88.5 days	350°C	nil
	Venus	1.0	108	225 days	460°C	nil
	Earth	1.0	150	365.25 days	20°C	1
	Mars	0.5	228	687 days	–23°C	2
OUTER PLANETS	Jupiter	11.2	778	11.75 years	–150°C	16
	Saturn	9.4	1427	29 years	–180°C	21
	Uranus	3.7	2870	84 years	–210°C	15
	Neptune	3.5	4497	164.77 years	–220°C	2
	Pluto	0.2	5900	248 years	–230°C	1

At Key Stage 3 pupils learn about the position of planets within the Solar System.

PLANT GROWTH

Plant growth is dependent on a number of factors:

Light intensity   normally the more intense the light the greater the rate of plant growth. The plant normally shows vigorous (healthy and strong) growth due to a high rate of photosynthesis. Light intensity can be measured simply using a photographic light meter. Alternatively, plants can be placed in cupboards (dark), corners of rooms (dim), on a window ledge or in front of a bright bulb.

Temperature   temperature affects the rate of photosynthesis taking place within a plant and thus affects the rate of plant growth. There is an optimum temperature range for different plants. A plant can be placed outside, in an unheated greenhouse or cold frame, or indoors. If possible this should be compared with the effect of placing a plant in a hot area, such as a boiler house. It is, however, difficult to control other factors which affect growth such as light, water and moisture levels.

Water availability   plants need a certain amount of water to sustain growth. Water is needed to transport materials around the plant and in the chemical reaction of photosynthesis. It is absorbed from the soil through the roots. It is easily possible to over-water plants which will then die because the roots cannot obtain sufficient oxygen. Investigations can be conducted which compare the effects of different volumes of water provided per day, for example 10 cm^3, 20 cm^3, 30 cm^3, 100 cm^3, etc., on plant growth.

Supply of minerals   plants need a supply of minerals, which includes nitrogen, phosphorus, potassium, magnesium and iron. These minerals are needed by the plant to make complex food substances, for example proteins. This supply of minerals is obtained from the soil and can be supplemented with fertilizers.

> Suitable plants for performing investigations on plant growth at Key Stage 2 include: fast growing brassica, tomato, chick pea, broad bean, runner bean, sunflower, geranium, wild oat, wheat and barley.

PLASTER OF PARIS

Plaster of Paris is a dry, white powder which reacts with water to produce a hard-set substance (plaster). In the process of setting, heat is generated. The powder is made from gypsum (hydrated calcium sulphate). The gypsum (a hard rock) is heated: this dehydrates the gypsum by driving off the 'water of crystallisation' (the water which is chemically 'locked' to the calcium sulphate in gypsum). The powder which is produced will form a hard solid again when water is added.

POLLUTION

Pollution can be created by a variety of activities. Atmosphere, seas, oceans, rivers, streams, ponds and land can all be polluted by chemicals. Noise and light can also be considered to be pollution.

Atmospheric pollution

Acid rain
'Acid rain' is produced when the oxides of sulphur and nitrogen, which are both gases, are released into the atmosphere. The burning of fossil fuels produces oxides of sulphur and car exhaust emissions contain oxides of nitrogen.

These gases react with water and other gases in the atmosphere to produce sulphuric and nitric acids which fall as rain. Acid rain acidifies ground water and washes harmful minerals, which are normally locked into the soil and rocks, into streams and rivers.

These minerals (such as aluminium) can kill fish and other organisms. Once these fish die other animals which feed on them are affected and the balance of the ecosystem is disturbed. Plants such as trees are also damaged by the effects of acid rain partly because the acid makes them less resistant to disease.

Smog
Smog is caused by particulate matter (dusts and smokes) which is released into the atmosphere and is then trapped by certain weather conditions (for example, when the smoke produced by industry is trapped by fog or in a layer of cold air). Smog particularly affects people with asthma and may trigger asthmatic reactions in previously healthy individuals.

Emissions from motor cars in large cities such as Los Angeles cause a 'photochemical smog' which hangs as a haze above the city causing sore eyes and throats. The oxides of nitrogen and hydrocarbons from exhaust gases react with oxygen in the presence of strong sunlight to produce ozone which is the cause of the photochemical smog.

Holes in the 'ozone layer'
Ozone is a gas found throughout the atmosphere and in high concentrations in an upper layer called the stratosphere (*see* atmosphere). This layer protects us from much of the Sun's more harmful ultra violet radiation which can cause skin cancers. Damage to the ozone layer is thought to be caused by chemicals such as chlorofluorocarbons (CFCs) which react with ozone, breaking it down.

Deposition
Smoke, dirt and dust particles resulting from the burning of fossil fuels, wood or waste, and other industrial processes can be deposited on plants. Soot for example can cover leaves, thus blocking light from the Sun and so preventing photosynthesis. These particles can also prove to be poisonous to some organisms, for example aphids which feed off the sap of plants. The disappearance of aphids would interrupt the food chain which in turn would disturb the balance of the ecosystem.

Natural pollution
Dust and oxides of sulphur are evolved from volcanoes, thus creating acid rain and depositions.

Water pollution

Oil spillage at sea
Birds and sea mammals are coated with oil. Oil is toxic to animals including fish, shellfish and molluscs. Oil spills destroy beaches.

Raw sewage in the sea
People swimming in the sea are liable to illness, for example upset stomach. This pollution also affects other animals within the sea. The high levels of minerals in sewage also increase the growth rate of algae, which disturbs the balance of the ecosystem.

Fertilizer
Fertilizer in rivers and streams causes rapid growth of pond weed, so choking water courses and also, in some circumstances,

starving the water of oxygen, thus affecting the survival of other organisms, for example fish.

Industrial pollution
Effluent from factories can cause rivers to become lifeless. This may be due to a number of toxins. Heavy-metal salts such as copper, lead and mercury have long-term cumulative effects and can be passed on from organism to organism in the food chain. Many organic solvents used in chemical processes have more immediate effects. Even hot or warm water deoxygenates the water and so affects the survival of organisms. A certain amount of oxygen from the air is naturally dissolved in water; this is extracted from the water by fish using gills. Hotter water contains less dissolved oxygen.

Nitrate
Nitrate is leached from the soil into water where it contributes to excessive growth of water plants and algae. The latter causes an unsightly scum on the surface. Too much nitrate in drinking water can make babies ill ('blue baby'), and some studies appear to show a possible link with stomach cancer, although more recent studies have shown no evidence for this.

Rain washes nitrates out of the soil so most nitrate leakage occurs in the winter from natural nitrates in the soil, especially when ploughed fields are left uncovered. Fertilizers applied in the autumn or winter are an additional source of nitrate.

Noise and light pollution
Noise
Noise pollution is created in a number of ways; obvious situations include airports, road and rail traffic. The pollution not only has an effect on humans but also on a number of animals, disturbing them and perhaps interfering with their breeding pattern and driving them from their habitat.

Light
Light pollution is serious at night above cities. Often it is now impossible throughout many parts of Britain to observe many objects in the night sky that were visible 20 to 30 years ago.

■ POPULATION

Population is the number of living things of a species within a particular habitat. Populations are normally counted by sampling techniques.

> The daisy population on a school field can be counted by sampling a few randomly-chosen metre squares, finding the average number per square metre and then multiplying by the area of the field in order to find an approximate value of the total daisy population. The size of a population is controlled by competition for resources such as the availability of food and light, and by the number of predators, as well as environmental conditions.

■ POWER

Power is a word which is often used interchangeably with force and energy in everyday speech. It has a definite meaning in science which is not the same as either of those. Power is defined as the rate of transferring energy or the rate of doing work:

power = energy transferred/time taken

Power is measured in units of joules/second or watts (1 watt (W) = 1 joule/second (J/s))

1 kilowatt = 1000 watts

A 2 kilowatt (2 bar) electric fire is more 'powerful' than a 1 kilowatt (1 bar) fire because it heats the room more quickly, i.e. it transfers energy more quickly.

■ PREDATION

Predatory animals are carnivores (meat eaters). The group includes birds of prey (owl and hawk), mammals (lions and wolves), and insects (dragonfly nymph and wasp). The population of a species of predators in a particular habitat is determined by the population of the prey available.

■ PRESSURE

If a force is exerted over a small area it will have a greater effect than over a much larger area where its effect is more spread out. This can be appreciated if one considers the damage that can be caused by stiletto heels on some types of flooring. The damage can be greater than if an elephant walked over the same floor. Snow shoes are used to reduce the effect of the force (body weight) on the snow by spreading the effect of the force over a much larger area. They reduce the pressure exerted on the snow.

Pressure is defined as the force per unit area:

pressure = force/area

The units of pressure are newtons/square metre (N/m^2).

Pressure is introduced at Key Stage 3 and an understanding of pressure is required at Level 6.

■ PRISM

Prisms are triangular-shaped blocks made of either plastic or glass. They refract (bend) light as it passes through. Depending on the angle at which light enters a prism, light can be refracted to such a degree that it is split into the colours of the rainbow. These colours are called the visible spectrum. Images viewed through a prism appear coloured around the edges; alternatively shining a beam of light through a prism (note the angle of the light entering the prism) produces a spectrum.

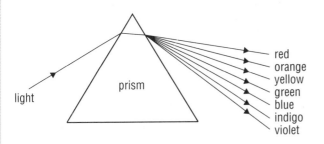

At Key Stage 2 children looking through a prism will observe an image of an object to the sides of the prism, as well as seeing an image that is coloured or has a 'rainbow' around them, indicating that light is being bent. Shining a single, sharply-focused torch beam through a prism can demonstrate this refraction (bending) more easily. Alternatively, light from a ray box (which produces a narrow beam of light) can be shone through a prism to show the effect clearly. Covering the glass of a torch with black paper in which a narrow slit is cut will produce a similar effect.

Prisms made from plastic and low quality (non-optical) glass are useful for most purposes but if a clear spectrum is desired a 'high dispersion' prism of good quality glass is required.

■ PROPERTIES OF MATERIALS

The characteristics of a substance depend on the material from which it is made and on the substance as a whole. Metals for example are considered to be strong whilst materials such as paper would be considered weak. An example of a property dependent on the whole substance is volume.

Properties dependent on the whole substance are:

- Colour.
- Roughness, smoothness.
- Shape (symmetrical, non-symmetrical, etc.).
- Volume.
- Weight.

Properties dependent on the material of which the substance is made are:

- Magnetic, non-magnetic.
- Conduction of electricity.
- Conduction of heat (feels warm/cold).
- Colour.
- Density (floats, sinks).
- Flexibility (bends, rigid).
- Solubility.
- Shiny, dull.
- Strength (tensile and compressive).
- Smell (nice, nasty).
- Tough, brittle.
- Taste (sweet, sour, salty, bitter).
- Waterproof, not waterproof.

Properties of a material can change when the material changes state, for example when it melts, solidifies or vaporises. When a metal melts it no longer can be considered to be strong. A chemical such as salt does not conduct electricity in the solid state but when it is heated sufficiently to make it molten it does conduct (*see* classification of materials).

■ QUALITATIVE

Treating something qualitatively means not involving measurement. Speeds of toy cars can be described in qualitative terms with such statements as *The red one goes faster than the* *blue one which goes faster than the green one*, etc. Other examples include *After 5 days this plant has grown the most*, or *Steeper slopes make cars travel further*.

■ QUANTITATIVE

Treating something quantitatively means assessing its qualities by measuring it. The quantification of variables referred to in the Programme of Study means that the variables (*see* variable) within an investigation should be measured. In practice this means stating that a *plant has grown by 3 cm in a week* rather than simply saying that a *plant has grown taller this week*.

■ RAINBOW

A rainbow occurs when white light is separated into colours of the spectrum as it passes through water droplets, such as raindrops. As light passes through the raindrops it is refracted (bent), split into its constituent colours and internally reflected within the drop, before emerging. The raindrop is behaving in a similar way to that of a prism (*see* prism).

For a rainbow to appear there needs to be bright sunlight and moisture in the air, for example rain. The colours produced by the combined effects of millions of raindrops produces a circular effect similar to that produced sometimes around images when looking through other transparent objects.

A 'rainbow effect' can be produced by shining a strong beam of light onto a mirror placed at about 45° in a bowl half in and half out of water. The best effects can be seen with a large, good quality mirror, such as a glass mirror tile and a strong, single beam of light such as that from a slide projector. However, a lot of practice is required before a satisfactory effect is observed.

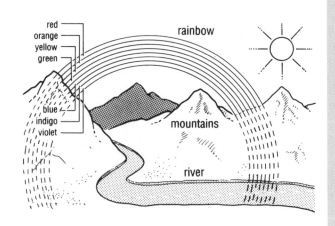

■ RAW MATERIALS

Many naturally occurring raw materials taken from the environment can be processed to produce other more useful materials.

Raw material	Process of manufacture	Product
gypsum	heating	wall plaster, plaster of Paris,
limestone	heating in kiln	lime for mortar, agriculture, etc.
sand	heating with limestone and sodium carbonate	glass
haematite (iron ore)	heating in blast furnace with coke (smelting)	iron

table continues

Raw material	Process of manufacture	Product
galena (lead ore)	heating in blast furnace with coke	lead
wood	wood pulp mixed with clay	paper
crude oil	distillation of oil into different fractions	petrol
crude oil	fractions of oil undergo polymerization reactions	plastics
china clay	firing in kiln	china plates etc.
clay	firing in kiln	pottery

■ RAY BOX

A ray box contains a light bulb and produces a narrow ray of light. It usually has facilities for conveniently fitting various lenses to focus the beam.

> Ray boxes can be purchased from scientific equipment suppliers. A similar effect can be produced using a sheet of black paper with a slit cut in it covering a good quality torch.

■ REFLECTION

All objects reflect light to some extent, some better than others. The eyes are sensitive to light reflected from objects.

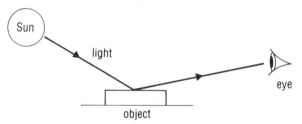

When light from the Sun or a light bulb strikes an object it is scattered in all directions by the surfaces of the object. Some of the light reaches the eyes.

> An understanding that this is why objects can be seen rather than the common children's ideas of *Light enters our eyes and then strikes the object* or that *Light comes from our eyes* is required at Level 5.

If a narrow beam of light (for example, from a torch) falls on a flat shiny surface it reflects off the surface at the same angle as it fell. This effect can be seen by bouncing a ball off a wall. The angle of the 'reflected' ball is the same as the angle of the incoming ball. With light this is known as the 'law of reflection', and the incoming beam is referred to as the incident ray and the reflected beam as the reflected ray. Sound too behaves in this way.

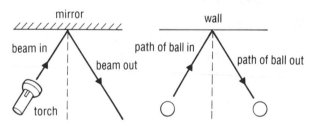

■ REFRACTION

Light travelling from one medium to another bends, and this bending is referred to as refraction. A medium is anything transparent through which light can travel, for example air, water, glass and plastic. Thus when light travels from air into glass it bends; when light travels from glass into air it also bends. This effect is seen by shining a narrow beam of light through a glass block or into a tank of water.

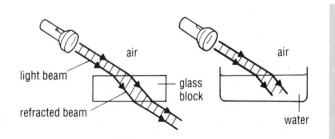

The refraction causes images to appear in unexpected positions, for example when looking into a swimming pool the floor looks closer than it really is because the reflected light beams from the floor are refracted or bent when they emerge from the water. Another effect is observed when looking through prisms or transparent blocks: images of objects appear in different places.

A fun and much-practised trick using this effect is that of the 'appearing coin'.

A coin is placed in the bottom of a non-transparent bowl. The child then gradually lowers his/her head until the coin is just obscured from view by the rim. Without moving, water is slowly poured into the bowl. As the water fills the bowl so the coin appears. The image appears in a different position enabling it to be seen.

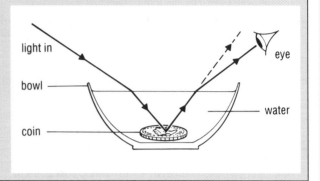

RENEWABLE ENERGY SOURCES

Renewable energy sources are those such as tidal, wave, wind and biomass (*see* energy sources).

REPRODUCTION

There are two types of reproduction, sexual and asexual. Both result in the formation of new individuals. Sexual reproduction involves fusion of two gametes (sex cells). These gametes are usually produced by different individuals called male and female. Each gamete contains half the normal amount of genetic material (chromosomes) carried by normal cells, hence the new individual inherits characteristics of both parents.

There are some animals and many plants where both kinds of gamete are produced by the same individual; these are called hermaphrodites.

Asexual reproduction

For asexual reproduction to occur only one individual is needed and there is no fusion of cells. Some familiar examples of asexual reproduction in the plant world include strawberry plantlets produced from runners, new bulbs or corms growing, for example crocus or daffodil, and some houseplants such as bryophyllum producing plantlets at their leaf edges. Taking cuttings of plants, budding and layering are also examples of asexual reproduction.

Sexual reproduction

In mammals sexual reproduction occurs when a male gamete (sperm) fertilises a female gamete (egg). Egg and sperm are brought together through the act of copulation. Internal fertilisation is essential for mammals since the fertilised egg develops inside the female body in the uterus. During copulation the male releases many millions of sperm which swim through the uterus to the fallopian tubes to meet with an egg. Very few sperm reach the egg and only one will finally penetrate the egg and fertilise it. Once the egg is fertilised it continues its journey from the ovary, where it was released, through a fallopian tube to the uterus where it becomes embedded in the lining. Here the embryo develops into a foetus.

In flowering plants sexual reproduction also takes place. The male genetic material is contained in pollen grains and the female genetic material is contained within ovules, in the ovary. Fertilisation begins with the process of pollination. Flowers do not normally pollinate themselves because inbreeding may weaken a plant stock. In order to prevent this the male and female parts of the flowers often mature at different times. Pollen is transferred from the stamen (male organ) of one flower to the stigma (female organ) of another, for example by a bee. Once pollen arrives on the surface of the stigma a pollen grain produces a tube which grows down through the style ('neck' of the stigma). As this occurs the male gamete develops within the tube tip. The tube penetrates the ovule discharging the male gamete and the ovule and gamete then fertilise. The embryo then develops into a seed. Each seed contains genetic material from both parents (*see also* life processes).

■ RESULTANT FORCE

When more than one force acts on an object, the net effect is referred to as the resultant force. The size and direction of the resultant force depends on the relative sizes and directions of the individual forces. The net effect of these forces can be readily accepted when throwing a ball high in the air on a windy day. The direction in which the ball falls depends on the strength and direction of the wind.

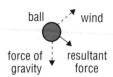

Other situations where the combinations of forces can be readily appreciated are kite flying, sailing boats, tug-of-war, swing ball, being pushed from the side whilst running and being pushed on a skate board.

■ ROAD SAFETY

Road safety can provide a useful context for exploring issues relating to forces and movement.

Road safety	Ideas to explore
stopping distance of a car (from *Highway Code*)	effect of speed on braking distances, grip, tyres, smooth and rough surfaces, grip in wet and grip in dry (friction)
crash barrier	energy absorbing design, barrier needs to be able to bend
seat belt	forces on a body in a car when it is suddenly brought to rest, in which direction does the body move, how can it be best restrained?
car safety design	crumple zone in a car
car seat design	headrest to support head and prevent whiplash
car bumper	energy absorbing design, needs to bend on contact and not be too rigid, since this will only transmit the energy

■ ROCK CYCLE

Rocks are constantly recycled and reformed. Rocks in the Earth's crust can be classified into three broad types according to how they were produced.

Igneous rock

Igneous rock is 'new' rock that results from the cooling of magma (molten rock) brought to the surface by volcanoes and through movements on ocean floors. The rock is characterised by being very hard, sometimes glassy in appearance and often contains crystals. Large crystals are a result of slow cooling, whereas small crystals are a result of rapid cooling. Typical igneous rock is granite, basalt and pumice.

Sedimentary rock

Sedimentary rock is produced by the laying down of sediments in rivers, streams and seas over many millions of years. The sediments arise from weathering, erosion and transport of materials from older, existing rock. The pressure of increasing layers of sediments compresses the particles to form rock. Sedimentary rock is characterised by banded layers (often visible as different coloured bands), visible grains, can contain fossils and is frequently soft. Typical sedimentary rock is limestone, chalk, sandstone and shale.

Metamorphic rock

Metamorphic rock is formed from existing rock which has been subjected to change under the Earth's surface by agents such as heat, pressure or chemicals. This rock is typically hard and uniform in shape. Typical metamorphic rock is marble, slate and gneiss.

■ SALTS

A salt is a substance which can form in a reaction between an acid and an alkali (a neutralisation reaction) and in a reaction between a metal and an acid. Metal salts are often crystalline and it is from this group of substances that large crystals can be grown (for example, crystals of copper sulphate or alum).

Naming salts

There is a systematic method of naming salts with chemical names, although many salts, particularly those which can be found as minerals in the Earth's crust, also have common names.

In the chemical name, the first part of the name is a metal (or ammonium) and the second part is dependent on the acid from which it is formed.

Sulphates can be derived from sulphuric acid, for example:

Chemical name	Uses	Chemical formula
ammonium sulphate	fertilizers, smelling salts	$(NH_4)_2SO_4$
calcium sulphate (gypsum, plaster of Paris)	making wall plaster and setting broken bones	$CaSO_4$
magnesium sulphate (Epsom salts)	a laxative	$MgSO_4$
aluminium sulphate	water purification	$Al_2(SO_4)_3$
copper sulphate	fungicide	$CuSO_4$

Chlorides can be derived from hydrochloric acid, for example:

Chemical name	Uses	Chemical formula
calcium chloride		$CaCl_2$
magnesium chloride		$MgCl_2$
potassium chloride (muriate of potash)	fertilizer	KCl
sodium chloride (table salt or common salt)	salting roads, flavouring	$NaCl$
copper chloride		$CuCl_2$

Nitrates can be derived from nitric acid, for example:

Chemical name	Uses	Chemical formula
ammonium nitrate	fertilizers	NH_4NO_3
calcium nitrate		$Ca(CO_3)_2$
magnesium nitrate		$Mg(NO_3)_2$
potassium nitrate (saltpetre)	fertilizers, explosives	KNO_3
copper nitrate		$Cu(NO_3)_2$

Carbonates can be derived from carbonic acid, for example:

Chemical name	Uses	Chemical formula
ammonium carbonate		$(NH_4)_2CO_3$
calcium carbonate (found as limestone, chalk, marble, coral and in eggshell)	roadstone, building	$CaCO_3$
sodium carbonate (washing soda)	water softener	Na_2CO_3
sodium hydrogencarbonate (bicarbonate of soda)	raising agent in baking	$NaHCO_3$
magnesium carbonate		$MgCO_3$

Phosphates can be derived from phosphoric acid, for example:

Chemical name	Uses	Chemical formula
Ammonium phosphate	fertilizers	$(NH_4)_3PO_4$
calcium phosphate	water softener (used in washing powders)	$Ca_3(PO_4)_2$

Certain salts are more complex and are referred to as 'double' salts:

Solutions of salts conduct electricity showing that they contain charged particles or ions. The name of a salt describes the particles (ions) which make it up.

Chemical name	Common name
potassium aluminium sulphate	potash alum
chromium aluminium sulphate	chrome alum
iron ammonium sulphate	ferrous alum

■ SATELLITE

A satellite is something which orbits a planet. The Moon is a natural satellite to our planet Earth. The Moon is not a planet. The Moon is travelling at a speed of about 1000 metres per second and would continue in a straight line if it were not for the gravitational pull of the Earth which makes it follow a circular path. The effect is the same as that produced when a stone tied to a piece of string is whirled around above the head.

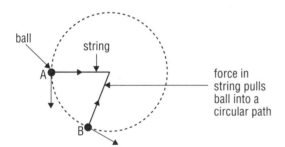

ball
string
A
B
force in string pulls ball into a circular path

At present there are many man-made satellites in orbit around Earth, performing a variety of functions such as communication, spying, weather data collection, land survey and experimentation (Spacelab is a satellite).

The speed at which a satellite orbits the Earth is determined by its height above the Earth. The gravitational pull of the Earth produces a downward acceleration (towards Earth). The satellite has to have a forward speed which is sufficient to balance the downward force. The higher the orbit, the less the effect of the pull of gravity so the slower the satellite needs to travel. Most satellites which are in orbit just above the atmosphere are travelling at about 8000 metres per second. Some however are needed to remain in position over a certain area (communications satellites, for example satellite television). These are said to be in geostationary orbit. Their speed has to match the speed of the Earth's rotation; this in turn will determine how far above the Earth they need to be placed in orbit (*see also* night sky).

■ SEASON

Seasons are caused by the tilt of the Earth's axis. As the Earth orbits the Sun, the Northern hemisphere is at times inclined towards the Sun and at other times inclined away from the Sun. The same, of course, is true for the Southern hemisphere. The part of the Earth's surface tilted towards the Sun receives more intense sunlight because the Sun's rays strike at right angles, whereas the Sun's rays strike the part of the Earth's surface tilted away from the Sun at a more oblique angle so the sunlight is less intense.

This effect can be illustrated by using a torch with a narrow beam and shining it onto a large ball on which the axis is marked.

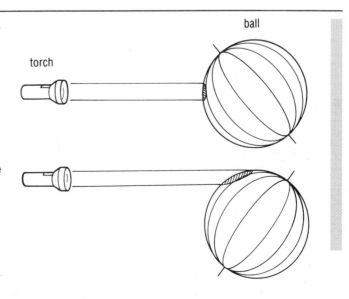

ball
torch

SEASONAL CHANGE

See environmental conditions.

SEDIMENT

Material which is deposited by water (for example, streams and rivers) as a result of weathering, erosion and transport is called sediment. It is usually found building-up in the parts of a river or a stream that flow slowly; for example, in a wide estuary or on a bend.

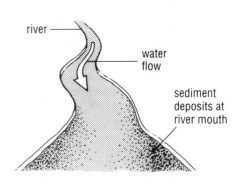

SELECTIVE BREEDING

Selective breeding is a process by which the characteristics of animals and plants are enhanced. Certain characteristics of plants and animals may be inherited. For example, colour in flowers, number of petals, amount of juice in a tomato, resistance to disease or the leanness of meat in cattle are all inherited characteristics. Sexual reproduction results in offspring having a variety of characteristics inherited from one parent or another because of the different genetic information provided by each parent (*see* gene).

Breeding selectively between individuals can produce animals and plants with desirable features. For example, lean meat in cattle is a desirable feature. Breeding from cattle which have been selected for the leanness of their meat increases the chance of their offspring possessing that characteristic. If lean cattle from a second generation are selected and interbred with similar lean cattle then this will increase the chance still further of all the offspring inheriting 'leanness'.

This type of selective breeding, continually selecting for one characteristic, can produce new 'varieties' or 'strains'. In this way man has created many varieties of roses, and other plants such as cereal crops, as well as domesticated dogs, and thoroughbred horses.

SEPARATING AND PURIFYING MIXTURES

Mixtures can be separated using a variety of techniques. These separating techniques include:

Key Stage 1   sieving, decanting.
Key Stage 2   filtering, chromatography and evaporation.
Key Stage 3   distillation, filtering, chromatography, evaporation, and use of variation in solubility.

Examples
Muddy water can be filtered using filter papers, different coloured inks can be separated using chromatography, salt can be separated from salty water by evaporation (*see also* physical processes).

SEWAGE DISPOSAL

In the 19th century sewage was often spread on fields where microbes in the soil broke it down into harmless materials. This gave rise to the term 'sewage farm'.

In a modern treatment works, sewage is first fed into a large settling tank, which allows the liquids and solids to separate. The solids are then heated in a 'digester' to about 40 °C where in the absence of air microbes convert them into material suitable for use as fertilizer. Methane gas is given off in the process.

Liquid sewage is treated differently. It is exposed to the air (air is blown through it). This helps a different set of bacteria to grow and break down harmful compounds. After passing through a biological filter, the pure water is then fed to a river.

It is the action of micro-organisms which break down the harmful substances in sewage into harmless ones.

SHADOW

Shadows are formed when light from one direction strikes an opaque object. The formation of shadows and the straight edges of shadows provides evidence that light travels in straight lines. Shadows can be formed by light from the Sun striking trees or sticks in the ground. Longer shadows are formed when the Sun is low in the sky, for example at the beginning or end of the day and during the winter months. Conversely shorter shadows are formed at midday and in the summer months when the Sun is high in the sky. When the Moon moves between the Sun and the Earth shadows are produced which fall on the Earth. This event is called an eclipse.

SHADOW STICK

A vertical stick, metre stick, climbing frame, swing or a post can be used as a shadow stick. Shadow sticks can be used to compare the length of the shadow cast by the Sun at different times of the day and year.

Long shadows are formed when the Sun is low on the horizon (i.e. at sun rise and sunset and during the winter months). The shadow is longer because the Sun's light strikes the Earth more obliquely so the heat is more spread out. It is cooler in the mornings, evenings and in the winter. A shadow stick can also be used to track the Sun's position every hour, so that the time taken for the Sun to travel across a portion of the sky can be determined (*see also* sundials).

SOIL

Soil is produced as a result of weathering and erosion of rocks, together with the action of plants and animals.

If a soil is examined closely it is seen to contain particles which are the result of weathered rocks and humus (the result of the decay of dead plants and animals). Soil can be separated by shaking a small sample in a jar of water. The larger, heavier particles will settle first, with the lighter particles above. Humus will float on the top. Soils also contain water, air and mineral salts and are habitats for micro-organisms, insects, and other soil minibeasts.

The proportion of different particles determines the characteristic of a particular soil:

Sandy soil contains relatively large particles and is very light, drains easily, is warmed easily, traps a lot of air and is easy to cultivate, although it can easily be eroded – the minerals (chemicals available for plants) being easily washed out.
Clay soil consists of mainly small particles and is usually heavy, does not easily retain heat, is sticky and easily becomes waterlogged.
Loam soil contains a mixture of sand and clay particles and has properties consistent with the proportion of clay to sand.

SOLAR SYSTEM

The Solar System consists of nine planets and a belt of asteroids orbiting the Sun in elliptical orbits. All planets orbit the Sun in the same direction, and all orbits are in the same plane with the exception of Pluto the orbit of which is slightly offset.

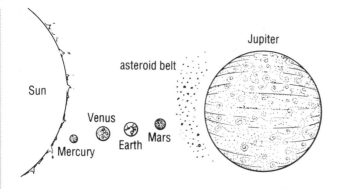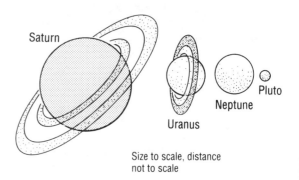

Size to scale, distance
not to scale

When comparing planets within the Solar System the following scales are useful:

Planet	Scale diameter (mm)	Scale distance from Sun (paces)
Mercury	5	1
Venus	12	2
Earth	13	3
Mars	7	4
Jupiter	140	14
Saturn	110	25
Uranus	50	53
Neptune	50	82
Pluto	6	109

It is not fully understood how the Solar System was formed but many scientists believe that the planets (and Sun) were formed from a swirling condensing mass of hot dust and gas which gradually separated into bands, the matter in the bands gradually coagulating to form the planets. Some evidence to support this idea or 'theory' comes from the fact that all planets orbit in the same direction and within the same plane. (In addition when matter is spinning in this fashion it would be expected that the larger bodies would be formed in the position of the larger planets.) (*See* planets.)

■ SOLID

At Key Stage 2 the following characteristics of solids can be explored:

- Solids have a definite shape and volume.
- Solids such as ice, wax and solder can be heated to show them melting.
- Strips of paper, card, pottery, wood, metal and plastic can be compared for strength and flexibility.

- Blocks of polystyrene, metal, wood and plastic can be compared for compressibility.
- Solids such as sugar, salt, Epsom salts, washing soda, bicarbonate of soda, pepper, flour, metals and wax can be compared for solubility in water.

■ SOLUBILITY

The extent to which one substance dissolves in a solution is dependent on the nature of the substances involved and the temperature. For example, table salt (sodium chloride) dissolves readily in water but not in liquids such as petrol, whereas candle wax does not dissolve in water but does dissolve in petrol. Sugar dissolves in both water and petrol.

Temperature will also affect the solubility of substances. Generally the higher the temperature the greater the solubility, although this is not always the case.

Water is a good solvent (*see* solution) in which many substances are soluble.

Solubility of common substances:

Soluble	Slightly soluble	Insoluble
salt (table)	sodium	wax
Epsom salts	bicarbonate	chalk
sugar	carbon dioxide	flour
washing soda		
methylated spirit		

Different types of salts (*see* salts) vary in solubility:

Chlorides   most are soluble.
Carbonates   most are insoluble.
Sulphates   most are soluble.
Nitrates   all are soluble.

SOLUTION

A solution is a liquid in which a substance is dissolved. Usually solids are thought of as dissolving in a liquid, but it is important to realise that solutions of liquids in other liquids or solutions of gases in liquids also exist. For example, alcohol dissolves in water to produce a solution as in beer or wine and carbon dioxide dissolves in water to produce a solution as in lemonade or Coca-Cola (the fizz is the gas carbon dioxide).

A liquid in which a substance dissolves is called the solvent and a substance dissolved in it is called a solute:

solution = solvent + solute

In a salt solution the solvent is water and the solute is the salt.

Bottled waters have a number of substances (salts) dissolved in them; the label usually provides a list of these substances. It is because of these dissolved substances that bottled waters taste different. Tap water also has small amounts of salts dissolved in it. Salts of magnesium and calcium are often present because as water travels through rocks into the ground it dissolves the more soluble minerals.

Water is only one solvent and solutions can be made using other solvents, for example methylated spirits, cooking oil and nail-varnish remover. Water is a good solvent because it can dissolve many different types of substances. Methylated spirits and nail-varnish remover are good at dissolving greasy substances but do not dissolve many of the substances which water can, such as salt, citric acid crystals and copper sulphate.

> A useful demonstration at Key Stage 2 is as follows.
>
> A saturated solution is one in which no more solute can be dissolved in the solution at a particular temperature. The preparation of a saturated solution is often the starting point for growing crystals. In order to make a saturated solution of alum, first warm the amount of water required and then carefully stir in alum a teaspoonful at a time, ensuring that the alum dissolves. Continue this process until no more will dissolve and a little alum is left in the bottom of the solution. Leave to stand, allowing to cool to room temperature. As the solution cools a little more solid will precipitate from the solution. Filter this solution to leave a saturated solution. If a tiny crystal on a cotton thread is now suspended in the solution and left for a few days the crystal should grow in size as the water in the solution slowly evaporates causing more alum to precipitate out.

SOUND

Sound is produced by vibration. Objects that vibrate fast produce high notes whilst slow vibrations produce low notes (*see* pitch). The human ear can sense vibrations within the range 20 vibrations per second (20 hertz (Hz)) and 20 000 vibrations per second (20 000 Hz). Sound produced by frequencies of less than 20 Hz are called subsonic whilst those above 20 000 Hz, the limit of human hearing, are called ultrasonic.

Sound is a way by which energy is transferred from one place to another. Sound travels through the air in the form of waves, the vibrating air carrying energy. A vibrating object (for example, a tuning fork) causes the air particles to move in a similar way moving backwards and forwards. This wave motion carries the sound (vibrations) in all directions, some of which reach the ear.

Sound can also travel through solids and liquids; in fact sound travels better through these media because the particles making up these materials are closer, making it easier to transfer the vibration energy between 'neighbours'. This can explain why the sound of whales carries over many miles across oceans, why submarines have to 'rig for silent running' to avoid detection from underwater microphones and why Red Indians were said to put their ears to the ground to hear the sound of horses a long distance away.

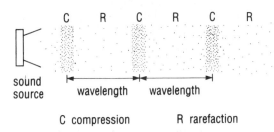

A vibrating object pushes air backward and forward causing compressions and rarefactions. The compression (pressed air) corresponds to a crest in a water ripple; the rarefaction (rarefied air) to a trough in a ripple.

SPECTRUM

The visible spectrum is formed from the colours which make up white light and is usually regarded as containing seven colours: red, orange, yellow, green, blue, indigo and violet; the colour of the rainbow. A useful mnemonic for the order is *ROY-G-BIV*. Alternatively remember Richard Of York Gave Battle In Vain. This visible spectrum can be formed by passing white light through a prism (*see also* electromagnetic spectrum).

SPECIES

Species is the name given to a group of animals or plants that have a set of common characteristics and are only able to breed amongst themselves. Examples of species would be man, dog, lion, rose and buttercup. It would not be possible for pollen from buttercup to fertilise a rose or for lion and zebra to breed. There are exceptions to this and some breeding across species does occur although it is rare. One example of inter-breeding is the mule, a sterile animal resulting from breeding from a horse and a donkey.

SPEED

Speed is the distance travelled by an object in a unit of time and is measured in units of kilometres/hour (km/h), metres/sec (m/s) and miles per hour.

$$speed = \frac{distance}{time\ taken}$$

At Key Stage 2 in most cases children can discuss change of speed in terms of going faster or slower. Children are introduced to the measurement of speed at Key Stage 3, an understanding of which is required at Level 6.

SPEED OF LIGHT

Light travels at a very fast speed (approximately 300 000 km/sec or 186 000 miles/sec. So fast in fact that on Earth it can be regarded to be almost instantaneous. Nevertheless light from the Sun takes about 8 minutes to reach Earth and light from the nearest star takes $4\frac{1}{2}$ years to reach Earth.

SPEED OF SOUND

Sound travels at a speed much slower than that of light. The speed of sound in air is about 344 metres/sec. Sound travels more slowly in gases than in liquids and more slowly in liquids than in solids.

A thunderstorm provides evidence that sound travels slower than light since the flash and the sound are produced at the same time but we often hear the sound after the flash because the sound takes longer to reach us. How long after depends on how far away the storm is. A rule of thumb for estimating the distance of a storm is to count in seconds the time for the thunder to be heard after seeing the flash. Roughly a mile is equivalent to 4 seconds. Evidence that sound travels slower than light is also provided by observing a person hammering a stake into the ground across a large playing field. You will often hear the sound after you see the person striking the stake with a hammer.

STAR

A star is a tiny point of light in the night sky. Each star is a glowing ball of gas, and gives off its own light. The light emitted by a star originates from a nuclear fusion reaction. This reaction generates intense heat and light. Our Sun is a star.

Life history of a star
Stars are thought to originate from a mass of interstellar gas which gathers together and begins to collapse under its own gravity. As it does so its temperature rises until enough nuclear reactions begin to convert hydrogen

gas to helium with the release of enormous amounts of energy. Once the hydrogen is converted to helium it is thought that new reactions begin and heavier elements are gradually formed. The star may then shrink in size. At this point the star may become unstable and become a supernova, or a pulsating star. Its ultimate fate depends on its size. A low-mass star is thought to become a white dwarf, an intermediate star a neutron star and a high-mass star collapses in on itself because of its high gravity to form a black hole. As stars pass through this cycle so their temperature changes: the hotter the star the more brightly it shines. Red stars have surface temperatures of about 3000 °C, yellow stars (like the Sun) about 6000 °C and white stars temperatures in excess of 20 000 °C.

■ STRENGTH

Strength is an ability to withstand tensile (pulling or stretching) forces and compressive (pushing or squashing) forces.

Metals are strong because of their internal structure (the way their atoms are bonded together) and as a consequence can be pulled into wires without breaking, will resist being squashed and can carry heavy loads without breaking.

The tensile strength of materials can be compared by suspending a strip of the material and progressively hanging weights on it until it breaks.

At Key Stage 2 suitable materials to test are: different types of metal wire, thread, hair, different paper, card, plastic strips, plastic carrier bags.

The compressive strength of materials can be compared by loading thin 'beams' of materials. When there is a load placed on a bridge beam it bends. The top layers of the bridge will be in compression whereas the lower layers will be in tension.

The loads on such beams can be weights that are progressively added until the beam breaks. Suitable materials to test are: different types of wood, plastic, card and concrete beams made from different types of concrete.

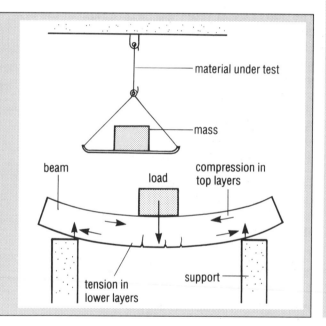

■ STRUCTURE

The shape of a structure has an effect on its strength. Paper can be folded to make different shaped beams, which can then be tested for strength by loading with different masses.

circular

square

triangular

Triangular cross-sectional shapes are stronger than square cross-sectional shapes. Straws can be used to make cubes or pyramids. Masses can be suspended from the structures as a test of strength.

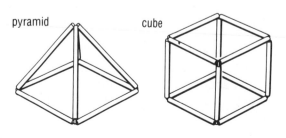

Forces involved with different bridge shapes:

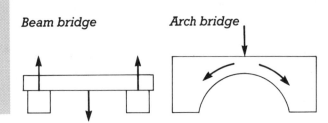

Beam bridge   *Arch bridge*

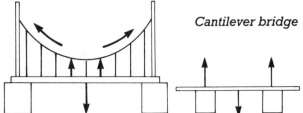

Suspension bridge

Cantilever bridge

SUCCESSION

When organisms in an environment compete they can bring about changes so that the ecosystem changes. For example, the introduction of foxes into an enclosed area inhabited by rabbits will bring about a decline in the number of rabbits which in turn will mean that the grass is not grazed to such an extent, which in turn will create longer grass. These conditions may be more favourable to certain types of plants and insects. These changes are referred to as succession.

SUN

The Sun is a star radiating its own light at the centre of the Solar System which contains nine orbiting planets. It is at a distance of about 150 million kilometres from Earth. The Sun appears to move across the sky because of the Earth's rotation. The Earth rotates on its axis from West to East, making the Sun appear to rise in the East and set in the West when viewed from the Northern Hemisphere. The height of the Sun in the sky varies because the Earth's axis is tilted.

This can be readily visualised using a narrow beam torch and a globe. The height of the Sun in the sky affects the length of shadows (*see* shadow stick, seasons).

The heat and light radiated by the Sun is generated by nuclear reactions where the element hydrogen is converted into helium (*see* stars). The surface temperature of the Sun is about 6000 °C. Some of this energy is radiated towards the Earth. The Sun is regarded as the ultimate source of energy for the Earth:

Photosynthesis enables the Sun's energy to be transferred to vegetation. This then becomes an energy store, for example food or fuel as in wood.

Fossilization of living things stores energy as coal, oil and gas (*see* fuel).

Warming of the Earth and the atmosphere drives the water cycle, the Sun providing energy to evaporate water thus enabling the formation of clouds, rainfall and the flow of water in rivers and streams. This energy can be used to generate electricity (hydroelectric power) or turn water wheels.

Uneven heating of the Earth's surface gives rise to wind and water waves.

SUNDIAL

The ancient Egyptians used obelisks such as Cleopatra's needle as sundials, the shadows falling on marks on the ground below. They were the first people to divide the day into a fixed number of hours. The length of shadows that form during the day vary according to the season, but their direction is always the same. The Earth rotates so that a shadow will move through 15° every hour (*see* day and night). Hour lines on sundials are thus drawn at an angle of 15°. The shadow is formed by a triangular shaped pointer called a 'style'. The angle of the pointer is the same as the angle of latitude (sundials are designed to work in particular latitudes).

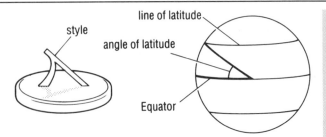

When in use sundials are aligned so that the leading edge of the style is parallel with the axis of the Earth's rotation.

When viewed in the Northern hemisphere the Sun appears to rise in the East, follow a course across the Southern sky and set in the West.

SURVIVAL

Survival is affected by availability of food supply, predation, adaptation to habitat and changes in environmental conditions such as temperature and rainfall. Human influences and pollution also affect the survival of living things (*see* pollution, environmental conditions, habitat).

TEMPERATURE

The temperature of something is its 'hotness'. Temperature is measured in degrees Celsius, degrees Fahrenheit or on the Kelvin scale. It is not sufficient therefore to quote temperature as being *x* degrees without qualifying this with the unit:

> freezing point (of water):
> 0 °C on the Celsius scale
>> =32°F on the Fahrenheit scale
>> = 273 K on the Kelvin scale.
> boiling point (of water):
> 100 °C on the Celsius scale
>> = 212 °F on the Fahrenheit scale
>> = 373 K on the Kelvin scale.

These temperatures only hold true at sea level and for pure distilled water since both the boiling point and the freezing point of water is affected by the presence of dissolved substances (as in tap water) and atmospheric pressure. Dissolved substances lower the freezing point of water (this is why salt is added to roads in winter) and raises the boiling point of water (this is often why tap water will boil at just above 100 °C). The atmospheric pressure will also influence boiling point since the lower the atmospheric pressure the easier it is for the water particles to escape from the surface of the water, hence the lower the boiling point. Water boils at a lower temperature up a mountain where the air pressure is less.

The 'hotness' of an object depends on the kinetic energy of its particles (atoms or molecules). As objects are heated their particles acquire more energy, they vibrate more and move around faster. 0 Kelvin (–273 °C) is regarded as Absolute Zero, the temperature at which particles are motionless and have no energy.

THERMOMETER

Thermometers measure temperature and are calibrated in degrees Celsius (°C).

Traditional mercury or alcohol thermometers work because substances expand when heated. They can be purchased covering a number of different temperature ranges. A suitable range for general purpose work is –10 °C to 110 °C. Forehead thermometers can be purchased which have a limited range (35 °C to 39 °C). They rely on liquid crystal changing colour within different temperature ranges. These are good thermometers to use when taking body temperatures. Clinical thermometers placed in the mouth are not advisable since they must be thoroughly sterilised before and after each use.

Soil thermometers are those which have a metal protective shield around them so can be placed into the ground. Soil thermometers can be purchased in garden centres and rely on a thermocouple effect. A thermocouple is a join between two different metal wires. The ends of the wires are connected to an electric meter. If the joint is heated a small electric current is generated which travels through a circuit causing the needle in the meter to move. This is called the thermocouple effect (thermo = heat, couple = two wires). The electric matter is calibrated to read in degrees Celsius. Thermocouple-type thermometers are very robust and can record temperatures over wide ranges.

Thermocouples are usually found in ovens, kilns and deep freezers.

Maximum and minimum thermometers are U-shaped thermometers often filled with mercury that are able to record the maximum and minimum temperatures over a period as the thread of mercury expands and contracts. As the thread of mercury moves it pushes a small metal pin along in front of it which will remain in place as the thread of mercury retreats.

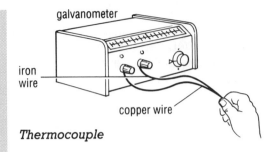

Thermocouple

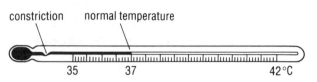

Clinical thermometer

Measuring temperatures

Often the only thermometer that a child will have experienced is a clinical thermometer, which has a restriction or 'kink' in the tube carrying the mercury, so that once it has expanded it cannot return. Thus the thermometer may be withdrawn from the patient's mouth and the mercury will still remain at its position. Shaking will return the mercury to the bulb below the constriction.

> When children first take temperatures using ordinary thermometers they will not know that they have to read it *in situ* and will assume that the reading stays the same even when they take it away from the source of the heat. Another common mistake is that they tend to hold the bulb of a thermometer when they are reading it, not realising that this affects a reading. Children need to be shown how to use and read thermometers correctly.

THUNDERSTORM

A thunderstorm is caused by a discharge of static electricity. Static discharge can also occur when a nylon sweater is removed – the crackling noise is the static discharging. In the dark it is possible to see flashes of static electricity discharging itself when a sweater is removed.

A thunderstorm forms when warm, moist air rises into cold air. As the warm, moist air rises, the water vapour condenses. The water droplets that are formed together with ice crystals rub against each other as they move, giving rise to a separation of charge so that the top of clouds becomes positively charged and the bottom negatively charged. This effect is similar to that produced when a plastic ruler is rubbed with a dry cloth. The ruler and cloth will become charged with opposing positive and negative charges. The charge distribution depends on the type of plastic and type of material from which the cloth is made. Once sufficient negative charge builds up at the bottom of the cloud it 'jumps' the gap to Earth and discharges itself as lightning. As this stream of electric charge flows between the Earth and the cloud it heats the air around it, causing a rapid expansion of the air which is heard as a 'crack'.

TIDES

Tides are caused by gravitational attraction between the Earth, the Moon and the Sun. On the sides of the Earth which face and are opposite to the Moon, the oceans' waters are raised into a bulge relative to the floor. The Sun, because of its greater distance from Earth, exerts a lesser pull.

A spring tide is an unusually high tide created when both the Earth and the Sun are in line so their gravitational effects are combined. A spring tide is nothing to do with seasons but does occur at periods of New Moon and Full Moon.

A neap tide is the lowest tide and occurs when the tidal bulges produced by the Sun and Moon are at right angles to each other.

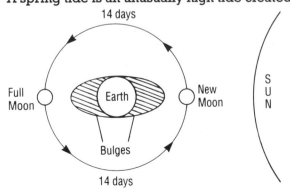

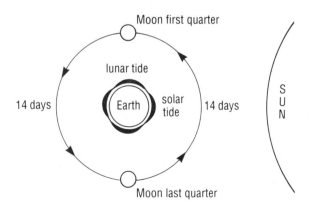

■ TIMBRE

Timbre is the characteristic quality of sounds produced by different instruments. When middle C is played on a guitar, it sounds different to that of middle C played on a piano. This is because different instruments produce different overtones. When the guitar or piano makes a sound, a string vibrates. Middle C is produced by strings vibrating at 256 vibrations per second (256 Hz). The string will also produce secondary vibrations in harmony with this vibration; in addition the body of the instrument will also vibrate and these additional vibrations produce overtones. The way in which the string is made to vibrate will also have an effect, giving rise to different overtones. For example, in a piano the string is struck whereas on a guitar the string is plucked.

■ TISSUE

Cells which have similar functions are arranged together within living organisms to form tissue. Muscle is a tissue, as are the different layers of skin. Often different tissues are grouped together to form an organ (*see also* cell, organ).

■ TOBACCO

Tobacco contains the addictive drug nicotine usually taken into the body by smoking (*see* drug).

Tobacco smoking:

- Impairs foetal development in pregnant mothers.
- Is a major cause of lung cancer and heart disease.
- Produces safety hazards in the home through increased risk of fire through accident.
- Causes addiction.
- Has an adverse effect on taste, appetite and metabolic rate.
- Impairs body health.
- Causes harm to others through passive smoking.
- Is expensive.

■ TRANSPORT

This is a geological term to describe the transfer of weathered or eroded material from its original site. For example, the transport of rock fragments from mountains to a river estuary by water or the transport of sand particles being blown by the wind.

■ UNIVERSE

The Universe contains all matter that is known to exist. It contains galaxies (gigantic clusters of stars), individual stars, nebulae (clouds of dust and gas), interstellar matter, rocks, ice, comets and above all vast tracts of space or vacuum. The Universe is thought to be expanding, i.e. galaxies are moving away from each other. This leads to one theory about the origin of the Universe called the 'Big Bang', which considers that all the material present in the Universe was generated at one point in a gigantic explosion, a big bang. This would account for the expanding nature of the Universe. This is the favoured view at present although there are others, for example the steady state theory which suggests that things stay more or less as they are with new stars and galaxies being formed and replacing those that 'die'.

The distances between stars and galaxies within the Universe are vast and are measured in light years. A light year is the distance travelled by light in one year. Light travels at about 300 000 kilometres in one second. The nearest star to the Solar System is Alpha Centuri and is about 4.5 light years away, whereas the Milky Way, our own galaxy of which we are a part, is about 100 000 light years in diameter. Distances between galaxies are measured in millions and billions of light years. As a consequence of this the Night Sky is in effect a 'time machine', since we are seeing stars and galaxies not as they are now but as they were thousands or millions of years ago when the light first left them.

VARIABLE

A variable is a characteristic which can have different qualities or values. For example, within the context of an investigation concerning bouncing balls (*What factors affect the height that a ball will bounce?*), possible variables that might affect the result include:

- The height from which the ball is dropped.
- The type of surface onto which the ball is dropped.
- The size of the ball.
- The material from which the ball is made.
- Whether the ball is inflated or not.

- The degree to which the ball is inflated.
- The weight of the ball.

Within an investigation the **independent** variable is the one which the investigator chooses to change systematically, for example height from which the ball is dropped, weight of the ball, etc.

The **dependent** variable is the one which may be affected by a change in the value of the independent variable. In this case the height of bounce is the dependent variable.

VARIABLE RESISTOR

A variable resistor is used to control the amount of electric current flowing through a circuit. A dimmer switch is an example of a variable resistor, as is a volume control on a radio.

One simple type of variable resistor allows the current to flow through either longer or shorter lengths of wire. Each wire carrying an electric current offers a small resistance to the flow of that current: the longer the wire the greater the resistance.

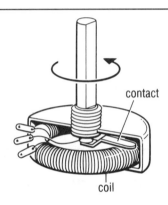

contact

coil

VARIATION

Variation describes the difference in characteristics which appear within a species. For example, clover leaves are all essentially the same shape; however there exist a variety of patterns on the leaves.

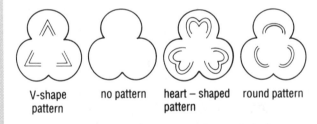

V-shape
pattern   no pattern   heart – shaped   round pattern
pattern

This example of variation is inherited, being passed on from one generation to the next. It is possible, however, for variation to be caused by environmental factors. Some plants will grow variegated leaves in bright sunlight, but revert to a green colour when growing in a dimly lit area.

Examples of variation in plants:

Seed size and weight of one species can be compared by measuring the length of the seed or measuring the weight on electronic kitchen scales to the nearest gramme (g).

Suitable seeds are sycamore, runner bean, butter bean, broad bean, sunflower.
Seed coat markings for example, the number and pattern of stripes on sunflower seeds.
Number of peas in a pod.
Length of seed germination within one species try sowing 20 pre-soaked seeds of one type and counting the number which germinate on any one day. Suitable seeds are sunflower, chick pea, broad bean, mustard, cress.
Height of plant sunflowers (do bigger seeds produce bigger plants?).
Length or width of leaf dandelion, plantain, oak, willow, beech can be used.
Variegations on coleus plants.

Examples of variation in animals:

Shell size of one species can be compared by measuring the length or width of the shell. Suitable shells collected from the beach include: scallop, mussels, oysters, periwinkle or, on land, snails.
Shell markings or colour for example, stripes on snail shells, or bands on seashells (for example, slipper shells) or colour in scallops.

Height, weight, eye colour, hair colour, foot size, hand spans, fingerprints, ability to roll the tongue, ability to waggle ears the teacher needs to approach the investigations of such variations with sensitivity and care, however, since children can often be very sensitive about their differences which may single them out, for example their ability to waggle their ears or their size.

Wing size for example, cabbage white butterfly.

■ VIBRATE

Sound is caused by vibrations. The speed of vibration is measured in hertz (Hz) and is the number of vibrations per second.

1 Hz = 1 vibration per second

Strings on instruments such as guitar, violin and piano can be seen and felt to vibrate as they produce sound. The pitch of the note is caused by the rate of vibration. Middle C is produced by a string vibrating at 256 Hz, whereas top C (one octave above middle C) vibrates at twice the rate, i.e. 512 Hz.

Examples of vibrations within musical instruments:

Instrument	Vibrating part	Method of causing vibration	Pitch of note changed by
guitar	strings body air in sound box	plucking	length of string tuning by tension
violin	strings body air in sound box	bow and plucking	length of string
drum	skin air inside	striking	changing vibrating area tuning by altering tension
recorder	air in tube	blowing	changing length of vibrating column of air by placing fingers over holes, the more holes covered the longer the column of air

■ VINEGAR

Vinegar is a solution of acetic acid (ethanoic acid). It has a pH of approximately 3 (i.e. it is weakly acidic). It is made either from malt or from wine. White wine vinegar (or other colourless vinegar) is the most suitable vinegar to use when exploring the effect of acids on indicators. Vinegar will turn red cabbage indicator red (*see* indicator) and will react with sodium bicarbonate or baking powder to produce a fizz. This fizz is the gas carbon dioxide, which is given off when an acid reacts with a carbonate. Vinegar can be used to test different rocks to see which are carbonates. Vinegar will, for example, fizz with chalk, showing that the chalk rock contains carbonate. Chalk is calcium carbonate. Limes one and eggshell also contain calcium carbonate.

■ WASTE DISPOSAL

Household waste in Europe contains approximately:

- 30% food and garden waste.
- 25% paper and card.
- 10% glass.
- 10% textiles.
- 10% dust ashes.
- 8% metals.
- 7% plastics.

This waste can be disposed of in three ways:

Landfill waste can be buried and allowed to decay. Glass and plastic will not be broken down. Over long periods of time metals will corrode, some more quickly than others. Escaping gas (methane) resulting from the decay of some materials has been known to cause explosions. In addition, as the material decays so the ground can subside.

Incineration Waste can be burnt in an incineration plant, the heat generated being used to generate electricity. Metals, glass, ash and dust will need to be removed beforehand and disposed of separately.

Recycling Waste can be sorted into different groups of materials and recycled. Glass, metals, textiles, paper, and some plastics can be recycled. Sorting is difficult and waste food and garden refuse will have to be disposed of separately.

■ WASTE PRODUCTS

When fuels burn, waste products are produced, in addition to heat. These waste products can be a nuisance and can cause pollution.

Fuel	Waste product	Pollution problems
natural gas	water	
	carbon dioxide	can contribute to greenhouse effect and hence global warming
coal	ash	disposal in landfill sites
	soot	covers and damages plant life
	water	
	carbon dioxide	can contribute to greenhouse effect and hence global warming
	sulphur dioxide (from sulphur impurities in the coal)	contributes to acid rain
	smoke	
oil	water	
	carbon dioxide	can contribute to greenhouse effect and hence global warming
	sulphur dioxide (from sulphur impurities in the oil)	contributes to acid rain
	unburnt hydrocarbons	can contribute to greenhouse effect and hence global warming
wood	water	
	carbon dioxide	can contribute to greenhouse effect and hence global warming
	ash	

■ WATER CYCLE

Water from the seas, rivers and lakes and leaf surfaces of plants evaporates continually due to the action of the Sun. The evaporated water vapour gathers in the warm air of the atmosphere. When this moisture-laden warm air meets colder air the moisture condenses and clouds form. The water condenses further and falls as rain, sleet, hail or snow when it becomes even colder. This often happens when drifting clouds are forced upwards on approaching mountains or hills.

The effect is exactly the same as that produced by the boiling kettle, when the at-first-invisible steam (near the kettle spout) meets the colder air (further from the spout) and becomes visible. When this now-visible steam meets an even colder surface like a window it condenses further and runs down the window pane as water.

The water that has fallen (called precipitation by weathermen) then travels back through soils and rocks into rivers and streams dissolving some minerals from the rocks as they pass. The rivers eventually reach seas and oceans. Water is evaporated from the seas leaving the dissolved salts, which is why the sea is salty, and is steadily becoming saltier.

Plants contribute to the cycling of water because they take up water through their roots, a small part of which is used by the plant (1%), the majority of which, however, is lost through the leaves during transpiration. A single birch tree in summer can recycle 400 litres of water a day.

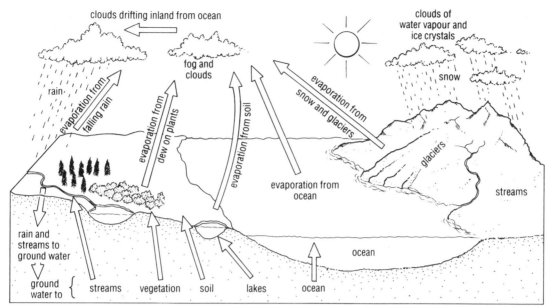

Water cycle

■ WEATHER

Weather is the state of the atmosphere at any given time over any given region. Temperature, wind, air pressure, humidity, cloud cover and precipitation are used as descriptions of 'weather'.

The main cause of different weather is the effect of the Sun's differential heating of the Earth's surface.

The heating effect of the Sun's rays is more intense at the equator than at the poles. At the equator the Sun is directly overhead, thus the rays strike the surface at right angles and have to travel through less atmosphere. Nearer the poles the Sun's rays strike the Earth obliquely, thus the rays are more spread out and travel through more atmosphere. Hence the heating effect is reduced since less energy reaches each square metre of the surface.

This results in the heated air in the tropics rising causing convection currents (hot air rises). These currents move rising hot air towards the poles and surface cooler air towards the equator. The effect of the spinning Earth causes these air currents to swing slightly.

As a result, in the tropics north of the Equator the surface winds are North East whereas south of the Equator the winds are South East.

These general movements are interfered with by the different land masses which influence the wind direction.

Land heats up and cools down more quickly than sea. The land is therefore hotter in summer, whereas the sea is warmer in winter. This uneven heating of the earth's surface in

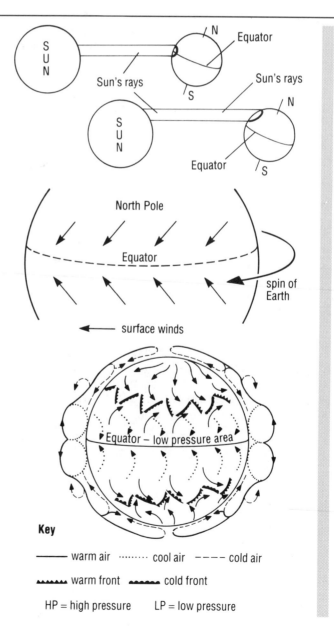

Key

— warm air ⋯⋯ cool air – – – cold air

▲▲▲▲ warm front ◼◼◼◼ cold front

HP = high pressure   LP = low pressure

the middle latitudes gives rise to cyclones and anti-cyclones which have a major influence in the weather. Cyclones are regions of low pressure, a result of warm air expanding and rising. The surrounding cooler air spirals inwards (in an anti-clockwise direction in the northern hemisphere and clockwise in the southern hemisphere), again caused by the spin of the Earth. Anticyclones are regions of high pressure caused by cool sinking air (air contracts as it cools). This produces a spiral of winds outwards.

In addition around coastal areas the land is hotter than the sea in the day and cooler than the sea at night, which in itself gives rise to sea breezes. During the day wind blows inland; during the night the breeze blows out to sea. This effect is particularly significant in the tropics.

The interaction of all these influences gives rise to the different weather conditions we experience.

The following weather factors can be explored by children at Key Stage 2.

Air pressure

Pressure is a measure of how much force is acting on a particular area of an object. The Earth's gravitational pull holds a layer of gases (the atmosphere) around the surface of the planet. The weight of the air pressing down on a unit area of the surface is the air pressure. Air pressure is measured using a barometer in units called bars or newtons per square metre. The air pressure is about 10 newtons per square centimetre (10 N/cm^2). This unit is also known as 1 bar or 1000 millibars.

Cloud cover

The degree of cloud cover can be estimated and is a useful measure of weather.

Children will need to design a scale for cloud cover before it can be considered as a quantitative observation.

Humidity can be recorded using a simple hygrometer. These can be purchased or simply made from a piece of spiral card.

Rainfall

Rainfall is measured using a rain gauge usually in millimetres (mm). Any container will do but those you buy have sloping sides funnelling the rain caught in the wide opening into a narrow bottom. The purpose of this is to make the reading of small quantities of rain easier and they are calibrated accordingly.

Sunshine

Recording accurately the hours of sunshine without specific measuring equipment is difficult. However, it is possible to record the light levels using a simple photographic light meter and to use this as a measure of the light intensity and hence sunshine.

Temperature

Temperature is measured in degrees Celsius. Suitable thermometers are readily available in garden centres; so too are soil thermometers. Soil thermometers are constructed so that they can be easily pushed into the ground. Maximum and minimum thermometers are useful since they can record the lowest and highest temperatures reached over a period, for example day/night.

Wind direction

Wind direction is measured by a weathervane which is an instrument which can be designed by the children themselves. They will need to decide how to make the vane so that it will catch the wind and turn, and what scale to use: N, NE, NNE, etc.

Windspeed

Windspeed is measured in knots, and can be measured using a simple hand-held anemometer; equally at Key Stage 2 children could be asked to design their own. One could be calibrated by holding it outside a car window, or even on a bike with a speedometer whilst travelling at 10 mph, 20 mph, and 30 mph, etc.

Much of this weather recording equipment can be easily obtained from garden centres.

WEATHERING

Weathering is the action of wind, rain, water, ice, frost and chemicals in rain on rocks. There are two broad types of weathering.

Chemical weathering

This involves a chemical reaction between rock and dissolved substances in water. The result of this is the production of a new material which is often soluble and can easily be transported away.

Rainwater, for example, naturally contains a small amount of dissolved carbon dioxide, which causes the water to be weakly acidic. Acids readily react with some rocks to form soluble products. One example is the action of acid on limestone, which gradually dissolves away the rock. Another example is the action of rainwater with dissolved carbon dioxide on feldspar, a constituent of granite. Feldspar is dissolved away leaving the other minerals in granite. This dissolved material eventually ends up as clays deposited by rivers. This action is very, very slow in temperate climates but is more rapid in hot, tropical climates.

Note Acid rain, often referred to as a form of pollution, is rainwater which additionally contains dissolved gases such as sulphur dioxide and oxides of nitrogen, emitted from power stations and cars, and is quite strongly acidic. It is wrong, however, to assume that unpolluted rain is neutral: in fact it is weakly acidic (*see* acids, and acid rain).

Physical weathering

Physical weathering usually begins along lines of weaknesses in rocks and results in fragmentation of rock:

Water may penetrate cracks in the rock and freeze. When water freezes it expands, and so it can force rocks apart, breaking them up just as it can do with water pipes that are not protected from the cold.

Plants may grow in the cracks the growth of roots forcing cracks further apart.

Wind gradually erodes the surface of a rock, even more rapidly if it contains small abrasive particles of rock, for example sandstone.

Although strictly erosion rather than weathering; water running over the surface of a rock can gradually wear away the particles of which it is composed. This happens more quickly if the water itself contains rock fragments which in turn have an abrasive effect.

In another example of erosion, glaciers wear away the surface of rock, again more rapidly if they contain fragments of rock. Glaciers are responsible for U-shaped valleys, whilst rivers and streams cut V-shaped valleys into the hillside (*see* erosion).

WEIGHT

The weight of an object is the effect of the Earth's gravitational field (the pull of gravity) on the object. It is therefore a force and is measured in units of newtons. Weights of objects can be measured using spring balances. Often however the spring balances which are used are calibrated in units of mass such as kilogrammes or grammes. To a scientist there is a difference between the weight of an object and the mass of an object.

At Key Stage 2 the Programme of Study requires children to relate the properties to the everyday uses of materials and makes no distinction between mass and weight: 'Properties such as . . . mass (weight) . . . should be investigated related to everyday uses of the materials.' (Programme of study AT3 (i) KS2.)

For an explanation of the difference between mass and weight, *see* mass.

WORK

Work is done when a force makes something move. The amount of work done depends on the size of the force and the distance moved:

work done = force × distance moved

When force is measured in newtons and the distance is measured in metres the unit of work is the joule. The work done is also a measure of the energy transferred in joules: they are the same (*see* energy).

■ YEAR, YEAR LENGTH

A year is determined by the time taken for the Earth to orbit the Sun and is 365.25 days. For convenience, the year is taken to be 365 days, a small correction being made every 4 years by adding an extra day on the 29th February (leap year).

Appendix Summary tables of investigations, by strand

■ ATTAINMENT TARGET 2 LIFE AND LIVING PROCESSES

KS2 SC2 Strand (i) **life processes and the organisation of living things**		
Programme of Study	Starting points for investigations	Statements of Attainment
Pupils should be introduced to the major organs and organ systems of mammals and flowering plants. They should explore some aspects of feeding, support, movement and behaviour in themselves and other animals. They should explore ideas about the processes of breathing, circulation, growth and reproduction. They should investigate the factors that affect plant growth, for example *light intensity, temperature* and *amount of water*. They should study how microbes and lifestyle canaffect health, and learn about factors that contribute to good health including the defence systems of the body, diet, personal hygiene, safe handling of food, dental care and exercise. They should be introduced to the fact that while all medicines are drugs, not all drugs are medicines. They should begin to be aware of the harmful effect on health resulting from an abuse of tobacco, alcohol and other drugs.	**Early in Key Stage 2** What will happen if we do not water this plant/keep this plant in the dark? What makes some people jump higher/run faster, etc.? What do you think plants need to stay alive? How could we find out? **Later in Key Stage 2** What affects how plants grow? What affects how fast plants grow? What affects how much weight we can lift? What affects how fast we can run? What affects breathing rate/pulse rate? What factors affect germination rate of one variety of seeds?	**Pupils should:** 2a Know that plants and animals need certain conditions to sustain life. 3a Know the basic life processes common to humans and other animals. 4a Be able to name and locate the major organs of the human body and of the flowering plant. 5a Be able to name and outline the functions of the major organs and organ systems in mammals and flowering plants.

KS2   SC2   Strand (ii) **variation and the mechanisms of inheritance and evolution**

Programme of Study	Starting points for investigations	Statements of Attainment
Pupils should investigate and measure the similarities and differences between themselves, animals and plants and fossils. They should be introduced to how plants and animals can be preserved as fossils. They should have the opportunity to develop skills in identifying locally occurring species of animals and plants by observing structural features and making and using simple keys. They should be introduced to the idea that information is passed from one generation to the next.	**Early in Key Stage 2** What is the most common eye colour/hand span/hair colour? How could we find out? Is there a connection between shoe size and height? Is there a connection between eye colour and hair colour? Can you find a way to sort these pictures of living things into groups? **Later in Key Stage 2** What affects how tall we are? Will the size of a seed have any affect on its growth? Does our size have any affect on how we move? What variations might influence seeds? What differences in seeds themselves might affect their gemination rates?	**Pupils should:** 2b Be able to sort familiar living things into broad groups according to easily observable features. 4b Be able to assign plants and animals to their major groups using keys and observable features. 5b Know that information in the form of genes is passed on from one generation to the next.

KS2   SC2   Strand (iii) **populations and human influences within ecosystems**

Programme of Study	Starting points for investigations	Statements of Attainment
Pupils should explore and investigate at least two different habitats and the animals and plants that live there. They should find out how animals and plants are suited to these locations and how they are influenced by environmental conditions including seasonal and daily changes and measure these changes using a variety of instruments. They should develop an awareness and understanding of the necessity for sensitive collection and care of living things used as the subject of any study of the environment. They should study aspects of the local environment affected by human activity, for example farming, industry, mining or quarrying, and consider the benefits and detrimental effects of these activities. They should be made aware of competition between living things and their need for food, shelter and a place to reproduce. They should study the effects of pollution on the survival of living things.	**Early in Key Stage 2** What will happen if we do not water this plant/keep this plant in the dark? How might the length of daylight affect how well a plant grows? Where do you find daisies? Clover? Where do the biggest plantain plants grow; in the bright light or in the shade? **Later in Key Stage 2** What affects where moss grows? What conditions do woodlice prefer? What might affect the size of plants in a wood or field? Why do you think cress seeds bend when they grow? Near smoky factories what might affect how well plants grow? What differences might the time of day make to conditions either side of a hedge?	**Pupils should:** 2c Know that different kinds of living things are found in different localities. 3b Know that human activity may produce changes in the environment that can affect plants and animals. 4c Understand that the survival of plants and animals in an environment depends on successful competition for scarce resources. 5c Know how pollution can affect the survival of organisms.

KS2   SC2   Strand (iv) **energy flows and cycles of matter within ecosystems**

Programme of Study	Starting points for investigations	Statements of Attainment
Pupils should be introduced to the idea that green plants use energy from the Sun to produce food and that food chains are a way of representing feeding relationships. They should investigate the key factors in the process of decay such as temperature, moisture, air and role of microbes. They should build on their investigations of decay and consider the significant features of waste disposal procedures, for example in sewage disposal and composting, and the usefulness of any products.	**Early in Key Stage 2** What sorts of things decay? How could we make something decay more quickly/more slowly? What would happen if we left these plants in the dark? **Later in Key Stage 2** What affects how quickly something decays? What affects how many aphids are found in a garden?	**Pupils should:** 2d Know that some waste materials decay naturally but do so over different periods of time. 3c Know that green plants need light to stay alive and healthy. 4d Understand food chains as a way of representing feeding relationships in an ecosystem. 5d Know about the key factors in the process of decay.

■ ATTAINMENT TARGET 3 MATERIALS AND THEIR PROPERTIES

KS2 SC3 Strand (i) **the properties, classification and structure of materials**

Programme of Study	Starting points for investigations	Statements of Attainment
Pupils should investigate a number of different everyday materials, grouping them according to their characteristics. Properties such as strength, hardness, flexibility, compressibility, mass (weight), volume and solubility should be investigated and related to everyday uses of the materials. Pupils should be given opportunities to compare a range of solids, liquids and gases and recognise the properties which enable classification of materials in this way. They should test the acidity and alkalinity of safe everyday solutions such as lemon juice using indicators which may be extracted from plants such as red cabbage. Pupils should know about the dangers associated with the use of some everyday materials including hot oil, bleach, cleaning agents and other household materials. Experiments on dissolving and evaporation should lead to developing ideas about solutions and solubility. They should explore ways of separating and purifying mixtures such as muddy water, salty water and ink by evaporation, filtration and chromatography.	**Early in Key Stage 2** Which is the best washing up liquid? Which is the best carrier bag? Which is the strongest carrier bag? Which is the best material from which to make a kite? Can you find a way to dissolve sugar in tea more quickly? How sweet can you make tea? Which ball is the best bouncer? **Later in Key Stage 2** What affects how well sugar dissolves? What affects the strength of the material in a carrier bag? What affects how stiff bed springs are? What affects how stretchy hair is? What affects how well balls bounce?	**Pupils should:** 2a Be able to group materials according to observable features. 3a Be able to link the use of common materials to their simple properties. 4a Be able to classify materials as solids, liquids and gases on the basis of simple properties which relate to their everyday uses. 5a Know how to separate and purify the components of mixtures using physical processes. 5b Be able to classify aqueous solutions as acidic, alkaline or neutral using indicators.

KS2 SC3 Strand (iii) **chemical changes**

Programme of Study	Starting points for investigations	Statements of Attainment
Pupils should explore the origins of a range of materials in order to appreciate that some occur naturally while many are made from raw materials. They should investigate the action of heat on everyday materials resulting in permanent change. These might include cooking activities and firing clay. They should explore chemical changes in a number of everyday materials such as those that occur when mixing plaster of Paris, mixing baking powder with vinegar and when iron rusts. They should recognise that combustion of fuel releases energy and produces waste products including gases.	**Early in Key Stage 2** What do you think will happen if you heat these materials? How can we change these back? Can you find a way to make clay strong? **Later in Key Stage 2** What affects how quickly potatoes cook? How can we cook potatoes more quickly? What affects whether an egg is hard boiled or soft boiled? What conditions are needed to make things rust? Which is the best material for keeping soup hot? What affects how quickly dough rises?	**Pupils should:** 2b Know that heating and cooling everyday materials can cause them to melt or solidify or change permanently. 3b Know that some materials occur naturally while many are made from raw materials. 4b Know that materials from a variety of sources can be converted into new and useful products by chemical reactions. 4c Know that the combustion of fuel releases energy and produces waste gases. 5c Understand that rusting and burning involve a reaction with oxygen.

KS2 SC3 Strand (iv) **the Earth and its atmosphere**

Programme of Study	Starting points for investigations	Statements of Attainment
Pupils should have the opportunity to make regular, quantitative observations and keep records of weather and the seasons of the year. This should lead to a consideration of the water cycle. They should investigate natural materials (rocks, minerals, soils), sort them by simple criteria and relate them to their uses and origins. They should be aware of local distributions of some natural materials (sands, soils, rocks). They should observe, through fieldwork, how weather affects their surroundings, how sediment is produced and how soil develops. They should consider the major geological events which change the surface of the Earth and the evidence for these changes.	**Early in Key Stage 2** Do you think all soils look/feel the same? What do you think causes brickwork to crumble? Can we grow things equally well in different soils? Can you find a way to make a vibration (earthquake) detector? Is damp seaweed a good predictor of rain? Is there a connection between wind and rain? **Later in Key Stage 2** What affects how well soils drain? What affects how much water soils can retain? What affects how well rocks absorb water? What affects how quickly a puddle of water evaporates?	**Pupils should:** 3c Understand some of the effects of weathering on buildings and on rocks. 4d Know how measurements of temperature, rainfall, windspeed and direction describe the weather. 4e Know that weathering, erosion and transport lead to the formation of sediments and different types of soil. 5d Understand the water cycle in terms of the physical processes involved.

■ ATTAINMENT TARGET 4 PHYSICAL PROCESSES

KS2   SC4   Strand (i) **electricty and magnetism**

Programme of Study	Starting points for investigations	Statements of Attainment
Pupils should have the opportunity to construct simple circuits. They should investigate the effects of using different components, of varying the flow of electricity in a circuit and the heating and magnetic effects. They should plan and record construction details of a circuit using drawings and diagrams. They should learn about the dangers associated with the use of mains electricity and appropriate safety measures. They should investigate the properties of magnetic and non-magnetic materials. They should begin to explore simple circuits for sensing, switching and control, including the use of logic gates.	**Early in Key Stage 2** What materials does a magnet attract? Can you find a way of sorting cans made of different metals? How can you measure the strength of a magnet? What can you find out about magnets? What affects whether two magnets push or pull? Which is the strongest magnet? Which materials allow electricity to pass through them? **Later in Key Stage 2** What affects how strong a magnet is? How does varying the current affect the strength of an electromagnet? What affects the strength of an electromagnet? What affects the brightness of a bulb in a circuit? How could you make a bulb dimmer?	**Pupils should:** 2a Know that magnets attract some materials and not others and can repel each other. 3a Know that a complete circuit is needed for electrical devices to work. 4a Be able to construct circuits containing a number of components in which switches are used to control electrical effects. 5a Know how switches, relays, variable resistors, sensors and logic gates can be used to solve simple problems.

KS2   SC4   Strand (ii) **energy resources and energy transfer**

Programme of Study	Starting points for investigations	Statements of Attainment
Pupils should investigate movement using a variety of devices, for example, *toys* and *models*, which are self-propelled or driven and use motors, belts, levers and gears. They should investigate the changes that occur when familiar substances are heated and cooled, and the concepts of 'hot' and 'cold' in relation to their body temperature. They should survey, including the use of secondary sources, the range of fuels used in the home and at school, their efficient use and their origins. They should be introduced to the idea that energy sources may be renewable or non-renewable and consider the implications of limited global energy resources. They should be introduced to the idea of energy transfer.	**Early in Key Stage 2** Why do some rooms feel colder than others? (Do some have more window space etc?) Are all parts of the room at the same temperature? How can we make a toy car travel faster across the floor? Which do you think would be colder, air, water in the pond or soil? Why? **Later in Key Stage 2** What affects how far a jar will travel when rolled down a slope? What affects how fast a cotton-reel tank can climb a slope? What affects how fast toy cars will roll down a slope? What affects how fast a sail boat will travel?	**Pupils should:** 2b Understand the meaning of hot and cold relative to the temperature of their own bodies. 3b Know that there is a range of fuels used in the home. 4b Understand that an energy transfer is needed to make things work. 5b Understand that energy is transferred in any process and recognise energy transfers in a range of devices. 5c Understand the difference between renewable and non-renewable energy resources and the need for fuel economy.

KS2   SC4   Strand (iii) **forces and their effects**

Programme of Study	Starting points for investigations	Statements of Attainment
Pupils should explore different types of forces including gravity and use measurements to compare their effects in, for example, *moving things and bridge building*. They should investigate the strength of a simple structure. They should be introduced to the idea that forces act in opposition to each other, that one force may be bigger than another, or equal to it, and that the relative sizes and directions of the forces can affect the movement of an object. They should investigate the factors involved in floating and sinking. They should explore friction and investigate the ways in which the speed of a moving object can be changed by the application of forces. This work should be set in everyday situations, for example, *road safety, transport (including cycling and sailing), balancing systems and hydraulic mechanisms in model making.*	**Early in Key Stage 2** What will happen if we wind the rubber band 10, 20, 30 or 40 turns in a cotton reel tank? When playing marbles how can you make a marble go the furthest? Which sorts of objects float and which sink? What do you think makes things float? **Later in Key Stage 2** What affects how well an object floats? What affects the strength of a bridge? What affects the strength of a piece of paper? What affects the 'pull' of a rubber band? Is there a connection between the size of a muscle and the force with which it pushes or pulls? What affects how strongly a training shoe grips?	**Pupils should:** 2c Understand that pushes and pulls can make things start moving, speed up, slow down or stop. 3c Understand that forces can affect the position, movement and shape of an object. 4c Know that more than one force can act on an object and that forces can act in different directions. 5d Know that the size and direction of the resultant force on an object affects its movement.

KS2 SC4 Strand (iv) **light and sound**

Programme of Study	Starting points for investigations	Statements of Attainment
Pupils should learn that sounds are heard because they travel to the ear and that they can do so via a variety of materials. They should learn that sounds are made when objects vibrate, and investigate how sounds are changed in pitch, loudness, and timbre by changing the characteristics of the vibrating objects, for example *by changing length, tension, thickness of material of the vibrating object, or the way it is made to vibrate as exemplified by using musical instruments.* They should be aware of the obtrusive nature of some sounds in the environment. They should learn about the reflection of both light and sound and relate this to everyday effects (mirrors, echoes). Pupils should learn that light travels faster than sound by considering natural events such as thunderstorms. They should explore the effects produced by shining light through such objects as lenses, colour filters, water, prisms. They should also investigate the formation of shadows and represent in drawings their ideas about how light varies in terms of brightness, colour and shade.	**Early in Key Stage 2** What do you think will happen if we shine light on things? Can you find a way to see behind you using mirrors? Can we hear some sounds better than others? Can you find a way to make your notes higher/lower (using a drinking straw whistle or bottles containing water)? **Later in Key Stage 2** What factors affect the pitch of a note (use a stringed instrument or a drinking straw whistle)? What affects the loudness of a note? What makes a good string telephone? (Which factors affect how well sound travels through the telephone?) What affects how well a surface reflects light? (or sound?) What affects how much light bends when it travels through things?	**Pupils should:** 2d Know that light passes through some materials and that when it does not shadows may be formed. 3d Know that light and sound can be reflected. 4d Know that light travels faster than sound. 5e Understand how the reflection of light enables objects to be seen. 5f Know that sound is produced by a vibrating object and travels as a wave.

KS2 SC4 Strand (v) **the Earth's place in the Universe**

Programme of Study	Starting points for investigations	Statements of Attainment
Pupils should track the path of the Sun using safe procedures such as a shadow stick or sundial. They should study, using direct observations where possible, the night sky including the position and the appearance of bright planets and the Moon. They should learn about the motions of the Earth, Moon and Sun in order to explain day and night, day length, year length, phases of the Moon, eclipses and the seasons. They should be introduced to the order and general movements of the planets around the Sun.	**Early in Key Stage 2** What affects how long a day is? What do you think happens to the Sun during the day? What affects how high the Sun is in the sky? What affects how brightly a torch shows up an object? What affects the length of shadow? **Later in Key Stage 2** What affects the size of crater? (On the Moon?)	**Pupils should:** 2e Know that the Earth, Sun and Moon are separate spherical bodies. 3e Know that the appearance of the Moon and the altitude of the Sun change in a regular and predictable manner. 4e Be able to explain day and night, day length and year length in terms of the movements of the Earth around the Sun. 5g Be able to describe the motion of planets in the Solar System.